# New International

## A MAGAZINE OF MARXIST POLITICS AND THEORY

Number 5

D1522449

## Contents

In This Issue                                                      1
The Coming Revolution in South Africa
  *by Jack Barnes*                                                 7
The Freedom Charter                                              63
The Future Belongs to the Majority
  *by Oliver Tambo*                                              69
Southern Africa: A Decade of Struggle
  *by Ernest Harsch*                                             85
Cuba's Internationalist Volunteers in Angola
  *by Fidel Castro*                                             119
ARSENAL OF MARXISM
What Were My Disagreements With Lenin on the
  Character of the Russian Revolution?
  *by Leon Trotsky*                                             137
ISSUES IN DEBATE
Semicolonial and Semi-Industrialized
  Dependent Countries
  *by Ernest Mandel*                                            149
Once Again on the Workers' and Peasants'
  Government and the Workers' State:
  A Self-Criticism
  *by Livio Maitan*                                             176

Editors: Michel Prairie and Mary-Alice Waters
Managing Editor: Steve Clark
Business Manager: Jim White

Printed in the United States of America
Fourth printing, 1990

This fourth printing has been issued with a redesigned cover and new advertising. Typographical errors have been corrected. No other editorial changes have been made.

Distributors:

United States:
  Pathfinder, 410 West Street, New York, N.Y., U.S.A. 10014

Africa, Europe, and the Middle East:
  Pathfinder, 47 The Cut, London, SE1 8LL, Britain

Asia, Australia, and the Pacific:
  Pathfinder, P.O. Box 153, Glebe, Sydney,
  NSW 2037, Australia

Canada:
  Pathfinder, 6566, boul. St-Laurent, Montréal, Québec, H2S 3C6

Caribbean and Latin America:
  Pathfinder, 410 West Street, New York, N.Y. 10014

Iceland:
  Pathfinder, P. Box 233, 121 Reykjavík, Iceland

New Zealand:
  Pathfinder, Box 8730, Auckland, New Zealand

Sweden:
  Pathfinder, P.O. Box 5024, S-12505 Älvsjö,
  Stockholm, Sweden

# In This Issue

THE STRUGGLE inside South Africa against the racist apartheid regime has accelerated sharply during the latter half of 1985. This issue of *New International* focuses on that revolutionary struggle, its impact throughout southern Africa and worldwide, and the tasks of opponents of apartheid in the labor movement in North America and internationally.

The upsurge in the South African freedom struggle, and the murderous response by the racist authorities, have spurred increased international solidarity actions against the apartheid regime. Protests are demanding a total boycott of economic, military, political, sporting, cultural, and all other ties with Pretoria. Demands are being raised for the freedom of Nelson Mandela and other leaders of the African National Congress, of the United Democratic Front, and of other organizations targeted by the white supremacist state.

In North America, anti-apartheid protests took place October 11-12 in more than thirty cities and on more than 100 college campuses — from Los Angeles to Montreal, from New York City to Houston. Some 5,000 people demonstrated in Stockholm, Sweden, that same day. In London, England, 100,000 people participated in a November 2 anti-apartheid march, followed by a rally addressed by ANC President Oliver Tambo and leaders of the British Labour Party and union movement. Demonstrations and meetings in solidarity with the South African freedom fight have been held from Burkina Faso to New Zealand, from France to Nicaragua, from Japan to Mauritius.

Not only has virtually every labor organization in the world adopted positions condemning apartheid, but unions have increasingly begun to move into action against this racist system in recent months. This fall leaders of South Africa's National Union of Mineworkers have been on speaking tours throughout North America — initiated in the United States by the United Mine Workers of America, and in Canada by the Canadian Labour Congress and the Quebec Federation of Labour. Dockers and other transportation workers in Britain, Australia, Sweden, and other countries have refused to handle goods bound to or from South Africa. Unions have established solidarity funds to aid the struggle, and

1

helped organize action coalitions drawing in forces inside and outside the labor movement.

Young people have been at the forefront of the battles for national rights and democracy inside South Africa, and their counterparts in other countries have moved into action to support these struggles. A November 1-3 National Student Conference on South Africa and Namibia held in New York City issued a call for nationally coordinated anti-apartheid protests over a three-week period next spring; these run from March 21, anniversary of the 1960 Sharpeville massacre of anti-apartheid protesters in South Africa, to April 6, seventh anniversary of the hanging of ANC fighter Solomon Mahlangu. Campus protests have forced administrations at a number of U.S. universities to withdraw at least some of their endowment funds from corporations doing business in South Africa.

The NAACP, Coalition of Labor Union Women, Coalition of Black Trade Unionists, National Black Independent Political Party, National Organization for Women, and many other organizations are also sponsoring programs and participating in campaigns to educate about apartheid and help mobilize opposition to it.

As the lead article in this issue of *New International* explains, mobilizing the most powerful and broadly based anti-apartheid movement necessitates an accurate and concrete understanding of the revolution in South Africa: its class character and leading social forces, the vanguard political role of the ANC, and the place of that revolution in the class struggle in southern Africa and the world. The articles and documents published here are aimed at helping anti-apartheid fighters in North America and elsewhere to equip themselves with the political foundations for such an understanding.

The Socialist Workers Party's national convention in early August came just on the heels of the apartheid regime's state of emergency measures, aimed at quelling the mounting freedom protests in South Africa. During the week that the delegates were meeting, an emergency union-initiated solidarity demonstration in New York City drew 30,000 participants. In response to this new situation, the SWP convention voted to give top priority to involvement in the anti-apartheid fight, along with the party's continuing participation in actions against Washington's deepening war drive in Central America and the Caribbean.

To better prepare the party for this effort, the SWP National Committee met immediately following the convention to discuss the revolution in South Africa. The feature article in this issue of *New International* is the report by SWP National Secretary Jack Barnes that was adopted by the National Committee at that meeting. We are also publishing two documents from South Africa: the 1955 Freedom Charter, championed by the African National Congress, and a 1984 speech by ANC President

Oliver Tambo; a ten-year overview by Ernest Harsch of the rise of the revolutionary struggle in southern Africa; and three excerpts from speeches and interviews by Fidel Castro explaining why Cuban internationalist volunteers are committed to help the government and people of Angola defend themselves from South African-organized attacks on their sovereignty and social progress.

*       *       *

THE REPORT by Jack Barnes on the South African revolution also makes a contribution to the discussion on a topic that has been featured in previous issues of *New International*: the revolutionary continuity of the communist movement in the fight for state power by the workers and exploited farmers. The report approaches this question from the standpoint of the national, democratic revolution to overthrow the South African apartheid regime, and to replace it with a nonracial democratic republic based on the exploited toilers.

Three other items in this issue of *New International* also address this ongoing discussion among revolutionists. Two of these — by Fourth International leaders Ernest Mandel and Livio Maitan — appear in a new "Issues in Debate" section of the magazine.

In his article, "Semicolonial and Semi-Industrialized Countries," Mandel argues that a number of countries in the colonial world — among them Mexico, Argentina, Brazil, and South Korea — have undergone such a major economic transformation in the post-World War II period that it is misleading to any longer approach them politically as semicolonial countries. In assessing political tasks with regard to these countries, Mandel states, revolutionists must take account of important changes "in the weight of the different tactical components in revolutionary strategy as a whole, which, itself, remains the same — i.e. determined by . . . the strategy of permanent revolution."

Maitan reviews the discussions in the Fourth International since World War II on the workers' and peasants' government and its relationship to the struggle to expropriate the capitalist exploiters and establish workers' states. The Fourth International "used the formula 'workers' and peasants' government' several times in analyzing revolutionary processes at the end of World War II and in the following decades," he concludes, but *"let us say . . . without flinching: this use was always wrong."* Maitan also explains why he disagrees with the positions adopted by the U.S. Socialist Workers Party on this question, as well as with reports and articles by SWP and Fourth International leaders Jack Barnes, Mary-Alice Waters, and the late Joseph Hansen.

A final item dealing with the discussion on the political continuity of communism is the 1927 manuscript by Leon Trotsky, "What Were My Disagreements With Lenin?" It is published for the first time in this issue of *New International*, along with an introduction by managing editor Steve Clark.

*       *       *

Since THE publication of our last issue, *New International* has been joined by a French-language sister publication, *Nouvelle Internationale: Une revue de théorie et de politique marxistes*, published in Montreal, Quebec. Its Autumn 1985 inaugural issue includes translations of two articles published previously in *New International*: "Their Trotsky and Ours: Communist Continuity Today" by Jack Barnes [Fall 1983], and "The Workers' and Farmers' Government: A Popular Revolutionary Dictatorship" by Mary-Alice Waters [Spring-Summer 1984]; a 1969 report by Joseph Hansen on workers' and farmers' governments since World War II; an excerpt from a 1975 speech by Fidel Castro reviewing the first three years of the Cuban revolution; and documents on the workers' and peasants' government from the June 1923 meeting of the Executive Committee of the Communist International.

*Nouvelle Internationale* is published primarily for a readership among the nationally oppressed French-speaking population of Quebec. But it will also be of interest to many other French-speaking people in Canada and the United States, as well as in other parts of the world. This includes the growing numbers of Haitian immigrants now living in North America.

*       *       *

*New International* is one of a number of revolutionary publications that will benefit from a $125,000 fundraising drive that was carried out by socialists across the United States this fall. The Socialist Publication Fund was launched in mid-August and officially ended November 15. These funds will help finance the weekly *Militant*, the Spanish-language biweekly *Perspectiva Mundial*, the biweekly *Intercontinental Press*, as well as *New International*. The monies raised will also help produce books and pamphlets published by Pathfinder Press, such as its recent collections of speeches and interviews by Maurice Bishop, Fidel Castro, and Sandinista leaders, and its new book *Cosmetics, Fashions, and the Exploitation of Women* by Joseph Hansen and Evelyn Reed, with an introduction by Mary-Alice Waters.

Some readers of *New International* will not previously have been informed about this important fundraising effort, since both this current issue and our last one fell outside the dates of the three-month-long drive. But you can still help promote the circulation of socialist ideas in the United States and elsewhere around the world. If you find what you read in the following pages valuable in your political work in the labor movement, the anti-apartheid fight, Black rights organizations, or other progressive social struggles, then you should consider doing your part to help us meet the rising costs of putting out this magazine. In doing so, you will also be helping in the production and circulation of other socialist publications.

Make your check payable to *New International*, and send it to 14 Charles Lane, New York, N.Y. 10014.

*      *      *

Translators who helped in the production of this issue are Michael Baumann, Sonja Franeta, Will Reissner, John Riddell, and Susan Wald.

# The Struggle Is My Life

## BY NELSON MANDELA

"I cannot sell my birthright, nor am I prepared to sell the birthright of the people to be free. I am in prison as the representative of the people and of your organization, the African National Congress, which was banned. . . . Your freedom and mine cannot be separated."

*Nelson Mandela, February 1985*
Speeches, writings, and documents spanning a forty year period that record the struggle against apartheid in the words of its most well-known opponent. 249 pp., $10.95

## Apartheid's Great Land Theft: The Struggle for the Right to Farm in South Africa

by Ernest Harsch
The forced dispossession of Africans from the land is central to the origins of the apartheid system. The fight to have access to the land is key to forging an alliance of exploited producers to overthrow the apartheid state. 50 pp., $2.50

## Thomas Sankara Speaks
### THE BURKINA FASO REVOLUTION 1983-87

Thomas Sankara, president of the West African country of Burkina Faso (formerly Upper Volta), was assassinated in an October 15, 1987, coup. Sankara's speeches and interviews tell the story of the democratic, anti-imperialist revolution that unfolded in one of the world's poorest countries. Internationalism, health care, literacy, and support for the struggles of peasants, workers, and women were hallmarks of his revolutionary leadership. 260 pp., $16.95

# The Coming Revolution in South Africa

## by Jack Barnes

*The following report was adopted by the Socialist Workers Party National Committee in August 1985.*

THE UNITED States is the mightiest imperialist exploiter and chief world cop. For this reason, politics here is directly affected by revolutionary struggles anywhere they develop. Because of the depth of the revolutionary struggle in South Africa, and the immense stakes in its outcome for the imperialists and for working people throughout the world, it is having a deep impact on this country.

Important new responsibilities and openings exist to build support for the demand that Washington break all ties with the apartheid regime. To respond to these opportunities, revolutionists in the United States need a clear understanding of the character of the revolution that is unfolding in South Africa today. To be effective in helping mobilize support here for that revolution, we have to understand the line of march of the different classes in that revolution.

We in the Socialist Workers Party need to strip away remnants of sectarian and ultraleft obstacles that might hamper our ability to continue to turn our party outward along a working-class axis. Equipped with an accurate understanding of the South African revolution today, party members in the industrial unions will be better able to work together with all those workers who want to bring the weight of the labor movement to bear in the campaign for a free South Africa. The goal is for the labor movement to join this fight, add power to it, help lead it forward — and change and strengthen itself in the process.

This report will take up four aspects of the South African revolution.

• First, what is the historic character of the revolution in South Africa?

It is a revolution to overthrow the apartheid state and tear apart the apartheid system.

It is a revolution to open the door to forging, for the first time, a nonracial South African nation-state.

This new nation will incorporate the African people from various tribal backgrounds, the descendants of those who lived there and worked the land before the white colonizers arrived, and who are the vast majority of the population of South Africa today. It will incorporate those the apartheid system classifies as Coloureds and Indians, who, together with the Africans, constitute the oppressed Black population. And it will incorporate those whites who will accept living and working as citizens with equal rights — no more, no less — in a democratic South Africa.

It is a revolution to conquer the right of the Black majority to own, work, and develop the land from which they have been expelled by the apartheid regime. To win the right of Africans to become free farmers, producing cash crops for an expanding home market. To carry out a real Homestead Act, opening the land to those who want to work it.

It is a revolution to abolish all restrictions on the rights of Black South Africans to live, labor, and travel where they choose. To establish full equality in the job market. To guarantee full trade union and labor rights.

It is a revolution aimed at replacing the state of the white minority with a democratic republic based on one person, one vote. Its goal — in the words used by the African National Congress — is a single, united, nonracial, and democratic South Africa.

It is a revolution in which the toilers are seeking to replace minority apartheid rule with rule by the working people, the great majority. They will then use that new revolutionary power to ensure that not a single brick of the apartheid system is left intact and that the democratic program of the revolution is put into practice.

From the historical standpoint, the South African revolution today is a bourgeois-democratic revolution for these goals. It is a democratic revolution, a national revolution. The working people are striving to lead it to victory and to create for the first time a true South African nation-state.

The South African revolution today is not an anticapitalist revolution. It will open the road to the transition to an anticapitalist revolution, but no one can predict how long, or short, that road will be. That will be determined by the relationship of class forces in South Africa and internationally that will emerge from the revolutionary overthrow of the apartheid state.

• Second, this report will look at the role of the South African working class and of the peasantry in this revolution.

The working class is striding forward to lead the national, democratic revolution to overthrow the apartheid state and replace it with a democratic dictatorship of the South African workers and peasants. This democratic revolution cannot be carried through to victory under the leadership of any wing of the South African capitalist class or liberal political forces.

This leadership role has been thrust upon the working class by the development of South African capitalism itself. As a result of the special oppressive forms through which the apartheid system mobilizes labor power, South African and foreign capitalists have squeezed superprofits from the labor of Black workers. But in the process they have brought into being a large and powerful South African working class, the vanguard of the gravediggers of apartheid.

• Third, the report will look at the organization of the struggle against apartheid in South Africa today, and in particular at the leadership role of the African National Congress (ANC).

The ANC has conquered, in struggle, its place as the vanguard organization of the democratic revolution in South Africa. Revolutionists in the United States and around the world must act on the basis of this fact in participating in the fight against apartheid.

• Finally, the report will place the South African revolution in its international context. It will analyze the impact of this revolution not only on southern Africa and throughout the African continent, but also on the class struggle by workers and farmers against imperialism — both here in the United States and around the world.

This will tie together our understanding of the South African revolution with the tasks of the Socialist Workers Party in the campaign for a free South Africa. We will look at how these tasks fit in with building a revolutionary workers' party in the United States today.

## I. THE REVOLUTION IN SOUTH AFRICA: A NATIONAL, DEMOCRATIC REVOLUTION

THE APARTHEID system is more than an oppressive legal structure with far-reaching social and economic consequences. When we talk about the apartheid system, we are also talking about a *state*.

The continued existence of apartheid is completely dependent on the existence of the apartheid state, and vice versa. The entire state structure is designed to mobilize the force and violence necessary to impose and preserve a particular organization of the exploitation of labor, based on the special oppression of the great majority of working people.

This state in South Africa — this capitalist state — is not a nation-state, at least not in a meaningful sense of the term. Only a small minority of the population in South Africa has any real rights of citizenship.

This minority — some 5 million out of a total population of about 33 million — is defined by law as persons "of the white race."

There is no South African *nation-state*; there is a state of the "white race." In the geographical territory that the apartheid state controls, in what is today the *country* of South Africa, the overwhelming majority of people have no constitutional rights to speak of. Blacks are effectively denied the right to citizenship in the country in which they live and work.

The Black majority is itself made up of a number of peoples, none of which constitutes a nation. Within the Black population there are important differences in legally enforced social positions, which the apartheid rulers perpetuate and seek to increase through legislation, economic policy, and other means. By far the largest group of Blacks are the Africans, 24 million direct descendants of the original inhabitants of what is now South Africa. They have even fewer rights than other components of the Black population and are the center of the target apartheid aims at. Those the apartheid rulers refer to as Coloured number 3 million. There are also 1 million Indians — many of whose ancestors were brought to Africa from the Indian subcontinent as indentured laborers to work on the sugar plantations.

In the past, the term *Black* was most often used to refer only to Africans. But since the 1970s Africans, Coloureds, and Indians — those whom the apartheid state brands as "nonwhite" — are increasingly identifying themselves as Black. This evolution of the meaning of the term *Black* reflects the development of unity and consciousness among those fighting against the apartheid state.

The apartheid system has one central and overriding purpose: to organize and perpetuate the superexploitation of African labor by capital. It denies Africans the right to own and work land, and it denies them the right to compete freely and equally with whites in the sale of their labor power.

Apartheid has turned the African population into what, for lack of a better word, we can call an estate. By *estate* we mean in this case a part of the population whose legal and social rights are drastically limited in comparison to other sections of the population, a status enforced by the ruling power. It is a term we are most used to in connection with feudal society, not capitalist society. Nonetheless, it expresses the reality of apartheid. And it underscores the fact that apartheid is a qualitatively different phenomenon from the racial oppression that exists today in the United States.

Under apartheid, almost all Africans have been driven off the land and are denied the right to own land. They are without juridically recognized claims for equal protection under the laws of the state. To be born an African is to be born into that permanent social position, codified in law and enforced by the organized force and violence of the state.

That is what we mean when we speak of Africans as constituting an estate under apartheid. It is an estate similar to — though not the same as — the peasant estate in tsarist Russia as late as the second decade of the twentieth century.

This fundamental underpinning of the apartheid system is part of a broader structure of laws and institutions that define the economic, social, and political rights not only of Africans, but also those categorized as Indian and Coloured in South Africa. Coloureds and Indians, too, hold a juridically established subordinate position in South African society. Every African, Indian, and Coloured person in South Africa has a social and legal status that deprives them of equality with any white person, of any social class.

The apartheid system blocks the creation of a South African nation, a modern nation with modern producing classes. Apartheid attempts to perpetuate and institutionalize tribal differentiations through the Bantustan system (the reservations that the regime calls "national homelands") and other means. Apartheid blocks modern class development and differentiation, whereby some Africans — as part of a South African nation — would become free farmers, producing and selling their commodities on the market, while others would be able to sell their labor power on an equal basis with all other wage workers.

A South African nation does not yet exist, but it is in the process of being forged through the freedom struggle for liberation from apartheid. It will be forged from Africans, Coloureds, Indians, and those whites who will stay to live and work as equals in a nonracial, democratic South African republic.

A true nation-state in South Africa will be brought into being only as a result of the revolutionary overthrow of the apartheid state and the establishment of a new state power. It is in this sense that the South African revolution can accurately be termed a national revolution. It is important to keep this content in mind, because in today's world the term *national revolution* is almost exclusively used in connection with a struggle for liberation from colonial or neocolonial domination by another country. In South Africa, the obstacle to forging a nation isn't occupation by a foreign imperialist power; it's the apartheid state itself. To make the national, democratic revolution in South Africa, apartheid rule has to be overthrown.

## Development of apartheid system

THE ROOTS of the apartheid system go far back in history, to the establishment of the colonial-settler state, which entrenched white minority rule over the African majority. The emergence of this state was intertwined with the extension of capitalist property relations, which had become dominant by the beginning of the twentieth century.

But the apartheid state against which the battle is now raging was not completely put together until after World War II. It was born under the aegis of U.S. imperialism, which had emerged triumphant over imperialist rivals at the end of that war. The apartheid state was consolidated under the protection of what the Sandinistas accurately call "the enemy of humanity" — the Yankee ruling class. With the backing of the United States and its "democratic imperialist" allies, who were the victors in what was supposedly a war to rid the world of fascism, the Nazi-like rulers of South Africa emerged in their full glory. Rule by the *sjambok* — the whip — was enshrined.

The full-blown apartheid structure — a universal, top-to-bottom system that controlled every aspect of economic, social, and political life — was put together after the war. With the victory of the National Party in the 1948 elections, apartheid was established as official policy. This was the response of the white South African rulers to the relatively rapid industrialization in the 1930s and during the war years, with the resulting growth of the Black working class and its increasing concentration in urban areas.

It was only in the period after World War II that South Africa emerged as the junior imperialist power it is today. The South African capitalist class achieved a high degree of industrialization and monopolization. Finance capital — the merger of banking and industrial capital — emerged to play the leading role. The South African bourgeoisie began to invest large amounts of capital in other countries. The apartheid state began taking its place as the military enforcer of imperialist domination throughout southern Africa.

### Weakest link in chain of imperialist powers

AS AN imperialist power — albeit a qualitatively weaker one than the major European and North American powers and Japan — South Africa is a link in the world imperialist chain. It is a bastion of reaction and military might against the peoples of an entire subcontinent — from Namibia and Angola through Zaire and across Zimbabwe and Tanzania; from the South Atlantic well into the Indian Ocean.

This chain of imperialist world rule is threatening to break at its weakest link, just as it broke in 1917 at what was then its weakest link: backward, absolutist, imperialist Russia.

South Africa is part of the world police force of the imperialist system. As a junior cop it both defends its own interests and carries its load in the division of labor with the other imperialist powers. And the world should never forget that South Africa is one of the nuclear powers of imperialism.

But the Pretoria regime pays a price for wielding its imperialist power. That price is the deepening interpenetration of the world revolution and South African politics. Every advance for the Namibian liberation struggle is a blow at apartheid's rulers. Every step forward in Burkina Faso, in Ethiopia, in the Seychelles — or anywhere else in the region of the world in which South African imperialism plays a major role — helps weaken the South African state.

Nowhere has this fact of political life been driven home more emphatically than in Angola. Over the past decade, the Angolan people and armed forces — supported by Cuban internationalist volunteers — have united to defend Angola's sovereignty and inflict defeats on South Africa's imperialist army. A key turning point for the revolution in southern Africa was the defeat of the apartheid regime's invading army in late 1975 and early 1976. The consequences of that unanticipated disaster for the South African state included the upsurge of youth that began in the Black township of Soweto and rocked the entire country later in 1976.

President P.W. Botha likes to boast publicly that the South African state can stand alone, if necessary, against the entire world. The reality is the opposite. The image of self-sufficient invincibility — political, military, and economic — that the apartheid regime seeks to create is false. The fate of the apartheid regime is totally intertwined with that of its fellow imperialist powers.

Far from being invincible, the apartheid state is vulnerable. This is what causes so much concern in Washington, London, Paris, and the other imperialist capitals, in the face of the advance of the South African revolutionary struggle. The concentration of power in the hands of the white supremacist state and the consequent contradictions and one-sidedness in the development of South African imperialism are measures not of the strength, but ultimately of the weakness, of the South African link in the imperialist chain.

## Parallels to Jim Crow system

The Jim Crow system in the U.S. South offers a useful analogy to apartheid. That may seem to contradict what we noted earlier about the unique character of apartheid. But it does not, if the analogy is used correctly. The Jim Crow parallel is particularly useful for us in the United States, since it relates the struggle in South Africa to the historic battle that working people here lived through, fought, and won only recently — in the 1950s and 1960s.

The Jim Crow system at its fullest development was the attempt in the states of the old Confederacy to institutionalize, codify in law, and make permanent the expropriation and oppression of Black people — the freed slaves and their descendants — by separating them from all economic, social, and political activity engaged in by white people. It was, by its very nature, intended to be all-encompassing. Its purpose was to make it as difficult as possible for Blacks to become free farmers, and to make it impossible for them ever to compete on an equal basis with white workers in selling their labor power to the capitalists.

Jim Crow segregation was imposed and perpetuated through force and violence organized both by the state and by extralegal means, such as the Ku Klux Klan terror units. From the smashing of Radical Reconstruction in the late 1870s to the victory of the civil rights movement almost a century afterwards, it was hard to find a sheriff in the U.S. South who was not also an organizer of the local Klan. The state-authorized force and violence and the extralegal force and violence went hand-in-hand.

Denial of citizenship rights — centered around denial of the right to vote — was essential to the maintenance of this legally sanctioned tyranny over Black workers and farmers. This, too, was enforced by a combination of legal institutions (such as poll taxes, literacy tests, and segregated jury lists) and night-riding terror against those who tried to break through these barriers. That is why the battlecry of "One man, one vote!" became so central to the civil rights struggle — a slogan that is echoing back today from the cities, townships, and countryside of South Africa.

The civil rights movement used to stress the parallels between Jim Crow and apartheid, between Selma, Alabama, and Johannesburg, South Africa. This reflected a reality. South Africa was not really so far away.

The logic of the Jim Crow system was not to return to chattel slave labor. No, the logic of Jim Crow, fully developed, was apartheid: the subjugation of Blacks as an estate, with no right to own land, and no right to compete on an equal basis with white workers in the sale of their labor power. (Lenin stressed the "startling similarity" between the conditions of Blacks in the South at the beginning of this century and those of the peasant estate in tsarist Russia.[1] Black sharecroppers, he noted, were "exploited by former slave-owners in feudal or semi-feudal fashion."[2])

The parallels between the South African struggle and what workers and farmers in this country fought for, conquered, and today jealously guard help to explain the depth of the identification of many U.S. working people with the current battles in South Africa.

## Apartheid today

NONETHELESS, THE apartheid system goes beyond what the architects of Jim Crow in the South were able to implement. Unlike apartheid, Jim Crow segregation did *not* become completely intertwined with the entire state structure in the United States. It was the product of the bloody defeat of Radical Reconstruction in the states of the old slavocracy. As a result, the Jim Crow system could be smashed by mighty civil rights battles in the 1950s and 1960s without challenging the state structure of U.S. imperialism itself.

This is where the analogy between apartheid and Jim Crow reaches its limit. Apartheid is the legal institutionalization of the complete expropriation of the African people; it is state control over every aspect of their labor and life. The African peoples there had a history of thousands of years of productive life on the land, and development of culture. Their tools, their land, and their cattle were stripped from them first in bloody wars of conquest, and then by the institutionalization and enforcement of apartheid rule.

Having been forcibly robbed of their land and tools, the African peoples were swept into the mines and factories, and onto the capitalist plantations, as proletarians. But they were not free proletarians. They got all the worst that came with being made propertyless: they lost all they owned, and were driven from their land. But they gained none of the freedoms that under other conditions have historically accompanied proletarianization: freedom from being tied to the land; freedom to sell your labor power on the market on an equal basis with all other workers; freedom to change jobs, to pack up and move from one part of the country to another, or even abroad, seeking work under the best conditions and for the highest pay available; freedom from all the reactionary encumbrances, restraints, and prejudices of feudal society.

Where Africans can work, where they can live, how long they can stay in the "white" cities, where and when they can travel — all this is under the control of the state of the white rulers. For the big majority of Africans, permission to live outside the "homelands" is contingent on working a particular job with approval of the apartheid authorities. An African who quits that job, or is laid off or fired, has to return to the rural "homeland." Millions of Africans migrate from impoverished rural Bantustans to the mines and back again, from Bantustans to white-owned capitalist plantations and back again, from Bantustans to Black urban townships and back again.

Although there is a large Black working class in South Africa, only a relatively small percentage of these wage workers comprise a hereditary

African proletariat in the proper sense of the term. An African may work much of his life in the mines, yet constantly have to return to the rural "homeland" where his family lives. It is up to the apartheid authorities to decide whether, and for how long, his children will gain permission to leave the Bantustan to sell their labor power.

Every aspect of life in South Africa is dominated, shaped, and restricted by the apartheid system. Housing, health care, and education are strictly segregated by law. Licensing of professionals and of job occupations is by race. Whether or not you have the right to stay in a city after sundown depends on the shadings in color of your skin. Who you can socialize with and live with is restricted by the state.

If there is one thing that expresses this more than anything it is the pass system — the system of internal passports. If you are African you must have a pass and carry it at all times. Any cop can demand to inspect it at any hour of the day or night. It has to include everything from your tax receipts and work records to the signature of your current boss. The pass is a key instrument for controlling the life, employment, and movement of the African population. It turns even such acts as walking down the street into crimes if not carried out within apartheid's rules, subrules, constantly changing and recodified rules. It is truthfully said that it is impossible for Africans to walk from one side of town to the other without "breaking the law."

For these reasons, the pass system has been a particular target of struggle against white minority rule. Opposition to the pass laws was a central aspect of the ANC-initiated Defiance Campaign in 1952. There was an explosion of protests by women when the pass law was extended to cover them in the mid-1950s. Renewed protests against the pass system at the beginning of the 1960s was met with brutal repression by the apartheid regime — the Sharpeville massacre in 1960, the outlawing of the ANC and other organizations that same year, and the arrest and imprisonment of Nelson Mandela and other anti-apartheid leaders a few years later.

This apartheid system is not just "capitalism and racism" as we in this country understand it. Apartheid is not just racist segregation and inequality. It is not just racist cops. It is not just segregated schools. It is not just neighborhoods that are dangerous to walk in if you are Black. It is not just discrimination in employment and education. It is an entire state structure that institutionalizes and enforces the relegation of Africans to the condition of an estate.

Since the end of World War II, the apartheid state has become even more purely the state of the white race. It has developed beyond the white-settler state, beyond the already existing forms of racist oppression, beyond just the domination of capital over labor to reach the current reality. This history and reality have established the goals of the South African revolution today.

Two things exist side by side in South Africa today. There is the state of the white minority. And there is an emerging nation that is fighting its way into being by the only means possible: by struggling to overthrow the apartheid state and replace it with a democratic republic whose citizens will be all those who live in South Africa.

## Land and nation

T HE FREEDOM Charter, which was first drawn up in 1955 and is championed by the African National Congress (ANC), proclaims that "our people have been robbed of their birthright to land, liberty, and peace by a form of government founded on injustice and inequality." It demands an end to all racial restrictions on the right to own land.

When we think about how to advance the worker-peasant alliance in South Africa, we have to start from the fact that the great majority of Africans in South Africa cannot farm. This is not because they cannot make it economically, or they go deep into debt, or they are discriminated against by the banks, transport companies, and wholesalers. They *have no right to own land*. They can toil on white-owned plantations. Some can "illegally" grab a plot of land and "illegally" farm it for a while. But by law they have no landholding rights of free farmers.

This has not always been the case in South Africa. In fact, as recently as the nineteenth century and the early years of the twentieth, a substantial landholding African peasantry existed in some regions of South Africa, producing cash crops for the market. The wholesale expropriation of these African peasants was launched in 1913 with the Natives' Land Act — more accurately known as the "law of dispossession" by South African Blacks.

Today, Africans can own and farm a plot of land only on the 13.7 percent of South Africa's poorest soil that has been set aside by the apartheid regime as so-called independent Bantustans, and in a few and declining number of rural areas known in South Africa as "Black spots." And there overcrowding and soil exhaustion make it impossible for all but a handful to eke out anything more than a bare subsistence.

We get a false picture of South Africa unless we understand the economic and social consequences of this forcible denial of Africans' right to own and till the land. If we think of South Africa just in terms of its industry and mines, of what we know about the cities and the white farmers in the countryside, we get a false picture. We see only the South Africa of the white state, of the white minority. We don't see the South African nation-state that has not yet been born.

We can't see it, because the nation hasn't been developed. The wealth isn't being drawn from the land by the people, by the Black majority. Africans are virtually barred from producing cash crops for the market. Despite the weight of modern industrial capitalism in South Africa, elementary commodity circulation and the development of an internal market still exist only on a primitive level for the Black majority.

No matter how much money they save, no matter how hard they and their families are willing to work, no matter who would give them a loan — *Africans can't farm.*

Opening the land is inseparable from resolving the national question. Neither can be accomplished without the destruction of the apartheid state structure, which blocks the road to development of the South African nation-state.

This is what Black freedom fighters are pointing to when they say that the apartheid state has to be *overthrown*. The white supremacist rulers have, can, and will continue to be driven to make reforms. But the South African apartheid state can never be reformed out of existence. It will have to be brought crashing down, not modified.

## Full citizenship rights

THERE IS a third component to be added to the fight for the right to land, and the right to establish a nation and a nation-state: the fight for full political, civil rights for every human being. It is a fight for equal protection under the law; for equal claim to the rights and privileges of citizenship; for one person, one vote in a unitary South Africa. It is a fight for the rights historically established by the bourgeois-democratic revolution.

As the Freedom Charter puts it:

"Every man and woman shall have the right to vote for and to stand as a candidate for all bodies which make laws.

"All the people shall be entitled to take part in the administration of the country.

"The rights of the people shall be the same regardless of race, color, or sex.

"All bodies of minority rule, advisory boards, councils and authorities shall be replaced by democratic organs of self-government."

These rights have been and are being fought for and conquered by the peoples of the earth. They are among the rights that laboring people around the world have come to consider inalienable. They are the rights that Blacks are now fighting to wrest from the rulers for the people of South Africa as a whole.

Land, a nation, a democratic republic. They are totally intertwined.

**Freedom Charter**

The goals of the national, democratic revolution in South Africa are set forth in the Freedom Charter. This document was adopted in 1955 at a Congress of the People, which was convened by the ANC and its allied organizations and attended by delegates from a wide variety of groups across the country.

The Freedom Charter is a solid program for the national, democratic revolution in South Africa. It succinctly presents demands for political rights, for land rights, for trade union rights, for the right to equal pay for equal work, for the right to housing, medical care, and education, and other rights. It is the program of the revolutionary democratic movement in South Africa. And it is the minimum program of a revolutionary workers' party, of a communist party, in South Africa today.

With all of the further advances and development of the ANC in the three decades since the Freedom Charter was adopted — and there have been important political and programmatic clarifications and the emergence of a whole new generation of leaders — the ANC has not moved away from the Freedom Charter. Just the opposite: the development of the ANC has been toward a clearer class view of the leadership and methods needed to carry out the Charter, and toward even better ways of presenting the ideas in the Charter to all of the people of South Africa.

Today the Freedom Charter has also been adopted by many other South African political organizations, including ones playing a leading role in the United Democratic Front (UDF), an anti-apartheid coalition of some 600 organizations, representing 2 million members.

I stress the importance of the Freedom Charter because some of the material that we in the Socialist Workers Party have distributed and taken political responsibility for has had an ultraleft sectarian approach toward it. This was true, for example, of the first edition of the Pathfinder Press book *South Africa: White Rule, Black Revolt* by Ernest Harsch published in 1980.

This edition had the following to say about the Charter:

"The Freedom Charter, which the ANC officially adopted in 1956, marked a partial pullback from the African nationalist positions put forward several years earlier. While the earlier Programme of Action [of the second half of the 1940s] had stressed the attainment of self-determination and political independence 'under the banner of African nationalism,' the Freedom Charter glossed over the nationalist side of the liberation struggle. It refrained from advocating outright Black majority rule, speaking instead of a 'democratic state, based on the will of all the people' and emphasizing that 'South Africa belongs to all who live in it, Black and white.' "

What this paragraph is referring to, although not presenting accurately, is the fact that adoption of the charter was part of a process of clarification of differences inside the ANC with the "Africanist" current that would later split away and, in 1959 form the Pan Africanist Congress (PAC).

What was known as Africanism, or African nationalism had first been raised during the Second World War as the banner of a revolutionary-minded wing of the young generation of fighters in the ANC — among them Nelson Mandela, Walter Sisulu, and Oliver Tambo — who wanted to loosen the grip of conservative leaders and turn the organization toward more militant struggle. The African nationalism of these fighters was inspired by the upsurge of the independence struggle throughout the continent. It recognized the connection between the struggle to overthrow the white rulers of South Africa and the struggle of all African peoples to throw off colonial domination by the European powers. In this sense, the Africanism of these young revolutionaries was a deepening internationalism.

As they set their sights more clearly on the fight for political power, to overthrow the apartheid state, they also of necessity defined more clearly the need to unite *all* those in South Africa who were the targets of apartheid. They sought to forge a united struggle with Coloured and Indian organizations, and to include those whites who were prepared to join the revolutionary struggle.

THE CONGRESS Alliance, formed in 1955, united the ANC with the South African Indian Congress, the South African Coloured People's Organisation, and the Congress of Democrats. This latter organization was made up of whites who opposed apartheid rule. That same year, the South African Congress of Trade Unions, a nonracial labor organization, was formed, and joined the alliance.

Through this process of struggle and discussion, the "Africanism" of the emerging ANC leadership grew into the perspective of a revolutionary fight for power around the democratic program embodied in the Freedom Charter.

A minority within the ANC, however, opposed the Freedom Charter. It objected in particular to the Charter's statement, "that South Africa belongs to all who live in it, Black and white." These opponents of the Charter counterposed their notion of "Africanism" to the goal of uniting all sections of the oppressed Black population, as well as whites, in a revolutionary movement aiming at the destruction of the white supremacist state and the conquest of power by the working people. They failed to distinguish between the place of Africans in the forefront of this revolutionary struggle — a place assigned to them by the structure of South

African society — and the goal of a nonracial democratic republic, with full citizenship rights for all.

These opponents of the Freedom Charter perspective turned away from the course of seeking allies among all races and all progressive classes for the struggle for national liberation. They counterposed an Africans-only movement to a revolutionary-democratic movement struggling for state power as the road to winning land, nationhood, and a democratic republic. For them, "Africanism" was not a step toward internationalism, but a step toward an antiwhite, and anti–working class, orientation.

But the 1980 edition of *South Africa: White Rule, Black Revolt* favored this "Africanism" over the ANC's revolutionary democratic political approach. And that's not all. The commentary in the book went on to criticize the Freedom Charter on these grounds: "Although the Freedom Charter included a vague nationalization plank, Mandela took care to explain that 'it is by no means a blueprint for a socialist society.' "

That criticism is true ultraleft sectarianism.

(So there will be no misunderstanding, I should add that Ernest Harsch cannot be held personally or solely responsible for statements such as these, although, like the rest of us, he generally agreed with them at the time they were written. The book was edited by a team of editors. It reflected, if not where we really were in 1980, at least where we had come from.)

What is the Freedom Charter's "vague" nationalization plank? Under the heading, "The people shall share in the country's wealth," the Charter says, "The national wealth of our country, the heritage of all South Africans, shall be restored to the people;

"The mineral wealth beneath the soil, the banks, and monopoly industry shall be transferred to the ownership of the people as a whole;

"All other industries and trade shall be controlled to assist the well-being of the people;

"All people shall have equal rights to trade where they choose, to manufacture, and to enter all trades, crafts, and professions."

That's not vague, not at all. It is a concrete, specific plank in a revolutionary democratic program. It is not a socialist demand. It does not call for expropriation of industrial capital. It is not a call for the dictatorship of the proletariat. Correct. ANC leader Nelson Mandela was accurate when he said the Freedom Charter is no "blueprint for a socialist state."

And it shouldn't be.

First, all blueprints for a socialist state are sectarian schemes. Always. Second, a mass revolutionary movement in South Africa today cannot and will not be built around a socialist program. A communist party can and will be built around a socialist program, but it will also embrace the Freedom Charter as its minimum program. A communist movement in South Africa would be smashed on the rocks if it tried to impose its full, socialist program on the national, democratic revolution that is on the agenda in South Africa today.

Where were we wrong in 1980?

On the one hand, we were inclined to agree with those who criticized the ANC for not being more "Africanist," more nationalist. We tended to look at the national struggle in South Africa not as a profound expression of the class struggle, but as somehow more fundamental than the class struggle.

At the same time, we were attracted to those who criticized the ANC for leading the struggle around a democratic and national program, rather than a socialist program. We didn't look at the revolution in the framework of the fight for political power, the framework of the working class leading the whole people in the fight to bring down the apartheid state. We wanted to get on with the socialist revolution, the "real" revolution.

As if the battle to overthrow the apartheid state is not a real revolution! As if the bourgeois-democratic revolution in South Africa today is less worthy of support, or is of less world-shaking importance, than the future socialist revolution that it will open the transition to. And as if the proletarian vanguard could advance toward the socialist revolution in South Africa by any other road than doing everything in its power to carry through the national, democratic revolution in the most thoroughgoing, revolutionary way.

It is only through this struggle to lead the national, democratic revolution to victory that a revolutionary workers' party can be built in South Africa. It is from among the workers who are leaders of the democratic revolution that this proletarian vanguard party will be forged. Where else could communist leadership come from?

What was Mandela getting at when he said the Freedom Charter is not a blueprint for a socialist state? Here is what he said:

"Whilst the Charter proclaims democratic changes of a far-reaching nature, it is by no means a blueprint for a socialist state but a programme for the unification of various classes and groupings amongst the people on a democratic basis. Under socialism, the workers hold state power. They and the peasants own the means of production, the land, the factories, and the mills. All production is for use and not for profit. The Charter does not contemplate such profound economic and political changes. Its declaration 'The People Shall Govern!' visualizes the transfer of power not to any single social class but to all the people of this country, be they workers, peasants, professional men, or petty-bourgeoisie.

"It is true that in demanding the nationalization of the banks, the gold mines, and the land, the Charter strikes a fatal blow at the financial and gold-mining monopolies and farming interests that have for centuries plundered the country and condemned its people to servitude. But such a step is imperative because the realization of the Charter is inconceivable, in fact impossible, unless and until these monopolies are smashed and the national wealth of the country turned over to the people. To destroy these monopolies means the termination of the exploitation of vast sections of the populace by mining kings and land barons and there will be a general rise in the living standards of the people. It is precisely because the Charter offers immense opportunities for an overall improvement in the material conditions of all classes and groups that it attracts such wide support."[3]

What Nelson Mandela explained about the Freedom Charter showed a clear understanding of the class forces in the South African revolution (unless we believe that he includes South Africa's current capitalist rulers among the "classes and groups" that will benefit from the overthrow of apartheid!). In many respects, Mandela was clearer than the book we helped publish and distribute.

We should note what this reveals to us now about ourselves — about where we have come from, how we are developing our understanding, and where we are going. The first edition, the one I have just quoted from, was published only five years ago. When the first edition ran out in 1983, Ernest wanted to do a whole new edition with major revisions. Instead Pathfinder decided to make only limited changes, restricting the number of pages that could be revised in order to cut costs and save time. We didn't yet see the need for the more thoroughgoing political correction that we will now be able to make.

## Not a 'stage' of the socialist revolution

T HERE IS another error we can fall into, even as we try to correct past ultraleft sectarian misconceptions about the South African revolution. We could say, "Yes, the key tasks of the revolution in South Africa are clearly national and democratic in character. Yes, it would be completely ultraleft for South African revolutionists to wage the struggle around a socialist program. But, given the development of modern capitalist industry and mining, and the size of the Black working class, won't the overthrow of the imperialist apartheid state actually establish the dictatorship of the proletariat and open what we might call the democratic stage of the socialist revolution?"

The answer is, "No." What is on the agenda in South Africa is a bourgeois-democratic revolution, not the democratic stage of the socialist revolution. It is a bourgeois-democratic revolution that will be made and led by the working people, and it will open the road to the transition to the socialist revolution. But these are not merely stages of a single revolution; they are two revolutions.

Without clearly differentiating between the bourgeois-democratic revolution and the socialist revolution, the working-class vanguard will not be able to lead the toilers in making the first, and thereby will only wind up postponing the second. And without keeping clearly in mind the tasks of the working class in the bourgeois-democratic revolution, the communist vanguard won't be able to strengthen itself and draw toward it the proletarian leaders who will come forward and develop in revolutionary combat against apartheid.

What we have reviewed about the relationship between the classes in South Africa today should make it clear that the class character of the South African revolution is qualitatively different from the socialist revolution that is on the agenda in imperialist countries such as the United States, Japan, or Australia. It bears a closer resemblance to the character of the revolutionary struggle to topple the tsarist regime in imperialist Russia, which, as the Bolsheviks explained, was a bourgeois-democratic revolution. The socialist revolution was not yet on the agenda in Russia, Lenin explained. It would be placed on the agenda only by the proletarian vanguard leading the toiling people in a thoroughgoing democratic revolution, resulting in a democratic dictatorship of the workers and peasants.

## Bourgeois-democratic and anticapitalist revolutions

**W**E CAN bring the character of the South African revolution into still sharper focus by looking at what makes it different from the *anticapitalist revolutions* that have led to the establishment of workers' and peasants' governments in Cuba, Grenada, and Nicaragua over the past quarter century, and that are on the agenda in many — although not all — semicolonial countries oppressed by imperialism.

Let's take the example of Nicaragua. Both the struggle for power that culminated in the victorious July 1979 insurrection, and the measures implemented by the Sandinista-led government since, have been predominantly anti-imperialist and democratic in character.

In 1979, the Nicaraguan workers and peasants overthrew the U.S.-backed Somoza dictatorship and put an end to neocolonial domination by Yankee imperialism. As part of carrying out these tasks, the workers' and farmers' government expropriated the Somoza family and its direct ruling class collaborators, and nationalized certain imperialist holdings, including the nation's chief mineral resources.

The revolutionary government established broad democratic and labor rights. It initiated social programs to improve the health, education, living conditions, and political self-confidence of the toilers. It launched and has deepened a radical agrarian reform to provide land to propertyless farm laborers and to peasant families whose plots were too small to make a decent living and produce a surplus for sale on the market. State farms and cooperatives have been established, as well.

Washington has organized and financed a *contra* war, with the goal of bringing down the Sandinista government. As this war has escalated, defense of Nicaragua's sovereignty has become an increasingly central task of the revolutionary state power.

The Sandinista government expropriated the Nicaraguan bankers. It has put restrictions on foreign trade, and on how Nicaraguan owners of capitalist farms and industries can invest their capital. Nonetheless, some 60 percent of industry remains under capitalist ownership, as does a substantial portion of cotton, coffee, and other agricultural production.

These aspects of the Nicaraguan revolution are similar to what can be anticipated in the coming South African revolution. But there are also qualitative differences.

Despite the economic backwardness of the country and the weight of anti-imperialist and democratic tasks, the Nicaraguan revolution is an *anticapitalist* revolution. The revolution in South Africa is, by contrast, a *bourgeois-democratic* revolution. What are the differences? The answer brings us back to the character of the apartheid system and state structure.

In South Africa, the vast majority of the population has not yet been able to establish a nation-state. That is a central task of the South African revolution. This is not true of Nicaragua. The Sandinistas do confront the important task of fully integrating the Indian and Black peoples of the Atlantic Coast into the Nicaraguan nation, while guaranteeing them rights to their language and culture. This involves some 110,000 persons out of Nicaragua's total population of 3 million. Nonetheless, the Sandinista revolution begins with a Nicaraguan nation-state. Under the Somoza tyranny all Nicaraguans were citizens of the country, with formal rights to equal protection and treatment under the law. They had the formal right to vote, even though Somoza's elections were rigged.

The Nicaraguan toilers were exploited as workers and peasants, and faced discrimination and oppression on the basis of their class position, political views, and racial origin. But they were not restricted by law in their right to travel, in where they could live, in where they could work, in where they could be after nightfall. Nicaraguan workers were deprived of trade union and other labor rights. But they were not encumbered by a special, permanent legal status that restricted their job mobility and opportunities, their wage levels, and otherwise set them apart from some other legally established layer of the working class. There was no separate estate encompassing the vast majority of the toiling people.

In these ways, Nicaragua under the Somoza regime was a bourgeois republic, although an extremely repressive and undemocratic one, and one exploited by imperialism. The South African regime, however, is not a republic even in this sense. It bears more resemblance to some of the state structures of ancient Greece and Rome, where only a minority of the population had the right to own land, to vote, and to enjoy the other prerogatives of citizenship. The vast majority were slaves or other toilers without citizenship rights.

The land question in Nicaragua was different from that in South Africa, as well. Agricultural production in prerevolutionary Nicaragua combined large-scale capitalist farming, employing wage labor, with a substantial landowning peasantry. A majority of these peasants held tiny plots and could barely survive, but there was also a middle layer of more prosperous peasant producers, as well as a smaller layer of exploiting capitalist peasants. In other words, there was a modern class development and differentiation within the Nicaraguan nation, both in the city and countryside.

In South Africa, on the other hand, the development of modern classes and class relations in the countryside is blocked for the Black majority. Agricultural production by the white minority combines capitalist farms and landholding individual commodity producers, but the vast majority of the population is legally barred from owning land and engaging in agricultural production for the market.

The obstacles to the development of the South African nation are not primarily *precapitalist* survivals, such as the semifeudal relations that characterized the countryside in tsarist Russia, or the extremely undeveloped economic and social relations that still predominate today in numerous other African countries and many of the Pacific islands. The primary obstacles that must be cleared away by the national, democratic revolution in South Africa are the apartheid structures that have been *created* by the white capitalist ruling class.

The Nicaraguan toilers, too, confront many objective material difficulties to carrying through their national, democratic revolution against imperialist domination and its legacy of underdevelopment. But they have not had to clear away obstacles to the creation of a nation and the development of modern class differentiation such as the toilers in South Africa face.

For this reason, when the revolution triumphed in July 1979, an anticapitalist revolution was on the agenda in Nicaragua — albeit a revolution in which democratic and anti-imperialist tasks have predominated throughout the initial period.

The fact that the Nicaraguan workers and peasants have made an anticapitalist revolution, however, does not mean that Nicaragua is today a workers' state, with the dictatorship of the proletariat. It is not. The economic foundations of such a state are state property, the state monopoly of foreign trade, and a substantially planned economy on this base. These do not yet exist in Nicaragua.

The transition from the present workers' and peasants' government to the creation of a workers' state in Nicaragua will take place only through a major deepening of the organization and mobilization of the masses, culminating in a second qualitative turning point in the revolutionary process — the expropriation of the bourgeoisie. Given the low level of development of productive forces in Nicaragua, the relatively small size of the working class, and imperialism's military and economic pressures, the Sandinista leadership has correctly charted a course of avoiding any unnecessarily rapid moves toward that second qualitative turning point. They have done everything in their power to gain the maximum time to advance the consciousness and organization of the workers and peasants to prepare for the decisive challenge of the transition to a workers' state. This includes taking maximum advantage of the international relationship of forces — especially the decisive aid that this has made it possible for Nicaragua to receive from a number of workers' states.

Unlike Nicaragua, before South Africa can have its anticapitalist revolution it has to have its bourgeois-democratic revolution. To miss this qualitative distinction would be to ignore what the apartheid state has placed before the South African masses. It would be to misread the character of the South African revolution in an ultraleft sectarian way. The oppressed South African toilers have to bring a nation into being, guaranteeing universal citizenship rights to all who make up that nation. They have to establish a democratic republic. They have to draw the big majority of the toilers for the first time into commodity production and exchange.

ONLY BY successfully carrying through such a national, democratic revolution can the road be opened to the transition to the socialist revolution in South Africa. The point is not to try to anticipate how long a period that transition will take. The point is to understand South Africa as it really is, the whole of South Africa — the Bantustans as well as the industrial zones and Black townships around Johannesburg, Cape

Town, or Durban; the landless African toilers who want to farm as well as the white-owned capitalist farms; the migratory labor system and prisonlike dormitories as well as the modern gold and diamond mining operations. Only then can we understand the true character of the revolution that is unfolding in South Africa.

The fact that there is a large and increasingly combative working class in South Africa does not place the socialist revolution on the agenda. The weight of the proletariat doesn't determine anything, by itself, about the historic character of the revolution. What it does determine is the place of the working class in the leadership of that revolution. If the working class can forge a fighting alliance with the oppressed rural toilers, and if it charts a course toward the fight for power, not relying on bourgeois liberals, then it will play the decisive leadership role in the bourgeois-democratic revolution in South Africa.

How long will the transition period be between the opening of the democratic revolution and the beginning of the anticapitalist revolution? Nine months? That was Russian time — from the February 1917 revolution that overthrew the tsar, to the Bolshevik-led October revolution that brought to power the soviets of workers', soldiers', and peasants' deputies.

Maybe the period of time between the overthrow of apartheid and the opening of the anticapitalist revolution will be shorter in South Africa. Maybe it will be longer. It is worse than useless to try to make predictions about this.

What is decisive for the proletarian vanguard is not anticipating the timing, but understanding the relationship between the two revolutions. The working class, by allying with the peasants and popular masses, strives to lead the nation-in-becoming to make the democratic revolution in the most thorough and uncompromising way, culminating in the establishment of a nonracial democratic dictatorship of the South African proletariat and peasantry. In doing so, it opens the door to the transition to the socialist revolution. If the proletarian vanguard were to try to leap over that democratic revolution, to get more quickly to the socialist revolution, it would wind up being still further away from it. It has to go *through* the democratic revolution.

Lenin explained this time and again with regard to the revolution against the landlord-capitalist regime in tsarist Russia. "We cannot get out of the bourgeois-democratic boundaries of the Russian revolution," he wrote, "but we can vastly extend these boundaries, and within these boundaries we can and must fight for the interests of the proletariat, for its immediate needs and for conditions that will make it possible to prepare its forces for the future complete victory."[4] By pursuing this course, Lenin emphasized, "we are not putting [the socialist revolution] off, but are taking the first step towards it in the only possible way, along the only correct path, namely, the path of a democratic republic."[5]

What will be the character of the new state power that the democratic revolution will bring to power in South Africa? Will there be a provisional revolutionary government made up of a coalition of forces in which the representatives of the revolutionary workers will have won, or will be striving to win, the leadership? Will there be a kind of dual power? How will the contradictions be resolved between revolutionary democracy and the extreme concentration of wealth in the hands of white capitalist families? We can't predict the answers to these questions, any more than the Bolsheviks could have predicted that the February 1917 revolution would give rise to a power divided between the capitalist Provisional Government, on one side, and the soviets of workers', peasants', and soldiers' representatives, on the other.

What we can do, and what we have to do, is to keep clearly in front of us the goal of a revolutionary democratic dictatorship of the toilers of South Africa. Will the overthrow of the apartheid state lead to the coming to power of such a popular revolutionary government? That will be determined by the relationship of class forces within the revolutionary democratic movement. This movement will be led by the plebeian masses; and the proletarian forces within it will be in the forefront of the fight to overthrow the state, take the power, organize and arm the toiling people, and use the power of the majority to implement the Freedom Charter.

The relationship of forces that exists in South Africa today bodes well for the success of the national, democratic revolution, for carrying it through in the most thoroughgoing manner. And it bodes well for the struggles of the workers and peasants that will be led forward under the new conditions brought about by the downfall of the apartheid state.

## II. THE PLACE OF THE WORKING CLASS AND PEASANTRY IN THE SOUTH AFRICAN REVOLUTION

IN ADDITION to understanding the character of the revolution that is on the agenda, we have to understand the place of the working class and of the peasantry within the leadership of that revolution.

The decisive weight and power of the working class in South Africa determines the kind of leadership that can be built, and must be built, if the revolution is to triumph. It determines what kind of class alliances are possible. It determines the degree of confidence and power with which that leadership can reach out and draw in all those who are willing to act to bring down the apartheid state, while at the same time firmly rejecting reliance on and subordination to the liberal bourgeoisie.

The revolutionary crisis will reach maturity in South Africa because of the irreconcilable clash between the white rulers' dream of apartheid and the struggles of the Black working class that this "dream" has brought into being.

What was the apartheid dream? It sounds mad, to us. It is as though you brought the Confederacy into the twentieth century, added some Nazi theoreticians, sociologists, and urban planners, gave them some of the richest land and natural resources on earth, offered them the backing of the mightiest imperialist powers, and told them, "Go ahead, set up a society according to your dream."

Their dream was to keep the overwhelming majority of the population, the African people, from being part of the urban centers. Their plan was not only to prevent the development of a nation through a divide-and-rule strategy, including the establishment of the fake "national homelands," the Bantustans. It was not only to rob Africans of the land and therefore leave them no way to survive except by selling the only thing they couldn't be robbed of, their labor power. It was not only to drive down the value of that labor power by institutionalizing oppression at every level and in every sphere of life. It was not only to maintain all of this by excluding Africans from every civil right and every aspect of political life.

The dream was to do all of this — *and* keep the Africans out of the cities. The dream was that Africans would somehow come into the cities in the morning, cook the breakfast, change the diapers, do the laundry, labor in the factories and offices, produce all the wealth — and disappear by sundown.

That is what the architects of apartheid have tried to bring about, with violence and terror and elaborate legal structures and codes to enforce it. The goal was to build a state of the tiny white minority to enforce apartheid — through which the white owners of the land, the mineral resources, and factories would grow rich — while keeping the urban centers of wealth and capitalist culture the sole preserve of whites.

This may sound absurd. But it wasn't, given the logic of the dream. The National Party rulers of South Africa had no doubts about the problems of moving in the other direction: allowing all South Africans freedom of movement, the right to farm and to own homes, the right to vote, and the right to organize and fight for freedom.

But the dream has backfired. It has brought into being the very thing it was trying to prevent. To produce the wealth, the white rulers have had to create a labor force, a working class with a set of skills, with some continuity, with a measure of stability and growth. It has created more than 8 million Black workers, comprising more than 80 percent of the work force.

As this class was forged, the rulers had to devise more and more complex rules and regulations to limit its power, to try to keep it from bringing its growing economic leverage and social weight to bear. The apartheid bourgeoisie has evolved the most elaborate and extensive system of labor control seen on earth. They created the migratory labor system, forcing millions of Black workers to move constantly back and forth between the Bantustans and the "white" cities, without citizenship rights. These workers are at the mercy of the employers and the apartheid state authorities even for permission to stay overnight in the cities. Millions are denied the right to have their families live with them where they work. Mandatory registration with state labor bureaus, computer controls of labor supplies, enforced migration and relocation — the dream is a genuine nightmare.

Apartheid has created millions of "illegal aliens" in their own land. This is another way that we can relate an aspect of the apartheid system to the struggles of working people in the United States. We know how the "illegal alien" scheme works in this country. The ruling class is not trying to prevent more undocumented workers from joining the labor force. No capitalist class has ever been concerned about too many workers competing with each other to sell their labor power. Rather, the purpose of keeping the threat of victimization hanging over undocumented workers — both here and in South Africa — is to keep them in a pariah status in order to drive down the historically determined, or "moral," part of the value of their labor power. This gets internalized by individuals, and by the class as a whole, so that those who are "illegal" *expect* to get paid less, and *tolerate* getting paid less.

The Black proletariat of South Africa is fighting to become what Frederick Engels called "free outlaws" — workers who, having been robbed of their land and tools, have at the same time been liberated from all traditional fetters. Today, Black workers in South Africa are "unfree outlaws." They do not have the freedom that comes with the proletarian condition in most capitalist countries, even very repressive ones. The Black workers in South Africa today are demanding to be free to sell their labor power to the highest bidder, free to travel, free to live and work wherever they want.

The great proletarianization and urbanization of the Black population, the gigantic concentrations of capital and consequently of labor, have undermined the apartheid system itself. They are bringing the dream to an end.

### Organization of Black workers

OUT OF the experiences and struggles that this working class is going through, it has increasingly moved toward the leadership of the fight to overthrow the white supremacist state.

When the coal miners in Britain went on strike last year, one of the first contributions of money to their union came from the miners' union in South Africa. That tells us something about the level of consciousness of the Black proletariat in South Africa. It tells us something about the development of the labor movement there, despite all the obstacles, distortions, and special problems that apartheid imposes, including segregated unions and dual union structures.

In the last decade, Black-led and -organized legal and semilegal unions have won the right to exist. They take the legal openings the apartheid rulers have been compelled to give them, and they try to take another inch of legality. Since 1976, unionization of Black workers has exploded, from a few tens of thousands to more than half a million today. Unionization drives and strike actions have become the major new area of organization, education, and combat experience of the working class, increasing its confidence and cohesiveness.

Of course, the unions are not, and cannot be, political formations to organize the vanguard of the revolutionary democratic struggle. They are striving to become genuine trade union organizations of the working class as a whole. Their goal is to unite all the workers in each industry, not just the most conscious workers. Their aim is not to become revolutionary vanguard parties, but to strengthen themselves *as unions*, by defending the interests of the working class, by broadening their capacity to think socially and act politically.

The apartheid plan is not just to keep Blacks separated from whites. It is also to keep the Africans divided among themselves — the Xhosa divided from the Zulu, the Zulu from the Sotho, the Sotho from the Tswana — and to keep the Africans divided from the Indians and from the Coloureds.

The apartheid regime has extended some privileges to Indians and to Coloureds, relative to the Africans. It has gone to extreme lengths to divide Africans along lines of language differences, regional differences, and differences in tribal origins. It has bought off African collaborators who accept positions as part of the apartheid state structures. And it has developed networks of informers, an indispensable weapon for the kind of repressive regime apartheid has wrought.

But the development of the working class has helped to cut through all these divisions. It has brought African workers from different backgrounds into the same unions, the same industries, even sometimes the same plants — all suffering the same racist oppression, all forced into the same "estate." It has brought them into greater day-to-day contact with Coloured and Indian workers. In the course of the class struggles by these workers to defend their common interests, the differences have more and more given way to new and common ground.

## Workers and land rights

We also have to look at another side of the development of the working class. The African population has been proletarianized in the classical sense of the word, which is not identical to being turned into industrial workers. Their land, both family holdings and common lands, their cattle, their tools have been robbed from them. They have been expropriated. They have, to a large extent, been driven from the land.

One of the goals of the South African revolution is the "deproletarianization" of a part of this class, in the sense of winning the right to become property-holding farmers. The conquest of the right of all Blacks to toil on the land and produce cash crops is one of the central tasks of this revolution.

Thus from this angle we also come back to the national, democratic character of the revolution. A task of the alliance of workers and peasants in South Africa is to conquer the right of proletarians who want to be farmers, to become farmers. This can be conquered only through the revolutionary overthrow of the imperialist state. It is a concrete combination of tasks that the architects of apartheid have placed before the toilers of South Africa.

As the working class as a class has moved more into the leadership of the freedom struggle in South Africa, the place of women in the struggle has assumed greater importance. The confidence and explosive combativity of the youth has increased as they absorb the lessons of their experiences and keep fighting their way toward the working-class movement.

## Revolutionary democratic dictatorship of the toilers

THE PROLETARIAN vanguard of the revolutionary democratic movement in South Africa is fighting for the majority to come to power. It is fighting for a revolutionary dictatorship of that majority, to enforce and protect majority rule. It will mobilize the power of that majority to break all resistance of the old order and reorganize South African society. It will disarm the old state power, and it will raze to the ground all the old state structures. It will create the conditions in which human beings can break free of and advance beyond what the old structures forced them to be. It will make possible the development of the South African nation, opening the door to progressive class differentiation, allowing some to farm, some to become professionals, some to become retailers, and others to be wage workers — *all regardless of race*.

This is a genuinely revolutionary perspective. It draws together the democratic struggle to establish the South African nation, to open the land, to win the battle for one person, one vote. It points toward conquering these goals and defending them by any means necessary. It recognizes that no section of the bourgeoisie will grant these demands, let alone lead a struggle for them. A fighting alliance of workers and rural producers is the key to victory.

This revolutionary perspective rejects the liberal myth that the apartheid state can be reformed out of existence. It rejects the course of conciliation and compromise with the apartheid rulers. It rejects the course of relying on, or being led by, the liberal bourgeoisie. It is the perspective of working people, the popular masses, taking political power.

We shouldn't be surprised to see the fight for a revolutionary democratic dictatorship of the toilers, of the proletariat and peasantry, unfold in South Africa. It is not the first imperialist country where the revolutionary workers' vanguard tried to find ways of concretizing this goal. The Bolsheviks did it in tsarist Russia, the weakest link in the imperialist chain at the beginning of the century. They carried out a revolution whose victory has shaped world history ever since.

That is precisely what is going on in South Africa today. The goal of the vanguard of the proletariat is to forge the alliance of the toilers, an alliance that can take political power and will *use* the power of the majority to move forward and conquer every social, political, and economic goal of the people. The Black toilers of South Africa are not fighting to set up a new state based on exploitation and oppression, changing only the color of the skin of the ruling class. That is not the goal of this national, democratic revolution in South Africa, nor could it be.

### III. VANGUARD ROLE OF THE
### AFRICAN NATIONAL CONGRESS

THE SOCIALIST Workers Party recognizes that the African National Congress is the vanguard of the democratic revolution in South Africa. The ANC has conquered this position in struggle.

As a revolutionary struggle deepens, and the leadership evolves, one or another organization among those competing for leadership always establishes itself not merely as one of the vanguard groups, but as *the* vanguard. The ANC has done this.

Recognizing this fact does not mean that there are no longer divisions, weaknesses, and other problems that the ANC itself has yet to overcome. It does not mean that there will be no further evolution as the struggle develops. Neither is it the case that there are no other revolutionary organizations, or that we support only struggles led by supporters of the ANC. It simply expresses the reality that out of the revolutionary democratic struggle in South Africa, a democratic vanguard recognized by the vast majority of anti-apartheid fighters has been forged and is today increasingly organized within the ANC.

At a certain stage in Cuba the July 26 Movement became the leadership of the Cuban revolution. It wasn't just that the July 26 Movement was better known than other groups, or that it had a more elaborate public relations operation, as its opponents claimed. It became the organization that was leading the revolution. It won the vanguard position in the struggle. Every revolutionary in Cuba had to act accordingly. Every revolutionary current outside Cuba had to recognize that reality as well, and likewise act accordingly.

This didn't mean that there were no other revolutionary organizations in Cuba. There was at least one other, the Revolutionary Directorate. There was also the Stalinist party, the Popular Socialist Party, which presented itself as a revolutionary organization. The political approach of the July 26 Movement to other organizations that were revolutionary, or that claimed to be, was always one of the great strengths of the Castro leadership. It was a model from that point of view. This was true before the launching of the guerrilla war, and continued down through the revolutionary conquest of power and afterwards. The leadership of the July 26 Movement always worked systematically to draw into the leadership of the revolution all those who could be won to it. As it turned out, the fusion of the July 26 Movement with the PSP and the Revolutionary Directorate in the early 1960s was a decisive step for the revolution. But this fusion — initiated, led, and driven through by the July 26 Movement — merely confirmed that the July 26 Movement had indeed won the right to lead the Cuban workers and peasants in the revolution.

A moment came when that was also true for the National Liberation Front (FLN) in Algeria. The SWP took note of it and acted accordingly. There were differences of opinion over that conclusion at the time in the SWP leadership, and we had quite a debate about it.

There came a time in the Angolan war of independence from Portugal when the People's Movement for the Liberation of Angola (MPLA) emerged as the political vanguard of the struggle. The same became true for the Sandinista National Liberation Front in Nicaragua. In the case of both Angola and Nicaragua, we in the SWP were late in recognizing the reality of the leadership that had been forged in the course of the revolutionary struggle, and we have learned some important lessons as a result.

The ANC has won the leadership of the democratic revolution in South Africa. The Black masses look to the ANC to lead the South African revolution. The Freedom Charter has become the recognized platform of the revolutionary anti-apartheid struggle. That is what has been conquered. And this will remain true unless something changes in the struggle itself.

T HE ANC has earned the right to address the people of the world in the name of the freedom struggle in South Africa. It has earned the right to speak for South Africa at the United Nations. It has earned the right to be recognized by vanguard formations in every country as the leadership of the South African revolution. And that is what all people around the world who support the fight for a democratic South Africa must take into account.

We can give ourselves more time to become familiar with the history of the South African struggle before we seek to agree at what point over the past decades the ANC won this position. What we propose to settle on here is that this is unquestionably the case today. That is our judgment. That is how the SWP has been acting, and how we will continue to act.

There has been a long evolution of the struggle in South Africa. The ANC has changed over the decades, as the class structure and relationship of forces has shifted in South Africa. There has been a political evolution, an evolution of class orientation. There has been an evolution as younger generations have come forward. Part of this has been a very important development of the ANC's relations with vanguard communist forces around the world — from Cuba and Grenada to Vietnam and Kampuchea.

At the same time there has been an evolution, in a different direction, of currents opposed to the ANC. The biggest of these for some time was the Pan Africanist Congress (PAC), established in 1959 by a grouping that split from the ANC.

The PAC maintained a significant following inside South Africa in the 1960s, and played a major role in protest actions against apartheid. But it was marked from the beginning by anticommunist and anti–working class positions. We have already seen that the PAC founders strenuously objected to the Freedom Charter's perspective of a nonracial South African democratic republic, with equal rights for all, Black and white, who will live and work there. They counterposed to this an "Africans-only" perspective. They rejected collaboration with white revolutionaries, and with other South African whites who could be won to support the revolutionary democratic goals of the anti-apartheid struggle.

Prior to their split from the ANC, the PAC founders engaged in red-baiting of their opponents in the organization, denouncing those ANC leaders as communists. Some condemned the Freedom Charter as a document inspired by Moscow.

Today, the PAC has little or no following inside South Africa. It has undergone bitter internal splits, and exists almost entirely in exile. But this doesn't prevent its representatives from trying to speak in the name of the South African revolution on platforms across the United States.

There has also been an evolution among those who were part of the Black Consciousness movement and of the mass student struggles of the mid- and late 1970s. Many leaders and cadres have joined the ANC. The ANC has responded by working to integrate them into all aspects of its work and levels of its leadership.

Other leaders of the Black Consciousness Movement have formed the Azanian People's Organisation (Azapo) in opposition to the ANC. Azapo is the main initiating force of a grouping called the National Forum Committee. Azapo and the National Forum Committee condemn the ANC's policy of seeking alliances with white opponents of apartheid. And, from their ultraleft standpoint, they criticize the Freedom Charter for not raising socialist demands.

There have also been some splits from the ANC over the past fifteen years. There was a split in the early 1970s by a nationalist wing that sought to present itself in public as "ANC (African Nationalist)." There was a more recent split by an ultraleft wing that actually set up shop for a while as "The Marxist Tendency Within the ANC." Some things are the same the world over!

ANC leaders have fought, studied, and incorporated lessons from revolutionary experiences in other countries. Their political evolution has been part of an international evolution, through which a layer of revolutionary leaders on a world scale have come to understand the difference between the Pol Pots, Bernard Coards, Salvador Cayetano Carpios, and Aníbal Escalantes, on the one hand; and the Fidel Castros and Raúl Castros, the Maurice Bishops, and themselves, on the other.

There has been an evolution in understanding of the role of guerrilla warfare since ANC leaders took the initiative in 1961 to form the armed organization, Umkhonto we Sizwe (Spear of the Nation). Through their experiences, they have come to a clearer understanding of how to advance armed struggle as part of an orientation to the mass movement, to the labor movement, and to the urban areas, and how arming of the people will grow out of the determination of the masses to organize to defend themselves against the violence of the apartheid state.

The ANC has based itself on the workers and rural toilers as the only way to lead the national, democratic revolution to overthrow the apartheid state — a struggle that will be led by the working people or it will not succeed.

At the same time, it has also developed experience in building alliances with liberals in the churches and professional organizations.

There is a qualitative difference between seeking such alliances to compensate for weakness or to pursue a course of conciliation, and making such alliances from a position of strength built on the mass movement in order to advance a revolutionary course. The power of the mass movement of the toilers against apartheid gives the ANC leadership the confidence to encourage auxiliary organizations in which white as well as Black liberal forces can be successfully incorporated, even with all the problems and complications that accompany such a step forward.

The fact that some Black church leaders and white liberals in South Africa are supporting the fight is not something to fear. It is an indication that the victory of the revolution is nearer. When some bourgeois and middle-class liberals in Nicaragua began linking up with the struggle led by the Sandinistas, that wasn't a sign that the Sandinistas were giving up the revolutionary battle to overthrow Somoza. It was a sign that the triumph was closer. The same thing was true in Cuba leading up to the overthrow of Batista.

The point is not to put a time frame on the overthrow of the apartheid state. To the contrary. We are not on the eve of that historic event, and we don't know how soon it will be accomplished. The point is that there is a difference between a political leadership that bends or capitulates to liberalism, and a leadership that acts to draw toward the movement, through many forms, those of any race, of any class, who will support *in action* the revolutionary struggle.

Only a self-confident leadership can do this. Only a vanguard that is capable of forging a multinational leadership can, with complete confidence, accomplish this. The recent decision to open up ANC membership and leadership bodies to individuals of all races who are engaged in the struggle against apartheid registers an important gain for the ANC. This decision was taken at the national consultative conference of the ANC held in Lusaka in June 1985. The conference decided to expand the National Executive Committee from twenty-two to thirty members. There are now two Coloured members, two Asians, and one white on the NEC.

Throughout most of its history the ANC has forged alliances with organizations of Coloureds and Indians, as well as organizations of whites, who supported the struggle. The ANC itself, however, was an organization of Africans until the 1960s, when it began accepting Coloureds, Indians, and whites as members of ANC groups in exile. Membership in the underground organization inside South Africa and on all leadership bodies was still restricted to Africans only.

Now those restrictions have been removed, as well. These changes reflect the fact that the most politically conscious Africans, Coloureds, and Indians have come to see themselves as part of a common South African nation-in-becoming. While recognizing that the 24 million Africans are and must be the backbone of the struggle for liberation, the ANC is now seeking to build itself as a vanguard that reflects, in its membership and its leadership, the composition of the oppressed and of all those willing to fight uncompromisingly for the overthrow of apartheid.

## IV. THE SOUTH AFRICAN REVOLUTION
## IN WORLD POLITICS

**W**HEN WE look at the relationship of the South African revolution to the worldwide struggle against imperialism, what strikes us immediately is that a new ally of the Nicaraguan revolution, a new ally of Cuba, a new ally of the Salvadoran liberation fighters, has entered the battle. A new ally of the revolution in Central America and the Caribbean has marched with huge strides onto the field.

The South African revolution forces the Yankee enemies of humanity to divide their attention and resources. It deepens the tactical divisions in the U.S. ruling class over what course to take, and it decreases the options they have. It makes the Reagan administration pay a higher price for its most outrageous racist acts and statements.

We should always remember what the Cuban leaders have explained time and again about the role of the Vietnamese revolution in securing a breathing space for the Cuban revolution. Without the Vietnamese revolution, the Cubans remind the peoples of the world, the Cuban revolution might well have been overturned by Washington in the 1960s.

There is also a more direct connection between Cuba and the South African revolution. Cuban volunteers fought side by side with the Angolan army to push back the South African invasion of Angola in 1975-76. That military disaster for the South African imperialists encouraged and inspired renewed combativity among the youth of Soweto in 1976. It gave an impetus to the revolutionary movement inside South Africa. The apartheid state was not invincible!

A substantial number of governments spoke out against South Africa's naked aggression against Angola. But it was *Cuba* that responded to the Angolan government's appeal for aid and rushed combat units to fight against the invasion of the apartheid army. And for a decade since, the Cuban internationalist volunteers have remained at their battle stations in response to Angola's request. Despite all of Washington's pressure and threats, the Cuban government has refused to retreat from its internationalist aid to Angola. These facts have burned themselves into the consciousness of the Black revolutionaries of South Africa, Namibia, Angola, and of the toilers throughout Africa.

The connections of the South African revolution to the rest of the African continent are immediately felt both by the workers and peasants of Africa and by the imperialists. The South African state is the imperialist power whose particular role it is to help guarantee the continued subjugation of all of southern Africa to world imperialism. The prospect of the weakening, if not toppling, of that state has immense ramifications for the exploiters all the way from Washington to Paris and Tokyo.

The advance of the revolution in South Africa will also have an impact in Vietnam, helping it find a little more room to maneuver in face of the unrelenting pressure of U.S. imperialism. It will strengthen the Palestinian people's fight for national liberation against the Israeli state, which functions as an ally of the apartheid regime.

**Proletarian leadership**

The national, democratic struggle unfolding in South Africa is also decisive for the forging of a communist leadership there. The ANC is not a communist organization, and it does not strive to become one. It is a revolutionary democratic organization, the political vanguard of the national, democratic revolution in South Africa.

Out of the revolutionary struggle that is being led by the ANC, however, a growing South African communist vanguard will be forged and tested. This will occur as younger forces come forward in this struggle, as more and more leaders emerge from the ranks of the working class. And with this strengthening of a communist leadership in South Africa will come a strengthening of its convergence with communist forces on a world scale.

The advance of the South African revolution and its leadership marks a further objective shift in what is possible and what is necessary in the construction of a vanguard of the world revolution. It registers yet another step away from what Lenin — pointing to the bankrupt Second International — referred to as an International of the white race. It moves another step toward the kind of truly *world* revolutionary leadership that the Communist International sought to build in Lenin's time. And that has an important impact on the decisive question of building communist leaderships in every country where the construction of a multinational proletarian combat party is essential — from Brazil to Canada, from New Zealand to Britain, and of course, here in the United States.

The advance of the South African revolution will have an impact on the communist movement throughout the world. It is an opportunity for the vanguard communist forces in Eastern Europe to advance working-class consciousness by placing proletarian internationalism at the center of their program, and to find new opportunities to link up with workers and farmers on other fronts of the world revolution.

The revolutionary struggle in South Africa also opens up new opportunities for class-struggle militants around the world to absorb important political lessons. It helps the communist vanguard get rid of ultraleft sectarianism, which is a real problem in the imperialist countries especially, and which our movement is afflicted with.

Everywhere that workers are fighting for their own rights, they will be attracted to the freedom battle that is being waged today by the toilers in South Africa. British miners, Texas oil workers, New York garment workers, Toronto electricians, Bolivian tin miners, Brazilian auto workers, Bangkok textile workers — all are being encouraged by this revolution. Peasants struggling for land and freedom from the Philippines to Guatemala, farmers fighting debt bondage from the United States to Japan — all are being inspired by the struggle to overthrow the apartheid regime.

The struggle against apartheid deals a blow to every reactionary, and to every reactionary prejudice. Even his Holiness, who was recently in Africa, had to go so far as to humbly apologize for Christendom's role in the organization of the world trade in chattel slaves. Better late then never.

## Response in the United States

THE DEEPENING of the South African revolution, and what it opens up in the United States, is of immense aid to the SWP in advancing the construction of a multinational communist leadership of the working class. This historic task is completely interconnected with our response to the South African revolution.

There are virtually no limits on the breadth and depth of the support in this country for this democratic struggle of the South African people. We must put out of our thinking any idea that there are restrictions on what opponents of apartheid can do. We should think about what it means to pick up the newspaper this week and read about U.S. senators organizing their colleagues to raise money to rebuild Winnie Mandela's home, after it was firebombed by the racists. A bipartisan group of capitalist politicians is raising money to rebuild the home of the family the apartheid regime has branded as terrorists and communists! That's not a problem. Not for us. Not for Winnie Mandela. It is an opportunity.

The doors are wide open in the unions to help organize action against the apartheid regime. Given the current stage of politics in the United States, class-conscious workers cannot open doors on their own in the labor movement. The doors have to be opened by much more powerful forces — such as the impact of the revolutionary struggle in South Africa. But when these doors are opened, class-conscious workers can and must go through them. And once that happens, it gets that much harder for the class-collaborationist misleaders of the labor movement to close the door completely.

The developments in South Africa are having a profound impact on the working class in this country. Many union members, many working people of all kinds, are coming to the conclusion that they have to stand up and say "No" to apartheid. They have to do it out of basic human solidarity. They have to do it for themselves and their fellow workers. Most went along, not paying much attention to things in South Africa — that is a fact for most workers. But now the time has come. The struggle has been forced to our attention. The apartheid state has to be brought crashing down.

The Black masses of South Africa have won the right to freedom. The Black working people of Africa have taken this right. Nobody has a right just because they are oppressed. They may have a moral cause, but to win that right, to earn it, it has to be fought for. The South African people are winning the right to freedom — and workers in the United States, like everywhere else, have an obligation to fight alongside our South African brothers and sisters to bring down the slavocracy of our day and age.

Working people in this country, Black and white, see this revolution through the eyes of our own struggles, and correctly so. The South African revolution is a We Shall Overcome revolution. It is a Freedom Now revolution. One with enormous stakes. It will take a real Civil War to win, too. There happens to be a relationship of class forces and a history that makes it possible in South Africa for a leadership of the Malcolm X kind to become the vanguard of that revolution: a leadership that is proletarian, that understands the need to be internationalist, and that is committed to bringing down the apartheid state by any means necessary.

## Labor and the fight against apartheid

Union activists in the free South Africa movement don't need to be preoccupied with the motives of labor officials who are forced to march on a demonstration for a free South Africa. We don't care what their motives are. Some of them just wish every Black person would sit down and be quiet — in South Africa, and in their union, too. So what? Some of them simply hope — as do the liberal capitalist politicians they look to — that some reforms will enable the South African regime to find a way to put the lid back on the whole thing.

But we have to differentiate between what they want and what the current relationship of forces dictates that they can be convinced to *do* to aid the South African freedom struggle. That is what has changed, and that is what is decisive for workers who support the South African revolution.

When union officials say something that helps the fight for a free South Africa, union activists should quote them. Report it in local union meetings. Propose that South African trade unionists and ANC spokespeople be brought before a union meeting to explain their struggle, or that a movie or videotape on the anti-apartheid struggle be shown. Help get a motion adopted to endorse a protest action. Propose that the union allot some money to help build the movement, and provide office space and telephones. Build a union contingent in demonstrations.

Union opponents of apartheid have got to have the courage of their convictions and walk through those doors that are being opened in the labor movement today. There is virtually nothing around South Africa that can't be done right now through the unions. There is nothing that opponents of apartheid can't propose, can't urge others to do, or can't involve others in carrying through.

The whole movement is taking place under a simple banner: Release Nelson Mandela now! Freedom in South Africa, not slavery! Dismantle apartheid! One person, one vote! Free South Africa! These and variations on them will be the slogans of the movement, and rightly so. It is a political struggle, a struggle for political power.

## Break all U.S. ties!

**W**ITHIN THIS movement, we must do everything we can to stress the centrality of demands aimed at Washington. This is our obligation to the South African revolution. Above all, anti-apartheid fighters in this country have to keep the pressure on for one goal: a total boycott, a total break with South Africa. For an immediate halt to all economic, diplomatic, cultural, sporting, and military ties of any kind with the apartheid state!

Pretoria has become the outlaw regime of the world. It is a blot on the human race. It is the enemy of the most elementary rights of human beings. It is the modern-day Confederacy combined with the latter-day fascist state. It must be boycotted by everyone. Any government claiming the right to speak for its people should break all ties immediately.

Not only are the South African rulers who put together the apartheid regime having a hard time trying to reform apartheid. The U.S. rulers, the enemy of humanity, are also having a hard time, as they try to disentangle themselves from their South African counterparts. Their fortunes are intertwined.

It will take a gigantic struggle and mobilization in this country to force a break by the U.S. rulers with the apartheid regime. But the tactical divisions are already visible. The deepening of the struggle in South Africa will further widen them, as will the mobilization of those in this country determined to take action against apartheid.

### Free Nelson Mandela!

SOMETIMES A single human being, an individual, can represent a great deal. That is what is involved in the demand to free Nelson Mandela. It is a simple, clear, human demand. Free this man, who has given his life to the struggle for a democratic land for all who live in South Africa! Stop attacking his home! Let him go! And lift the ban on Winnie Mandela! Let her speak freely!

Our goal, as Marx explained to the International Working Men's Association, is to take the moral high ground, to set an example for the entire working class. Our goal is to lead the workers' movement to take this high ground and lead all of humanity in this struggle.

One of the obstacles to doing this is the sectarian tic of thinking that our contribution to this struggle is to explain that if the revolution really gets rolling in South Africa, then a lot of capitalist property is going to be taken over and we will all be fighting for socialism. No. Let the right-wingers and friends of apartheid in Washington keep trying to make that the issue. Let them try to shift the ground away from the democratic struggle to overturn apartheid.

Sometimes we can give our fellow workers the impression that we socialists only get really excited and committed to a struggle if it is for socialism, and that we just don't throw our full weight into a fight for democracy. That's wrong. That's not a communist approach, it's a sectarian approach. And it's an approach that will prevent a communist party from being built. What we are concerned about in South Africa today is the political fight to overthrow the apartheid state. Only that will make it possible for the fight for socialism in South Africa to be placed on the agenda.

We've got to get out of our heads any idea that this is "only" a democratic revolution. That "our role" flowers when the "real" revolution, the proletarian socialist revolution, begins. No. *This is our revolution.* This is the revolution of the working people of South Africa. No other force will lead it, will carry it through in a thoroughgoing and revolutionary way to advance the interests of the toiling majority. This is the revolution that communist workers everywhere should do everything in their power to aid, advance, solidarize with, and learn from.

### The truth, the facts about apartheid and the revolution

Our press can take the lead in bringing the truth about the white supremacist state to U.S. working people. Workers and farmers in this country need the basic facts to arm themselves for the fight to demand the U.S. goverment break all ties with apartheid. We have got to cut through the lies and coverups in the imperialist press.

Tell the truth about the denial of the right of Black people to own land.

Tell the truth about the pass laws.

Tell the truth about the Bantustans, the labor control schemes, the violence and terror that is inflicted every day on those who are fighting for freedom.

Tell the truth about the meaning of the fight for equal voting rights.

Tell the truth about the Freedom Charter, taking each of its planks and explaining what is involved.

Tell the truth about the denial of elementary trade union rights.

Tell the truth about the heroic fight of the youth, the schoolchildren who have shown their parents the way forward.

Tell the truth about the struggles of women in South Africa.

And never fail to tell the truth about the role of Cuba in coming to the aid of Angola, helping to defeat the imperialist army of South Africa in the field, and striking a blow for freedom of all of Africa in the process.

We have got to do all of this in clear language, with basic information. Our most important audience is our fellow workers, and others who are just coming into action around this question. Our concentration should not be on convincing radicals that they should support this revolution. That's not our problem.

We want our co-workers to look to the *Militant* and *Perspectiva Mundial* as regular sources of facts, of clear answers, of concrete explanations of every aspect of apartheid and the struggle against it. We've got to remember not to impose our consciousness on U.S. working people.

We must not think, for example, that workers and farmers understand the scam about "Black-on-Black" violence in South Africa. The rulers are trying very hard, and with some success, to convince millions of people in the United States that South African Blacks are a violence-ridden, tribal, backward people, and that whatever the problems may be with apartheid, Blacks will be slitting each other's throats by the millions if white rule is ended there. White liberals and middle-class people of all races — even those who find apartheid repugnant, and who can be won to support the struggle against it — are particularly susceptible to this specter of bloodshed and mayhem in the wake of apartheid's fall.

This scare campaign has an effect because, among other reasons, it taps a racist root in this country. It is our responsibility to take it seriously, to keep giving the answers, week after week, clearly and not agitationally. With facts. We should take an aspect of it and explain it each week. The truth about the killings over the last eleven months, over the last eleven weeks. Who has been killed, and by whom. We must untangle for the workers the deliberate confusion the reporters for the capitalist papers create. They say that when some cop who is Black tries to shoot you, and you shoot first, that is part of "Black-on-Black" crime.

We'll have to deal with the divisions and clashes among the different components of the Black population, divisions that the apartheid rulers try to use to maintain their rule. We must explain that the ANC is trying to lead the people to end this violence, end the murder, and establish a democratic South Africa. The ANC is waging a political battle against Bantustan official Chief Gatsha Buthelezi and his goon squads, who carry out attacks against Blacks, while collaborating with and apologizing for the apartheid regime.

We have to explain why Black informers for the apartheid regime are so hated by South African freedom fighters — and justly so. We have to explain how the apartheid regime, like all oppressive regimes both today and throughout history, has used informers not only to disrupt struggles of the oppressed, but to set up freedom fighters for imprisonment, torture, and murder at the hands of the authorities and extralegal terror squads.

It would be an error to underestimate the impact that the ruling class is having with this campaign around "Black-on-Black" violence in South Africa. It is one of the rulers' most effective propaganda weapons, and they wield it over and over again.

Answering this goes hand in hand with explaining the fight by Black South Africans to establish a democratic republic. It is part of finding popular ways to explain the content of the democratic dictatorship of the toilers that the South African revolutionary democratic movement is fighting to bring to power.

We must also not take for granted that our co-workers and others in this country understand why South African Blacks will benefit from a *total, unconditional* break of all U.S. economic, political, cultural, and other ties with the apartheid regime. The apologists for apartheid both in South Africa and in the United States crank out sophisticated arguments to try to convince U.S. working people that the Black majority would suffer from such a boycott — that it would cost them their jobs, that U.S. companies can set a "good example" of equal and fair treatment, and so on.

We need to take these arguments head on, and clearly explain why they are wrong. We have to explain that a total boycott of the apartheid regime is the demand of the leading anti-apartheid organizations in

South Africa, and that it represents the aspiration of the big majority of South African Blacks. We have to explain that the true interests of the Black population are advanced by each and every measure that weakens the South African apartheid state and brings closer its overthrow.

What we can accomplish by answering these questions will affect more than just those whom we can influence directly. Other forces in this country and worldwide — activists in the movement for a free South Africa, allies in the labor movement — will watch our press on this. They will see how we talk, the tone, our command of the facts. It will set an example and point the way for others.

Any windbag can denounce apartheid. But it takes hard work to dig out the facts, disentangle the ruling-class lies, and — week after week — present the case against the apartheid regime clearly and convincingly to workers, farmers, and young people in this country.

Part of this job involves shattering the myth of the invincibility of the South African apartheid state — the belief deep down that the struggle that is unfolding today won't be able to do what it set out to do.

The South African apartheid state is not invincible. The Cuban and Angolan troops who beat back the South African invasion in 1975-76 proved that the army of apartheid can be defeated. The Black South Africans who are fighting to bring down apartheid are proving, more and more each day, that this hated state is not invincible. They can win, and they will win.

Confidence in the revolution, confidence in the capacity of the toiling people of South Africa, confidence in the leadership of the class that is developing — this should set the tone for all supporters of the fight against the apartheid regime. People will come into action because they become convinced that it is a fight whose time has come. Yes, it can win. Yes, it will be victorious. Yes, it's right for me to support this struggle and become part of it.

# Summary of Discussion

**A**T THE beginning of the lunch break, Comrade Charles Aubin, who is here as a representative of the Bureau of the United Secretariat of the Fourth International, asked that I take some time during this summary to present my evaluation of the line on South Africa that has been carried in *International Viewpoint* [a magazine edited in Paris by the Bureau of the United Secretariat]. I told Comrade Aubin that I would take a look at some of the recent major articles in *International Viewpoint* and present some initial opinions. This assessment can't be complete, of course, since it was pulled together on short notice.

The purpose of this report to the National Committee was to outline the Political Committee's view on a number of the central questions of the South African revolution. We presented our position without polemicizing against alternative positions that have been put forward. We didn't try to prepare such a report, and we won't be voting on this part of the summary. But we will make sure that all the comrades here have copies of all the articles I am going to quote from, so that we all can take time to read through them over the next few weeks.

I'll start with one recent feature article in the June 3, 1985, issue of *International Viewpoint*. The article, appearing under the name Ndabeni, describes what it calls a sharpening rivalry between the United Democratic Front and the National Forum. The National Forum includes the Azanian People's Organisation (Azapo) and the Cape Action League, which consider themselves to be competitors of the ANC for the leadership of the anti-apartheid struggle.

This *International Viewpoint* article notes that both the UDF and the National Forum participated in the campaign against the elections to the apartheid legislatures held in August 1984. But, the article complains, "the UDF publicity machine was the more effective and they hogged most of the credit. Members of the Cape Action League and Azapo, affiliates of NF, who clashed with the police during the anti-election campaign, were particularly annoyed to read in the newspapers next morning or to see on the television screens that they were UDF."

**W**HAT WE see here is an effort by *International Viewpoint* to explain away the fact that the ANC and the UDF — not the National Forum — have the greatest following in the mass movement. This is consistent with other recent *International Viewpoint* articles, which seek to present the National Forum and the UDF as more or less equal competitors for the leadership of the struggle, with the National Forum having a better line and the UDF often on the verge of selling out. This is inaccurate on several counts.

The ANC has established itself as the vanguard of the broad leadership of the struggle against apartheid. This is reflected in, among other things, its ability to forge an alliance with the other forces that have rallied to the banner of the UDF. *International Viewpoint* must be the only serious publication in the world that argues that the mass support for the UDF and ANC — qualitatively greater than for the National Forum — is the result of public relations and connections with the bourgeois press.

Articles complaining that the UDF is "hogging the credit" make *International Viewpoint* seem not only sectarian, but also an unreliable source of information about South Africa.

The June 3 article then goes on to repeat violence-baiting slanders against the UDF. It claims, "It would appear from available evidence that most of the provocation [that is, physical conflicts between supporters of the UDF and supporters of the National Forum] has come from UDF who seem determined to establish itself as the only legitimate anti-apartheid organisation in the country. There have been physical attacks, not only on Azapo but also against members of FOSATU [the Federation of South African Trade Unions] and other unions."

But *International Viewpoint* offers not a hint of what this "available evidence" is, or where it comes from. This is absolutely unconvincing to anyone who does not already believe that the ANC is an obstacle to the advance of the South African revolution. We have never seen one piece of evidence for this accusation.

*International Viewpoint*'s hostile stance toward the ANC and UDF continued in the July 15, 1985, issue. An article under the name Peter Blumer takes up what it sees as a big problem represented by the involvement of religious figures and church organizations in the United Democratic Front. Under the subhead, "The moderates' game," the article talks about the divisions within the South African ruling class and among their imperialist allies over "what means to use to avoid a revolutionary explosion in South Africa.

"What is aimed at is not simply to put pressure on Pretoria to calm the situation down. It is to coopt a part of the Black movement and divert it. It is to divide the movement and hitch a section of it to a long-term perspective of a compromise solution.

"Such a project makes sense today only because a part of the mass movement is dominated by the churches, whose main personality is Bishop Tutu."

Desmond Tutu is one of the well-known public figures who have supported the UDF. This has helped open the door to greater involvement of church members in the mass struggles against apartheid. But, for *International Viewpoint*, this fact becomes an occasion to imply that those who are working to get church figures involved in the United Democratic Front are playing "the moderates' game."

*International Viewpoint* thus misses a very important fact about Desmond Tutu and the UDF. What is happening is that the revolutionary democratic forces in the UDF are winning people away from Tutu, away from his liberal perspective and toward a revolutionary perspective. This is clearly Tutu's view of every member of his church who goes too far. That is what he is worried about.

This *International Viewpoint* article continues: "The Churches are deeply involved in the United Democratic Front, where they share the real leadership with the pro-ANC 'Chartist' [Freedom Charter] current. They, however, have very little influence over the trade-union movement. . . .

"By using the South African opposition churches, the backers of this policy of division are trying to pull the UDF to the right. In so doing, they could also test the ANC, which would then have to choose between maintaining its influence in the UDF by making concessions or abandoning this coalition as a means of organizing its supporters."

Now we have the point: the UDF will move to the right. The ANC will be "tested." It will either move to the right or abandon the UDF. According to this analysis, if the ANC continues backing the UDF, that will prove that the imperialist powers and the South African rulers have succeeded in coopting the ANC.

But no evidence is offered that the UDF *is* moving to the right. The power of the revolutionary struggle is pushing more forces, including many church officials, into motion against apartheid. Some have joined the UDF. Does that mean that the UDF is moving to the right?

Look at the method. The ANC may sell out, says *International Viewpoint*. Well, yes. It could be that tomorrow everyone in the third row of this meeting hall will turn against the revolution. It's "possible," isn't it? But saying this is sort of jarring. What have these comrades in the third row done to make anyone think they are going to abandon the revolutionary movement? They are here today, taking part in the discussion. They are revolutionary fighters. Why single them out? Why start speculation about what they might do? What is there in their activity, their approach, their positions, that would lead someone to say that?

What is there that the ANC has said, published, or *done* that leads *International Viewpoint* to start speculating about unprincipled concessions?

*International Viewpoint* leveled some even more serious charges against the UDF and the ANC in connection with Senator Edward Kennedy's visit to South Africa early this year. Kennedy, a Democratic Party politician, visited South Africa in response to an invitation from Reverend Allan Boesak, one of the leaders of the UDF, who is Coloured. Azapo opposed the visit, attacking Kennedy and those who spoke on the same platform with him at anti-apartheid meetings in South Africa.

*International Viewpoint* makes a point of noting that, "Winnie Mandela, the wife of the imprisoned ANC leader, was also one of the supporters of this tour, and she accepted a bust of John F. Kennedy from the U.S. senator." (Let's leave aside the facts they get wrong — it was a bust not of John Kennedy, but of Robert Kennedy, who had made a highly publicized visit to Soweto nineteen years ago and who is held up by liberal Democrats as a hero of the U.S. civil rights struggle because he was U.S. attorney general during the high point of the mass civil rights struggles of the 1960s.)

Winnie Mandela "accepted" the bust. What should she have done with it? Rejected it? Should she have refused to talk to Kennedy at all?

*International Viewpoint* writes about the Kennedy visit under the subhead: "Splitting the movement of the oppressed." It says the Kennedy visit was an imperialist attempt to divide the anti-apartheid forces. "However, forces such as the Black Consciousness group AZAPO, a rival grouping to the UDF, the National Forum Committee, and some unions regarded the senator as an imperialist agent and did not support this operation." (*International Viewpoint* doesn't specify which unions, and what organizations other than Azapo and the National Forum, took this stance.)

Let's start with the simplest: Kennedy is a prominent bourgeois politician from a bourgeois family. He is not an "agent" for the imperialists, he *is* an imperialist. That's no secret.

*International Viewpoint* refers to this visit as an "operation," suggesting a disruption plot. But who is to be held responsible for this "operation"? Winnie Mandela? Allan Boesak? Other prominent figures associated with the UDF, who invited Kennedy? Says *International Viewpoint*, "When political debate is raging among the various currents, among the unions, between the unions and the UDF, etc., an operation such as the Kennedy trip was well timed to exacerbate the conflicts."

**Y**OU CAN agree or disagree with the tactics of Winnie Mandela and Allan Boesak and the others who invited Kennedy. But what was their purpose? To invite to South Africa a member of a bourgeois opposition party from another country who has publicly called on the U.S. government to impose sanctions on South Africa. Their goal was not only to further public activities against apartheid in South Africa, but also to find a way to reach the American people with a reminder that U.S. government support of the apartheid regime is being done with the agreement of Congress. The U.S. Congress has done nothing to tie Reagan's hands.

*International Viewpoint* omits mention of what Winnie Mandela said publicly about Kennedy's visit. "We have never really dreamed that our salvation lies with someone else," she explained. "We believe our salvation lies in our hands. We do not think [Kennedy] can necessarily bring about meaningful change as such, but we do believe he could use the visit positively when he goes back home to inform the American public about conditions in this country."

No serious person claims that Fidel Castro is participating in an imperialist operation when he invites bourgeois politicians, Democrats and Republicans, to visit Cuba and to meet with Cuban leaders. The Cubans hope that will encourage these politicians to say something in public supporting the normalization of relations between the United States and Cuba. No revolutionist has trouble seeing the value in such moves. But why can't Winnie Mandela do something similar without being smeared in the pages of *International Viewpoint* as a witting or unwitting participant in the "Kennedy operation"? Shouldn't the fighters against the apartheid state seek to take advantage of the divisions among bourgeois politicians — in South Africa and within the camp of its imperialist allies as well?

*International Viewpoint* presents Azapo as an organization with a claim to leadership of the South African revolution at least equal to that of the ANC. If this is not the way it looks to the Black people of South Africa and the rest of the world, it is because of the superior public relations facilities of the ANC. *International Viewpoint* goes on to spread accusations against the UDF of physical provocations, with no evidence offered. This is then carried still further with innuendos aimed at leaders of the ANC and the UDF about the "Kennedy operation."

What is the response of revolutionary fighters around the world who read these accusations in the pages of one of the major English-language publications of the Fourth International? What is the reaction of workers who are getting involved in the free South Africa movement? It isn't Winnie Mandela who is discredited by this kind of material. Her stature comes from her unbreakable determination to fight against apartheid until it is overthrown.

## Character of revolution

**W**HAT EXPLAINS *International Viewpoint*'s political hostility to the course and direction of the ANC, and its attraction to groupings such as Azapo? In my opinion, the explanation lies in the ultraleft and sectarian line of *International Viewpoint* over the past period on the character of the South African revolution. *International Viewpoint* has argued, though usually not directly or clearly, that what is on the agenda is not a bourgeois-democratic revolution led by the toilers, but a proletarian socialist revolution. Not a democratic dictatorship of the proletariat and peasantry, but the dictatorship of the proletariat.

A good example is a major article in the December 10, 1984, *International Viewpoint*, signed by Peter Blumer and Tony Roux.

One of the purposes of this article is to argue that South Africa is not an imperialist country in any sense, but rather a "dependent semi-industrialized country," a term that they would also apply to such semicolonial countries as Argentina or Mexico. You could say that whether or not the South African ruling class is imperialist is just a theoretical question. But this theoretical issue has a lot to do with the political questions we are talking about here.

According to the *International Viewpoint* articles, we have to begin by understanding that South Africa is "a semi-industrialized capitalist society dependent on imperialist investment and aid, one that despite a considerable industrial development, remains at the mercy of ups and downs in its gold exports."

The assertion that South Africa is dependent on imperialist economic aid is simply false. When did South Africa last get economic aid? Moreover, South Africa is not totally at the mercy of fluctuations in the price of gold. The South African economy is not a "monocultural" economy, facing the disaster that hits many semicolonial countries when the price of their sole major export commodity goes down.

*International Viewpoint* then tries to establish that the class structure of South Africa today dictates that a revolution there must be a socialist, not a bourgeois-democratic, revolution. "The industrial and mining proletariat," *International Viewpoint* states, "is now the driving force in the process of uniting the oppressed and exploited in the framework of the national struggle for winning the right to constitute a single united nation, which is today prevented by the apartheid policy and the Bantustans. In order to achieve this, it will, therefore, be necessary to sweep away apartheid and capitalist rule."

But this misses the point. In order to be able to achieve this, it will be necessary *to overthrow the apartheid state*. That will be the democratic revolution. That is what the ANC is fighting for. And that *will* sweep away apartheid.

But it won't sweep away capitalist relations. It will open a situation that, as one of the comrades accurately put it in the discussion here, will be an "awkward" one for the capitalists. It will indeed be awkward for them, because of the most uncricket distribution of wealth in South Africa. But that is the rulers' problem. It won't be awkward for the workers and peasants, who will tackle all that they are strong enough to tackle.

The connection between sweeping away apartheid rule and sweeping away capitalism is not simply an *and* in a sentence. The two tasks are not identical, and the first is not reducible to a "stage" of the second. If the vanguard isn't clear on the democratic character of the South African revolution, and the perspective of uniting the toilers in the fight for state power, then the democratic revolution will be defeated. In that case, the conditions in which the socialist revolution can be fought for won't exist.

The *International Viewpoint* article signed by Blumer and Roux makes its view more explicit in the next few sentences: "In this specific context, the liberation struggle of the Black masses cannot take the classical path of destroying a colonial government imposed by foreign rule. It cannot be limited to a fight for essentially democratic and national demands. It has to immediately incorporate social demands having an anticapitalist dynamic."

It is correct that the struggle in South Africa is not for independence from colonial rule. It is not a national, democratic revolution in *that* sense. The imperialist master is not in a metropolitan country somewhere else, but right there in South Africa. Nonetheless, the South African revolution that is on the agenda *will* be fought for democratic and national demands. That is what the struggle is about today.

Will this national, democratic revolution in South Africa incorporate "social demands having an anticapitalist dynamic"? Yes. The growing involvement of the labor movement in the democratic revolution means that demands for labor rights and improvements in the conditions of working people will be fought for and won in this revolution. And those aren't the only social demands that will be fought for. The Freedom Charter calls for a literacy campaign, free medical care for all, maternity leave with full pay, rent reduction, and so on. It proposes the nationalization of the entire mining industry of South Africa, and of all land that has mineral deposits beneath it. It also advocates the nationalization of monopolized sectors of capital and of the banking system.

THE FREEDOM Charter is not a socialist program. It doesn't advocate nationalizing all industry, the expropriation of the bourgeoisie, or the dictatorship of the proletariat. But it certainly does raise social demands affecting the welfare and organization of all working people.

That's what the ANC program calls for. It is the program around which the ANC has been built for thirty years, and which it has reaffirmed time and again. You can say that ANC leaders won't carry it out. But I submit that if they have the capacity and determination to lead the toiling people to overthrow the South African state — which will be one of the greatest victories for humanity in our lifetimes — then they probably will implement their program. Doing so will require a mighty revolution. But *not* a socialist revolution.

"In such a situation, therefore," continues *International Viewpoint*, "it is impossible to conceive of the organization of a national liberation movement of the classical type, comparable to those that have arisen out of anticolonial struggles in much less industrialized societies and which have generally been based on the peasant and plebeian masses."

But why can't the South African revolution be led by a movement like the July 26 Movement, which led the revolution that overthrew Batista's dictatorship and opened the road to a workers' and farmers' government in Cuba? Why not?

This same December 10, 1984, article in *International Viewpoint* argues that the "Chartist current" — those who stand on the program of the Freedom Charter — "proposes a democratic stage in the revolutionary process." In contrast, the National Forum and Azapo offer "a more radical, explicitly socialist program as an alternative to the Chartist current."

*International Viewpoint* sees a problem in the fact that the Chartists propose a "democratic stage in the revolutionary process." To be more precise, the ANC proposes a democratic revolution. So do we. A *democratic revolution.*

*International Viewpoint* rejects the possibility of a successful national, democratic revolution in South Africa. It suggests that only a revolution that establishes the dictatorship of the proletariat, a workers' state, can do away with apartheid. This leads to the conclusion that the ANC cannot and will not lead the struggle to overthrow the apartheid state, since its program is the Freedom Charter, not a socialist program.

But a communist leadership cannot be built in South Africa by trying to leap over the democratic revolution to get more quickly to the socialist revolution. It is only through the struggle to lead the democratic revolution, to carry out its minimum program to the end, that a communist party will be forged in South Africa.

The April 22, 1985, issue of *International Viewpoint*, in an article by Ndabeni, continues along the same lines: "While the liberation struggle is an end in itself to the Charterists, the National Forum is more concerned with a direct attack on the capitalist system. . . . Liberation in itself, the Forum argues, has done little to help the downtrodden workers in most African countries. The struggle against apartheid is no more than a point of departure in the liberation effort."

"Liberation in itself" doesn't help the "downtrodden workers"? The "downtrodden workers" who are fighting in the vanguard of the struggle for "liberation in itself" — in South Africa, Latin America, or Asia — don't see things that way. For Black South Africans, liberation from apartheid is a goal worth fighting and dying for. It is not merely a "point of departure," it is a historic conflict without whose triumph no progress for humanity in South Africa is possible. It therefore demands the full participation of every class-conscious worker in the vanguard of the democratic struggle.

The *International Viewpoint* article counterposes "a direct attack on the capitalist system" to the struggle to overthrow the South African state. Think about what is being mixed up here. The struggle for political power, the overthrow of the apartheid state, is a concrete political task. But what is a "direct attack on the capitalist system" in political terms? How does one go about doing that in South Africa? The logic is to counterpose the slogan of a socialist South Africa to the fight to bring to power a nonracial democratic republic based on the South African workers and peasants. That is pure ultraleft sectarianism in South Africa today.

These articles are consistent with the resolution adopted by the majority of the United Secretariat in January 1983 and published in *International Viewpoint*, March 7, 1983. I didn't agree with this resolution at the time, and I believe that the articles *International Viewpoint* has been publishing, which develop the approach of the resolution, provide convincing evidence that the line has to be corrected.

This resolution makes another serious error, which is also reflected in the *International Viewpoint* coverage. The resolution states that the ANC leadership is "[d]ominated by the Communist Party." I leave aside the factual inaccuracy of this accusation, which is intended to lend credence to the charge that the ANC "orient[s] itself towards collaboration with sections of the liberal white population." We have already dealt with that political issue.

But the error of saying that the ANC leadership is dominated by the Communist Party is of a different order. That can only strengthen the hand of the red-baiters. It is one of the charges repeatedly made by the opponents of the ANC. It is used by the regime to justify outlawing the ANC, and jailing Nelson Mandela and other ANC leaders. It is a charge that should never be repeated in the pages of a publication of the Fourth International, or of any other organization that opposes apartheid.

## Solving the land question

ONE OF the questions that was raised in the discussion was whether the revolution will take land away from the exploited white working farmers in South Africa. Is that the way that land will be made available to those dispossessed Africans who want to farm? No. The ANC does not propose to take land from the working white farmers. To the contrary. The ANC guarantees *not* to take land from exploited farmers, white or Black.

Where will the land come from? It will come from expropriating the expropriators, that is, from the large capitalist farmers and landowners who exploit farm labor. The revolution will not take land from any working farmer. The revolution will guarantee the land to everyone, of any race, who wants to work it and produce.

History never decides beforehand exactly how the land will be divided. But all of history has taught us one thing: peasants who want to farm will take the land to farm. The Black miners, factory workers, and farm laborers who want to farm will take land to farm.

The task of opening up commodity production in the countryside to those who want to farm and to raise cattle can't be bypassed. The revolutionary struggle to open up access to the land to make possible the development of the South African nation can't be leaped over. Any attempt to do so — for instance, by moving to immediate creation of state farms and compulsory cooperatives as the predominant forms of agricultural production — would be an ultraleft utopian disaster.

## ANC and the liberals

A second question that came up in the discussion concerns what is often incorrectly referred to as the alliance between the ANC and the liberals, particularly the white liberals. What divides the ANC from liberals, fundamentally, is that the ANC is out to overthrow the state. Liberals aren't. Ever. The program of the ANC is not a liberal program. It is a revolutionary democratic program. Let's not give too much credit to liberalism. Liberalism isn't revolutionary, even when what is involved is "only" a democratic and not a socialist revolution. The liberals weren't revolutionary in tsarist Russia, or in Batista's Cuba, or in Somozaist Nicaragua.

As the revolutionary crisis deepens, some liberals are impelled toward the mass movement. They can never lead the movement forward, but they can be drawn toward it. A vanguard political leadership of the democratic revolution has the task of finding ways to use that support, to organize it to strengthen the revolutionary struggle.

The ANC works with broader anti-apartheid organizations, of which the UDF is the largest. The ANC accepts support from anyone who is prepared to *act* to support the fight to implement the revolutionary democratic program. The UDF includes large numbers of liberals, including many church figures, who oppose the apartheid system.

The ANC works hard to recruit people from these other organizations and political currents involved in struggle. But the ANC is not a liberal organization. Some ANC members began as liberals, but, if they stick with the ANC, they wind up as revolutionaries.

The largely African leadership of the ANC has, as we have seen, reached the strength that it feels confident to open its ranks, inside and outside the country, to those of all races who demonstrate their capacity to function as part of a revolutionary organization. All of these individuals can aspire to leadership responsibilities, which they can earn by proving to their comrades that they are capable of shouldering them.

What we have to be alert to in this connection is the "new" idea that alliances with the liberals is now the key to the world revolution. Some who call themselves Marxists have argued that this is one of the main lessons to be learned from recent revolutionary struggles, notably in Nicaragua. They say that the most valuable contribution of the FSLN to Marxism is what they claim was the Sandinistas' policy of alliance with the liberal bourgeoisie, the liberal forces in the church, and so on. The Sandinistas are said to have dropped from their vocabulary such out-dated terms as "working class" or "peasantry" and "capitalist" or "land-lord." They found ways to speak more popularly than that, cemented an alliance with the liberals, and came to power.

This is not, of course, what actually happened in Nicaragua. The FSLN led the workers and peasants in a revolutionary struggle to over-throw Somoza. As the revolutionary crisis deepened, some liberals accepted the lead of the FSLN. The FSLN never gave political support to a capitalist party, let alone joined one. And neither does the ANC.

So when people talk about an "alliance with the liberals" in South Africa, we should demand that they be more precise. There is not, and cannot be, a political alliance between the ANC and liberalism. It was the rejection of any subordination to liberalism that made it possible for the ANC to begin taking the leadership of the revolutionary struggle in South Africa.

To deny that the ANC is the vanguard of the anti-apartheid struggle makes sense only if there is a fundamental problem with the ANC's strategic course. It simply can't be challenged on any other grounds — not size, influence, fighting capacity, or mass support. It can be seriously challenged only by those, such as Azapo, who disagree with the character of the revolution that the ANC is trying to lead.

## Role of the unions

Some opponents of the ANC have tried to counterpose the emerging leadership of the nonracial unions to the political vanguard role of the ANC. But this is a trap.

We reject any workerist or syndicalist notions that assign to the unions a role they do not play, and cannot play, as an *alternative* political van-guard of the national, democratic revolution in South Africa. These are labor unions, fighting for the right to represent the interests of the work-ers. They are fighting to transform themselves into instruments of strug-gle on behalf of their members, and on behalf of the entire working class and all exploited working people. They are fighting their way toward a broader political outlook.

They are not auxiliary organizations of a revolutionary democratic front. They are not branches of the ANC. They have emerged from the struggle of the Black workers, and are developing their relationship to the political struggle that is transforming the country.

The ANC doesn't claim to lead most of the major unions. It doesn't lead most of them. But neither does any single alternative political current exercise leadership over the nonracial unions. As the revolutionary democratic struggle deepens, the authority of the ANC in the labor movement will continue to grow. The unions themselves will develop, and new proletarian leaders will emerge from their ranks. That is the direction in which things are moving.

## Magnitude of the tasks

We have to come to grips with the magnitude of the tasks that face the leadership of the national, democratic revolution in South Africa. We have to get rid of any idea that these tasks can be accomplished in a short time.

The revolutionary democratic dictatorship of the South African proletariat and the peasantry will face the task of bringing a nation and nation-state into being. The land has to be opened to be worked by the people. That has been prevented by the imperialist, colonial-settler, apartheid state that has been built there. Imagine that the only farms in the United States were those held by the descendants of the original Puritan families, and that the immigrants who poured in for hundreds of years afterward have been driven off the land and barred by law from farming. That might help us to grasp the enormity of what apartheid has prevented from happening.

Without opening the land, the nation can't be born. It is this that makes the connection between the fight for the land and the national liberation struggle so important. And it is this that makes the worker-peasant alliance so decisive. It is this alliance of the proletarianized population, the alliance of the toilers of South Africa, that must be brought into being.

The bourgeois-democratic revolution in South Africa will open the door to solving these historic tasks.

### Break all U.S. ties to apartheid regime!

WHAT IS opening up before us now should help the Socialist Workers Party understand even better what we have conquered in the last five years. The party has gotten itself into position to meet these tasks through the turn to the industrial unions.

We have been able to do more than just get into the industrial unions. We have also been able to establish a framework of taking politics to the broader layers of our class and to the oppressed *through* the union move-ment, to base ourselves in the unions in order to reach out from there. It is from this base that we have begun to reach out in a modest way to working farmers and their organizations. It is from this base that we have been charting the strategic line of march that is dictated by the goal of overthrowing capitalist rule.

By carrying out this perspective in the United States, we have been deepening our relations with others around the world who are charting the same course. We have begun to strip away the obstacles we have car-ried from the semisectarian existence that was imposed on us with the onset of the cold war, the witch-hunt, and the political retreat of the labor movement. In doing this, we have begun to turn ourselves outward along a working-class axis.

The decisive political point is the one that was emphasized during the discussion here. *It will take a mighty battle to break the ties that bind the U.S. government to the South African regime.* Breaking those ties is the task of the people of the United States. It is a task of the communist van-guard in this country. We are better prepared today than ever before to understand, prepare for, and go into action to carry it out.

This will not be easy. The rulers are determined not to let it happen. They are on the offensive — in Central America, in the Caribbean, in their militarization drive, in their attacks on rights and living standards at home. Given the relationship of forces and what they have accomplished in the last few years, they are determined not to let their ties with the apartheid regime be broken. They understand that if this happens, it will affect not only South Africa, not only the African continent, but the whole world, including this country.

The U.S. rulers will fight the movement to force a break with South Africa. They will use their vast propaganda resources. They will employ red-baiting. They will seek to divide and disrupt the movement, and to play on every racist fear and prejudice about what "horrors" majority rule will bring.

We've got to set an example by answering their propaganda. We've got to organize ourselves to explain the truth — the concrete facts about apart-heid, the daily life of Blacks under apartheid. We've got to explain why every human being should support the fight to bring that system down.

We must always keep at the forefront the demand that Washington break its ties to the apartheid regime. Break economically. Break polit-ically. Break militarily. Break in every way. The government in Wash-ington must break from the apartheid state. Refusal to do so is intolera-ble to humanity. It is intolerable to the people of the United States.

The apartheid regime is the world outlaw. We are gearing into a worldwide struggle to concentrate on this simple, clear, popular, and historically decisive goal.

It is by fighting for that goal, along these lines, that we can accomplish the maximum both for the comrades in South Africa and for the struggles of working people and the oppressed here.

## Notes

1. V.I. Lenin, *Collected Works* (Moscow: Progress Publishers, 1974), vol. 22, p. 27.

2. Ibid., p. 34.

3. Nelson Mandela, *The Struggle Is My Life* (London: International Defence and Aid Fund for South Africa, 1978), p. 55.

4. Lenin, *Collected Works*, vol. 9, p. 52.

5. Ibid., p. 29.

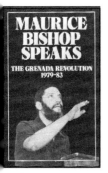

# The Freedom Charter

*The following is the text of the Freedom Charter, which was unanimously adopted by nearly 3,000 delegates attending the Congress of the People, held in Kliptown, near Johannesburg, on June 25–26, 1955. The congress was convened by the African National Congress, together with the South African Indian Congress, the Coloured People's Organisation, and the Congress of Democrats. At an ANC special conference in early 1956, the liberation organization formally adopted the Freedom Charter as its program.*

## Preamble

We, the people of South Africa, declare for all our country and the world to know:

• that South Africa belongs to all who live in it, Black and white, and that no government can justly claim authority unless it is based on the will of the people;

• that our people have been robbed of their birthright to land, liberty, and peace by a form of government founded on injustice and inequality;

• that our country will never be prosperous or free until all our people live in brotherhood, enjoying equal rights and opportunities;

• that only a democratic state, based on the will of the people, can secure to all their birthright without distinction of color, race, sex, or belief;

And therefore, we, the people of South Africa, Black and white together — equals, countrymen, and brothers — adopt this Freedom Charter. And we pledge ourselves to strive together, sparing nothing of our strength and courage, until the democratic changes here set out have been won.

## The people shall govern!

Every man and woman shall have the right to vote for and to stand as a candidate for all bodies which make laws.

All people shall be entitled to take part in the administration of the country.

The rights of the people shall be the same, regardless of race, color, or sex.

All bodies of minority rule, advisory boards, councils, and authorities shall be replaced by democratic organs of self-government.

## All national groups shall have equal rights!

There shall be equal status in the bodies of state, in the courts, and in the schools for all national groups and races;

All national groups shall be protected by law against insults to their race and national pride;

All people shall have equal rights to use their own language and to develop their own folk culture and customs;

The preaching and practice of national, race, or color discrimination and contempt shall be a punishable crime;

All apartheid laws and practices shall be set aside.

## The people shall share in the country's wealth!

The national wealth of our country, the heritage of all South Africans, shall be restored to the people;

The mineral wealth beneath the soil, the banks, and monopoly industry shall be transferred to the ownership of the people as a whole;

All other industries and trade shall be controlled to assist the well-being of the people;

All people shall have equal rights to trade where they choose, to manufacture, and to enter all trades, crafts, and professions.

## The land shall be shared among those who work it!

Restrictions of land ownership on a racial basis shall be ended, and all the land redivided amongst those who work it, to banish famine and land hunger;

The state shall help the peasants with implements, seed, tractors, and dams to save the soil and assist the tillers;

Freedom of movement shall be guaranteed to all who work on the land;

All shall have the right to occupy land wherever they choose;

People shall not be robbed of their cattle, and forced labor and farm prisons shall be abolished.

## All shall be equal before the law!

No one shall be imprisoned, deported, or restricted without a fair trial;
No one shall be condemned by the order of any government official;
The courts shall be representative of all the people;
Imprisonment shall be only for serious crimes against the people, and shall aim at re-education, not vengeance;
The police force and army shall be open to all on an equal basis and shall be the helpers and protectors of the people;
All laws which discriminate on grounds of race, color, or belief shall be repealed.

## All shall enjoy equal human rights!

The law shall guarantee to all their right to speak, to organize, to meet together, to publish, to preach, to worship, and to educate their children;
The privacy of the house from police raids shall be protected by law;
All shall be free to travel without restriction from countryside to town, from province to province, and from South Africa abroad;
Pass laws, permits, and all other laws restricting these freedoms shall be abolished.

## There shall be work and security!

All who work shall be free to form unions, to elect their officers, and to make wage agreements with their employers;
The state shall recognize the right and duty of all to work, and to draw full unemployment benefits;
Men and women of all races shall receive equal pay for equal work;
There shall be a forty-hour working week, a national minimum wage, paid annual leave, and sick leave for all workers, and maternity leave on full pay for all working mothers;
Miners, domestic workers, farm workers, and civil servants shall have the same rights as all others who work;
Child labor, compound labor, the tot system, and contract labor shall be abolished.[1]

## The doors of learning and of culture shall be opened!

The government shall discover, develop, and encourage national talent for the enhancement of our cultural life;
All the cultural treasures of mankind shall be open to all, by free exchange of books, ideas, and contact with other lands;

The aim of education shall be to teach the youth to love their people and their culture, to honor human brotherhood, liberty, and peace;

Education shall be free, compulsory, universal, and equal for all children;

Higher education and technical training shall be opened to all by means of state allowances and scholarships awarded on the basis of merit;

Adult illiteracy shall be ended by a mass state education plan;

Teachers shall have all the rights of other citizens;

The color bar in cultural life, in sport, and in education shall be abolished.

## There shall be houses, security, and comfort!

All people shall have the right to live where they choose, to be decently housed, and to bring up their families in comfort and security;

Unused housing space shall be made available to the people;

Rent and prices shall be lowered, food plentiful, and no one shall go hungry;

A preventive health scheme shall be run by the state;

Free medical care and hospitalization shall be provided for all, with special care for mothers and young children;

Slums shall be demolished and new suburbs built where all have transport, roads, lighting, playing fields, crèches, and social centers;

The aged, the orphans, the disabled, and the sick shall be cared for by the state;

Rest, leisure, and recreation shall be the right of all;

Fenced locations and ghettos shall be abolished, and laws which break up families shall be repealed.

## There shall be peace and friendship!

South Africa shall be a fully independent state, which respects the rights and sovereignty of all nations;

South Africa shall strive to maintain world peace and the settlement of all international disputes by negotiation — not war;

Peace and friendship amongst all our people shall be secured by upholding the equal rights, opportunities, and status of all;

The people of the protectorates — Basutoland, Bechuanaland, and Swaziland — shall be free to decide for themselves their own future;[2]

The right of all the peoples of Africa to independence and self-government shall be recognized and shall be the basis of close cooperation.

Let all who love their people and their country now say, as we say here:

"These freedoms we will fight for, side by side, throughout our lives, until we have won our liberty!"

## Notes

1. Contract laborers are migrant workers from abroad or from one of South Africa's ten Bantustans, the impoverished rural reserves. While employed in the cities, they must live in segregated, single-sex, barrackslike compounds. The tot system, practiced on some white-owned farms, involves giving wine rations to farm workers in place of part of their cash wages.

2. Basutoland (now called Lesotho) won its independence from Britain in 1966, Bechuanaland (now Botswana) also became independent in 1966, and Swaziland in 1968.

## MALCOLM X: THE LAST SPEECHES

These six never-before-published speeches and interviews shed light on Malcolm X's political evolution during the last months of his life and reaffirm his place among the outstanding revolutionary leaders of the 20th century. *$15.95*

## MALCOLM X SPEAKS

The classic collection of speeches and interviews from 1964 and 1965. Now available in a hard-back edition with photos and an index. *$14.95*

### By Any Means Necessary
Speeches and interviews from Malcolm X's last year. *$13.95*

### Malcolm X on Afro-American History
A 1965 speech focusing on Afro-American history, with brief excerpts from other speeches. *$7.95*

### Malcolm X Talks to Young People
Malcolm's December 1964 Harlem speech to visiting young civil rights activists, and his interview with the *Young Socialist* magazine. *$2.00*

### Two Speeches by Malcolm X
Includes two speeches at Militant Labor Forums in 1964 and 1965, and Malcolm's statement announcing his break with the Nation of Islam. *$2.50*

### The Assassination of Malcolm X
by George Breitman, Herman Porter, Baxter Smith
Explodes the government cover-up of the truth about Malcolm's assassination. *$13.95*

### The Last Year of Malcolm X
*The Evolution of a Revolutionary*
by George Breitman *$13.95*

# The Future Belongs
# to the Majority

### by Oliver Tambo

*The following message from African National Congress President Oliver Tambo is reprinted from the March 1984 issue of* Sechaba, *the official organ of the African National Congress of South Africa. The footnotes are by* New International.

**D**EAR COMPATRIOTS,
Brothers and sisters in the struggle,
Comrades,

Today, January 8, your organization, the African National Congress, is seventy-two years old. In keeping with established practice, we ask you to share with us today some thoughts on the tasks that confront us during 1984. Allow me to begin by extending to you all the wishes of the National Executive Committee and the general leadership of the ANC for great successes in the new year.

This time last year, when we marked the seventy-first anniversary of the founding of our organization, we pointed out that our long struggle had come to a point where the revolutionary ferment had reached unprecedented heights and had plunged the ruling racist clique into deeper and deeper levels of crisis. We went on to state that within the confines of the apartheid system there was no way out of this crisis situation. Apartheid cannot be reformed. The only real solution lies in the victory of the revolutionary forces, the dismantling of the apartheid machinery, and the transfer of political and economic power to the democratic majority.

Events of the past year have fully borne out the correctness of this assessment. The momentous struggles of the past year have taken us further upon the road to our cherished goal and have driven the racist rulers into further acts of desperation. For us, the future is brightening daily while for the Pretoria racist clique, the future is getting darker each passing day.

We commend you on the sacrifices and dedication by which, during 1983, you took our country significantly forward toward liberation. The past year can have left our enemies in no doubt that we have the determination to struggle, the ability to organize for victory, and the will to take power into our hands. The only question that confronts us all, singly and collectively, is how we should respond to the order of the day, "Mobilize and march forward to people's power!"

## The four pillars of our revolution

OUR REVOLUTIONARY struggle rests on four pillars. These are, first, the all-around vanguard activity of the underground structures of the ANC; second, the united mass action of the peoples; third, our armed offensive, spearheaded by Umkhonto we Sizwe; and fourth, the international drive to isolate the apartheid regime and win worldwide moral, political, and material support for the struggle.

Over the last few years, the guardians of reaction in our country have devised a program of action centered on the twin notions of so-called national security and total strategy. This program is based on the recognition that the apartheid system is immersed in a deep and permanent general crisis. The ruling group in Pretoria has therefore been addressing itself to the question of how to manage this crisis to ensure that it does not get out of hand.

The Bantustan scheme, the militarization of society, the offensive against the ANC, the new apartheid constitution, and other recent pieces of legislation, notably, those covering industrial relations, the so-called community councils, the press, and the economy, all are elements in this program of crisis management.[1] Coupled with the criminal war against the Namibian and Angolan people, and increased aggression against the rest of southern Africa, these measures point to the desperation of the regime as it battles for its survival.

The racists have decided, under mounting pressure from the revolutionary masses and the international community, to tinker with the apartheid system, but in such a way as to further entrench racism and consolidate this illegitimate and criminal system. Despite all these maneuvers, apartheid has no future.

In other words, the fascists recognize that they can no longer rule in the old way. We recall how, at the height of the Soweto uprising, J.B. Vorster made bold to declare, "there is no crisis" — no crisis for minority rule. But a few years later, P.W. Botha called on the whites to adapt to reality or perish with apartheid.

This was a public admission that there is a crisis threatening the destruction of the apartheid system. It is an imperative task of the revolutionary and democratic forces of our country to compound and further deepen this crisis by ever intensifying the struggle for national and social emancipation.

## Revolutions are about state power

The Black people of our country have challenged the legitimacy of the South African racist state from its formation in 1910 and throughout the ensuing decades.[2] As we fight the apartheid system today, we should all speak with one voice in declaring that the present regime, like all others before it, has no legitimate authority to rule our country. Indeed, its central purpose is to perpetuate the illegal rule of the white usurpers of power in our country.

All revolutions are about state power. Ours is no exception. The slogan, "Power to the people," means one thing and one thing only. It means we seek to destroy the power of apartheid tyranny and replace it with popular power with a government whose authority derives from the will of all our people, both Black and white.

The issue we have to settle together is what steps to take to attain that ultimate goal, what intermediate objectives we should set ourselves building on what we have achieved, and in preparation for the next stage in our forward march to victory. The answer to these questions relates directly to what we have already referred to as the illegality of the apartheid state.

We must begin to use our accumulated strength to destroy the organs of government of the apartheid regime. We have to undermine and weaken its control over us, exactly by frustrating its attempts to control us. We should direct our collective might to rendering the enemy's instruments of authority unworkable. To march forward must mean that we advance against the regime's organs of state power, creating conditions in which the country becomes increasingly ungovernable.

## We must hit the enemy where it is weakest

You are aware that the apartheid regime maintains an extensive administrative system through which it directs our lives. This system includes organs of central and provincial government, the army and the police, the judiciary, the Bantustans' administrations, the community councils, the local management and local affairs committees. It is these institutions of apartheid power that we must attack and demolish, as part of the struggle to put an end to racist minority rule in our country. Needless to say, as strategists, we must select for attack those parts of the enemy administrative system which we have the power to destroy, as a result of our united and determined offensive. We must hit the enemy where it is weakest.

The goal we are setting ourselves today is dictated by the logic of our revolution. Its realization is made possible by the fact that in our millions, we have already laid the basis for its accomplishment. Thus, through our efforts, the so-called Coloured Persons Representative Council ceased to exist;[3] as a result of extensive mobilization, the puppet South African Indian Council was brought in by a laughably insignificant minority; the entire Bantustan system faces overwhelming rejection and continuous resistance; and similarly, toward the end of 1983, we united in a massive rejection of the local management committees and community councils.

In certain areas and at different times, we have gone beyond rejection of this oppressive system of government, beyond a challenge to its legitimacy. In 1960, our people in Pondoland destroyed the regime's administration, and set up their own administration and people's courts.[4] Likewise in 1976, we caused the collapse of the Urban Bantu Councils.[5] In the recent past, in Sobantu village in Pietermaritzburg, we destroyed the newly installed community council and frustrated the plans of the Drakensberg Administration Board.

Our determined resistance at Crossroads and at KTC in the Western Cape has made it impossible for Koornhof to carry out his schemes.[6] He has been unable to govern at will. In Mdantsane our heroic struggle has shaken the puppet Sebe administration to its core.[7] Commenting on this situation, one South African political observer stated:

> The stakes are high because the issues have moved beyond those of a (bus) fare increase. The boycott has become a conflict of will between the Ciskei (puppet administration) and its many opponents in Mdantsane, the second largest black township in South Africa.

In the course of our struggle against rent increases and other facets of apartheid, such as the proposed incorporation of some townships into the KwaZulu Bantustan, we have gone further to destroy part of the Pretoria regime.

From these examples, it is clear that we have the ability to raise the struggle to greater heights. Having rejected the community councils by boycotting the elections, we should not allow them to be imposed on us. We do not want them. We must ensure that they cease to exist. Where administration boards take over their functions, then these must be destroyed too.

In the Ciskei, as with the other so-called independent Bantustans, we must take the battle further. In the conflict of will between ourselves and the murderous Sebe administration, our will must prevail. And it will, if we transform what began in Mdantsane as resistance to bus-fare increases into a nationwide offensive against the Pretoria regime's Bantustan system. In Mdantsane the people have said — "Sebe must go! Power to the people!" That call should spread throughout the Ciskei to galvanize the people into united action for the destruction of the instrument of oppression — the Ciskei Bantustan.

## Now is the time to choose

THE INTOLERABLE hardships and sufferings; the persecutions, detentions, and murders of patriots and democrats in other Bantustans call for the establishment of fighting organizations to organize and lead the struggle for the destruction of these racist institutions of oppression.

This year, Botha and Malan will be busy implementing the provisions of their apartheid constitution. In this regard, our democratic movement must mobilize to ensure that the so-called Coloured and Indian sections of the Black population refuse to be recruited to play the role of partners in apartheid tyranny. White South Africa alone should man the apartheid constitutional posts, which it alone has created, for its exclusive benefit. Those who elect to serve in these apartheid institutions must expect to face the wrath of the people.

We must go further to say that our white compatriots, with even a modicum of anti-apartheid feeling, have to abandon the delusion that they can use Botha's constitutional institutions to bring about any change. The forces struggling for a new order in our country are outside of these structures. It is within the ranks of these extraparliamentary forces that the anti-apartheid whites can make a significant contribution to democratic change in our country. Now is the time to choose.

It is essential that we continue to shift our posture from the defensive to the offensive. The enemy has failed to destroy us and never will. But invincibility is not enough. It is in the attack that we shall find victory. Nor should we wait for the enemy to take the initiative and then react to its plans and schemes. We have a purpose, a goal, an objective, a historic mission to accomplish for our country and for humanity. Our historic duty is to pursue it with relentless determination and persistence, whatever the enemy does or omits to do.

We must apply ourselves with more vigor in our efforts to organize the unorganized, to consolidate, defend, and expand existing people's action on all fronts. It is absolutely necessary to raise the standard of our organizational and educational work, as well as our psychological preparedness, to the level of the major and complex tasks facing our revolution today.

At this juncture allow me to single out the creation of the UDF [United Democratic Front] as a historic achievement in our people's efforts to unite in the broadest possible front for the struggle against the inhuman apartheid system. The formation of the United Democratic Front was a product of our people's determination to be their own liberators.

## The spirit of rebellion and politics of revolutionary change

THE GROWTH of the democratic trade union movement and its power to wrest recognition from both the regime and the employers, together with the determined efforts to form one national trade union federation, constitute one of the most significant advances of our struggle in recent years.

Everywhere in the country, our people and youth have courageously confronted the regime in numerous encounters, whether against rent increases, forced removals, or in military actions, among them, the [May 1983] attack on the Air Force Headquarters at Pretoria by Umkhonto we Sizwe.

This is the spirit that must guide and inspire the leaders, organizers, and activists of our democratic movement. We are talking of a spirit of rebellion and frame of mind which puts to the fore the politics of revolutionary change.

A special responsibility rests on the shoulders of the ANC and the most advanced members of our broad, democratic movement to act as revolutionaries — as such, to wage revolutionary struggle; and, basing themselves on the conscious and organized involvement of the masses of the people, to build a strong and disciplined revolutionary movement. In this context, the further mobilization and organization of the masses of our country assumes special importance.

Quite clearly, we have made great strides in these areas of work. This is evident in the strength of the UDF and the pace at which it continues to grow. It is evident also from the struggles we have conducted, in some areas for months on end. We can see it in the organizational growth of the trade union movement. There have been commendable advances in the development of the youth and students' as well as civic and women's movements.

We refer here in particular to the organization of the working class into a revolutionary trade union movement; the organization of the rural masses, inside and outside the Bantustans; the organization of the womenfolk of our country and the religious community into struggle.

Let us now take a brief look at each of these areas of work.

### The working class must lead

Millions of workers in our country, including the unemployed and those engaged in the agricultural sector, remain unorganized. We have to make determined efforts to reach these unorganized workers, bearing in mind that it is the historic responsibility of the working class to take the lead in our struggle for people's power.

The task of forming one federation to unite the democratic trade union movement has not yet been accomplished. We should pursue this goal with even more determination and speed because, apart from anything else, a united democratic workers' movement would give us greater possibilities to advance our struggle.

We do not believe, dear comrades, that there are insurmountable or even very serious obstacles on the way to the creation of such a federation. We do not agree with the school of thought which creates artificial barriers between the fight for trade union rights and the national liberation struggle under the racist conditions obtaining in South Africa. In our situation, the victory of the trade union struggle is unattainable except as an integral part of the victory of the political, ideological, and military struggle. The struggle of the working class is, therefore, and must be, an integral part of the national liberation struggle.

**The rural masses say, 'Seize the land!'**

The organization and mobilization of the rural population is clearly lagging behind those of our people in the towns and cities. And yet it is in these rural areas that the apartheid system has its most disastrous impact on our people. We have the organizational capacity to begin to tackle the rural areas seriously and continuously.

In the Freedom Charter we say that "the land shall be shared among those who work it." As you well know, the situation today is that our people in the Bantustans have been reduced to landless and jobless outcasts. Many are condemned to a slow and painful death in the so-called resettlement camps. On the commercial farms, the most merciless brutalization of our people, especially women and children, takes place, every day and every hour of the day at the hands of the landowners.

One of the fundamental elements for the solution of the problems facing our people in the countryside is the resolution of the land question in favor of the tillers. Our immediate task, therefore, is to mobilize the rural masses around the question of land. It is only when the countryside is organized that the rural masses will be able to respond resolutely to the call: "Seize the land!"

**Apartheid threatens peace**

In the past period we have seen the increased involvement of the religious community in our struggle for liberation. In this context, you are aware that at the National Conference of the Council of Churches last year, a proposal was made to convene a conference in 1986 to decide on the issue of the contribution of the Christian church to change in our country. It was then said: "When peace is broken or threatened by injustice, the Christian has a responsibility to work for peace, to work for righteousness, by striving to rectify what is unrighteous, unjust." Those words constitute a serious challenge not only to Christians, but also to people of other faiths in our country. While the evil and unjust apartheid system exists in our country, we cannot have peace, nor can the peoples of southern Africa.

The fraternal peoples of Namibia and Angola, especially, have for years now known no peace because of Pretoria's brutal colonization and occupation of their countries. Daily, our Namibian and Angolan brothers and sisters suffer death and destruction from the regime's bombs, bullets, and bayonets. This war of aggression is being conducted by a regime from our own country. We have a responsibility to ourselves and the children and people of Namibia and Angola, to raise our voices in condemnation of the aggression. We urge upon the people of South Africa to demand and fight for the immediate withdrawal of all South African troops, mercenaries, Pretoria-backed bandits, and special assassination groups from Angola, Namibia, and other affected countries of southern Africa. In this context, let the oppressed and democrats of our country assume their historic responsibility, recognizing that the struggle in South Africa is the hope of the subcontinent.

We are entitled to expect that people of all faiths in our country, including the Christian, the Jew, the Hindu, and the Moslem, will in fact act, and act now, in defense of justice, peace, and life, against a system that is totally evil and inhuman.

### Woman's place is in the battlefront

IT WILL be our special task this year to organize and mobilize our womenfolk into a powerful, united, and active force for revolutionary change. This task falls on men and women alike — all of us together as comrades in the struggle. We wish to stress the need, at the present hour, for the emergence on the political scene of a women's movement that is politically and organizationally united. Our struggle needs and demands this potentially mighty force.

Our struggle will be less than powerful and our national and social emancipation can never be complete if we continue to treat the women of our country as dependent minors and objects of one form of exploitation or another. Certainly no longer should it be that a woman's place is in the kitchen. In our beleaguered country, the woman's place is in the battlefront of struggle.

### People determined to be free

We have come a long way from the time, as in the fifties when we fought barehanded — disarmed and unarmed — against the military might and the trigger-happy army and police force of the apartheid regime. No Black hand was allowed to touch a firearm or possess any instrument more lethal than a penknife.

Today, the racist regime's army and police generals who occupy a central position in Pretoria's state machinery, through the State Security Council, are making frantic efforts to recruit and arm the "Kaffirs, Coolies, and Hotnots" of the fifties,[8] to serve as cannon fodder in the defense of a system that has fallen afoul of the times, a system that has enslaved and debased us these past seventy years.

It is not that the military might of the regime has declined. It is rather that the people, determined to be free, have taken up arms and, through their own army, Umkhonto we Sizwe, have moved on to the offensive.

Today, armed struggle is a vital, indispensable component of the struggle for national and social liberation in South Africa. Where the apartheid regime relies for survival on its fascist army and police, on Black mercenaries, and on puppet armies and murderous puppet administrations who slaughter men as readily as they butcher children, the democratic majority in our country supports the people's army — Umkhonto we Sizwe — whose rising sophistication will yet compound the survival problems of the apartheid system.

But the challenge confronting Umkhonto we Sizwe, in the face of current developments in southern Africa, has never been greater. Therefore, in commending its units and commanders on the sustained offensive of the past year, we charge them, and call upon our people, to carry the struggle to new heights, and sue for victory tomorrow rather than the day after tomorrow.

To this end, Umkhonto we Sizwe must deepen its roots and grow inextricably among the popular masses: among us — the workers, the peasants, the youth, the women; we, the unemployed, the landless, the homeless, and the starving millions.

Umkhonto we Sizwe must grow in size, in the spread and quality of its operations, and in the weight of every blow delivered. The armed struggle must grow. We shall achieve victory through a combination of mass political action and organized revolutionary violence.

We address a special message to the white youth. Your future is in issue. The apartheid regime has no future. Like Adolf Hitler and his war machine, after spreading death and destruction everywhere, the regime will be defeated and destroyed everywhere.

## The future belongs to the majority

The future belongs to the majority of the people of South Africa, Black and white, who, in struggle, are today laying the foundations of a united, nonracial democratic South Africa in what will then, but only then, become a peaceful and rapidly advancing region of Africa.

Your proper place is among these builders of a new order in our country. Join them. Refuse to join an army whose sole function is to murder, murder, murder African people everywhere.

It goes without saying that Black youth — African, Indian, and so-called Coloured — must under no circumstances serve in Pretoria's army of violent repression and criminal aggression. The democratic movement should immediately take up this issue with our youth throughout the country.

Our democratic movement, our movement for national liberation, is part of a multimillion-strong world alliance of forces which fights for national independence, democracy, social progress, and peace. On the other hand, the apartheid regime belongs firmly within the camp of imperialist reaction, and is active within this camp to further counterrevolutionary goals.

We therefore have an international obligation to be active in the struggle to defeat the counteroffensive that the imperialists, led by the Reagan administration of the United States, have launched. We too must raise our voice against the warmongers within NATO who have brought humanity closer to a nuclear holocaust by sabotaging all efforts at nuclear disarmament and who have, instead, unleashed a new arms race and heightened international tension and insecurity. We too must struggle together with the world peace forces, especially because the Pretoria regime itself possesses nuclear weapons and maintains secret military relations with the most belligerent circles on the world scene.

We too must speak out, and have spoken out, against the attempts of the United States to impose its will on the peoples of the world. This policy has already resulted in the criminal invasion of Grenada, the undeclared war against Nicaragua, and the direct intervention of the United States in El Salvador in support of a gang of murderers. It has led to a reign of terror against the people of Palestine and their organization, the PLO [Palestine Liberation Organization], as well as the people of Lebanon. It has helped Morocco to ignore the resolutions of the OAU [Organization of African Unity] and to maintain its colonial hold over the people of Western Sahara. This policy has further delayed the independence of Namibia and emboldened the Pretoria regime itself to seek to impose its will on the peoples of southern Africa by force of arms.

## Policy of military terror and economic strangulation

In this regard, through a policy of military terror and economic strangulation, the racists seek to compel the independent states of our region to surrender their independence and, as an important part of that surrender, to help evict the ANC from the whole of southern Africa. Never was there a clearer illustration of the relationship between the struggle to liberate our country and the struggle to defend the independence and sovereignty of the countries of southern Africa. The peoples of our region share one common destiny. Certainly, that can never be a destiny of subservience to the criminal regime of Pretoria.

As the Maputo Frontline States Summit of March 1982 agreed,[9] the only way forward for the peoples of our region is to support the ANC and SWAPO[10] in our common struggle against the Pretoria regime and to repulse the offensive of this regime against independent Africa.

For some time now, especially since the Maseru massacre,[11] spokesmen of the South African regime have repeatedly boasted of the intimate nature of their collaboration, and the happy relations they have, with the government of the Kingdom of Swaziland. The people of Swaziland, like most in the rest of Africa, will have resented that claim, especially if, as we suspect, Pretoria has in mind collaboration in the fruitless attempt to liquidate the ANC by assassinating and harassing its members and supporters in Swaziland.

The trouble about any alliance with apartheid is that the liberation struggle is growing and destined to grow and advance, no matter which or how many members and leaders of the liberation movement are murdered or arrested in the doubtful interests of either white minority domination or good neighborliness.

Of course the Botha regime is frantic about the emergence of the ANC as the alternative power on the South African political scene. The regime is frantic also because of its inability to block the powerful and evidently dangerous thrust of the ANC and the people towards the goal of liberation. The regime is therefore blackmailing African states into an alliance targeted on the destruction of the ANC.

### ANC — integral part of the world revolutionary process

BUT THE ANC has grown among the people of southern Africa in the past seventy years. It has always embraced and always will embrace them as allies and comrades-in-arms. It is a child of Africa's determination to achieve and enjoy human dignity, freedom, and national independence; it will never betray that parentage. It is an integral part of the world revolutionary process; it will stay in the revolution until final victory. The ANC is at once the life, the national awareness, and the political experience of the popular masses of South Africa. As the people cannot be liquidated, neither can the ANC.

We take this opportunity to give a stern warning to some of our people against the dangerous temptation to work as enemy agents for the liquidation of the people's struggle.

The indestructibility of the ANC should, however, not induce complacency on our part. In order for the ANC to pursue and accomplish its historic mission effectively, we must be unceasing in our efforts to strengthen and expand its underground structures, ensuring its active presence everywhere in this country.

## We support independent states of southern Africa

We hereby extend our unequivocal support to the independent states of southern Africa, including Seychelles, in the common struggle to defeat the aggressive policies of the Botha regime. The training, arming, and deployment of counterrevolutionary bandits into Mozambique, Lesotho, and Zimbabwe forms part of this aggression. We are greatly inspired by the heroic struggle of the people of Angola to expel the occupying South African forces from their country and to wipe out the puppet UNITA bandits.[12] We salute the internationalist Cuban forces which have contributed so decisively to frustrate the schemes of the Pretoria regime and its ally, the Reagan administration.

We extend our greetings to our comrades-in-arms of SWAPO, the People's Liberation Army of Namibia, and the Namibian people as a whole and pledge to fight side by side with them until our continent is rid of all vestiges of colonial and white minority domination.

As we enter this new year — we hail the firm and positive role played by the frontline states and the forward country of Lesotho, despite Pretoria's destabilization efforts and naked aggression against them. The dream of the total liberation of Africa is in sight.

We salute the resilience of the OAU in the face of concerted imperialist maneuvers and call upon both the OAU and the Nonaligned countries to increase their material and moral support for our struggle as well as that of SWAPO and the frontline countries.

## Socialist countries — pillar of support

The socialist countries remain a solid pillar of support to our national liberation struggle. We are assured of their continued internationalist solidarity till the triumph of our revolutionary struggle.

In the past year we have succeeded in widening and deepening our support in the Western countries. We are particularly cognizant of the consistent support we receive from Sweden and other Nordic countries, from Holland, Italy, and Austria to mention a few. We are happy to report the establishment of a new office in Australia, at the supportive invitation of the government and people of that friendly country.

Our efforts to win international support have been significantly sustained by a wide spectrum of anti-apartheid solidarity and mass organizations in almost all the Western countries as well as the countries of Asia, Africa, and Latin America. With respect to the latter continent, the bestowal of the Simón Bolívar International Award to our people's hero, Nelson Mandela, served the great purpose of laying a firm foundation for the future development of our relations with the peoples of Panama, Venezuela, Peru, Bolivia, Ecuador, and other South and Central American countries.

We pay tribute to the progressive forces in the USA for their valiant efforts to achieve wide-scale U.S. disinvestment in South Africa. On them rests the heavy responsibility to defeat the Reagan administration's racist "constructive engagement" policy with Pretoria, and to curb and confine the aggressive character of American imperialism.

We salute the heroic struggle of the Palestinian people, fighting for their birthright under the tried and tested leadership of the PLO, and commend those Arab countries who are making a positive contribution toward the achievement of genuine and lasting peace in the Middle East.

### We pay homage

O N THIS historic seventy-second anniversary of the ANC, we pay undying tribute to the many patriots who have fallen in action since January 8 last year. Among these we remember with great affection, especially Comrades Dora Tamana, Yusuf Mota Dadoo, Rev. James Calata — great stalwarts whose contribution to our movement shall be remembered by all future generations. We dip our revolutionary banner in tribute to the heroic combatants of Umkhonto we Sizwe, including Comrades Jerry Mosololi, Simon Mogoerane, and Thabo Motaung. We pay homage to the martyrs of our people like Saul Mkhize and Msize Dube — all of whom were murdered in cold blood by the Pretoria regime.

We salute all our leaders and activists incarcerated in Pretoria's dungeons, and greet all those who are banned and banished. We greet all our working people in the mines and factories; in the fields and highways; in offices, churches, schools, and hospitals; and in various other socio-cultural services.

We greet parents, and mothers, and fathers who managed to raise families against tremendous odds in the face of the genocidal apartheid polices. The loss of life resulting from the operation of this system is staggering. The progress and victory of our struggle will redeem the situation. In the meantime, as a people, we need to address the problem of lack of respect for human life which is manifest in the growing number of deaths from unnatural causes in the ghettos of our country.

We have just brought to its close a year we observed as one of united action. During this year, we built up the unity of our democratic forces as never before. We must defend and consolidate these gains. We must build on them as we move to the next stage of our struggle. The workers and peasants; women, youth, and students — all of us Black and white — must continue to engage in as ever broader and united assault on the racist regime and its policies.

## 1984 — the year of the women

One of the principal tasks we have to accomplish this year is, as I have said, the organization and mobilization of our womenfolk into struggle. For this reason, in the name of the National Executive Committee of the African National Congress, I declare 1984 "The Year of the Women," and charge the entire democratic and patriotic forces of our country with the task of joining in the effort to mobilize our women to unite in struggle for people's power!

To all true patriots of our country, we extend best wishes for success in our common struggle during this, "The Year of the Women!"

Mobilize and march forward to people's power!

Amandla ngawethu!

Matla ke a rona!

Power to the people!

## Notes

1. In the late 1970s and early 1980s, the apartheid regime embarked on a number of modifications in its system of rule. Some involved concessions, such as the 1979 decision to recognize the right of African workers to organize unions. Others were simply repressive (greater press censorship, provisions for the militarization of factories). Some "reforms" aimed at sowing further divisions among the African, Coloured, and Indian sectors of the Black population and at strengthening the layer of Black functionaries who collaborate in implementing apartheid regulations. The revised 1983 constitution, for example, set up new segregated and largely powerless Indian and Coloured chambers of parliament. In the Black urban townships, new Black-staffed community councils were set up to administer local township affairs on the regime's behalf.

2. In 1910, the four British settler colonies of the Cape, Natal, Orange Free State, and Transvaal were amalgamated into a single state — the Union of South Africa. By the same act, this white supremacist state was granted formal independence from British colonial rule.

3. Apartheid institutions set up by the government and staffed by Black collaborators, who claimed to "represent" different sectors of the Black population.

4. Peasants in the Pondoland region of the Transkei revolted in 1960 against the imposition of government-paid tribal chiefs, unpopular taxes, and arbitrary land "rehabilitation" schemes that only pushed even more rural Africans off their land. The peasants organized themselves into mass assemblies and elected their own leaderships.

5. The Urban Bantu Councils were the predecessors of today's Black community councils.

6. Crossroads and KTC are unauthorized Black shantytowns that had originally been slated for demolition by government minister Piet Koornhof; the government later backed down on its demolition plans.

7. Mdantsane is a large Black township near East London, but located within the borders of the Ciskei Bantustan, headed by the repressive administration of Lennox Sebe.

8. Racist terms for Africans, Indians, and Coloureds, respectively.

9. The frontline states are Angola, Botswana, Mozambique, Tanzania, Zambia, and Zimbabwe.

10. The South West Africa People's Organisation, which is leading Namibia's struggle for independence from South African rule.

11. On December 9, 1982, South African commandos raided ANC refugee houses in Maseru, the capital of Lesotho, murdering thirty South African refugees and twelve Lesotho citizens.

12. The so-called National Union for the Total Independence of Angola, a reactionary Angolan group that receives arms, training, funds, and direct logistical support from South African military forces based in neighboring Namibia.

# Southern Africa:
# A Decade of Struggle

### by Ernest Harsch

AGAINST THE mounting challenge to Africa's last white minority regime, the South African apartheid state is busy fortifying its defenses. South Africa's capitalist rulers have built up the most powerful military machine in Africa, with the goal of maintaining their racist domination over the whole southern end of the continent, through undisguised force when necessary.

Though it is several centuries since the initial white conquests of South Africa's indigenous African peoples, some of the methods remain the same. Not only is the whip still used to quell domestic unrest, but the near-mythical *laager*, or wagon encirclement, of the original land-grabbers is being resurrected. The regime revealed in early 1985 that it was projecting the construction of a fortified fence stretching from the Namibian border with Angola in the northwest to the Mozambique border in the east — a perimeter of more than 2,000 miles. Sections of the fence, composed of 20,000-volt electrified line and new "blade wire" that slashes anyone trying to cut it, have already been put up along Namibia's northern border and along the Limpopo River between South Africa and Zimbabwe. Gen. Magnus Malan, the South African defense minister, termed it "an integrated experiment with border control systems."

But this is a reactionary fantasy. The challenge to the apartheid regime in Pretoria is not a military one from beyond its borders. No African armies are marching on South Africa. Nor is it facing a "Communist onslaught" of Cuban and Soviet troops, as apartheid propagandists in Pretoria so frequently proclaim.

The real challenge is from within — the unfolding national, democratic revolution of the vast majority of propertyless and rightless Blacks, who aim to overthrow the apartheid state and establish a democratic republic that will smash all vestiges of racial oppression and return South Africa's vast wealth to its people.

Nevertheless, events beyond South Africa's immediate borders —

85

like those elsewhere in the world — have a big political impact on the course of this revolution. Victories in the anticolonial and anti-imperialist struggle in the rest of Africa embolden South African Blacks with the confidence that they too can win. And no electrified fence can stop that.

The impact of events elsewhere in Africa has been especially marked over the past decade. Since 1974-75, the "front line" of the freedom struggle has been brought to Pretoria's own doorstep. The people of Angola and Mozambique, arms in hand, won their liberation from Portuguese colonial rule. Invading South African troops were defeated in Angola with decisive assistance from Cuban internationalist volunteers. The Zimbabwean masses ousted the racist Rhodesian regime and won their independence from British rule. The people of South African–occupied Namibia have sharply stepped up their own fight for independence.

From one end of southern Africa to the other, the oppressed and exploited have taken big strides forward. Compared to the situation of ten or fifteen years ago, the relationship of forces throughout the region has swung in their direction, leaving the apartheid state — the bastion of imperialist domination over southern Africa — more isolated.

This transformation of southern Africa since the early 1970s helped set the stage for the outbreak, in mid-1984, of the most massive and sustained Black upheaval that South Africa has yet witnessed. Behind the recurrent scenes of tens of thousands of Blacks marching with banners and songs, of youths defiantly facing armed police, of factories idled by striking workers, there lies the conviction that the forward march of the African freedom struggle is irreversible. "The wind in the north has changed and it blows your way," a song by the popular South African band Juluka reminds its listeners.

For Pretoria, defense of its racist rule involves a battle on all fronts, both within South Africa and beyond its borders. That is why the apartheid regime constantly lashes outward, to defend its interests wherever they are threatened. Since the beginning of the 1980s alone, it has carried out scores of major attacks against neighboring Black-ruled states, including Angola, Mozambique, Botswana, Lesotho, and Zimbabwe, not to mention its escalating war in Namibia. Military invasions, sabotage, assassinations, commando raids, air strikes, and economic embargos are all part of Pretoria's arsenal. In September 1985, the South African regime brazenly admitted that it was providing direct assistance to counterrevolutionary terrorist bands seeking to overthrow the governments of Angola and Mozambique.

The South African regime is playing for high stakes. It is seeking to deny sanctuary and support to the South African and Namibian liberation organizations anywhere in southern Africa, punishing those governments that give them assistance. Stymied by the military capabilities of the Cuban troops in Angola, and fearing the political impact throughout the region of Angola's continued resistance, Pretoria is pushing for the expulsion of the Cubans from that country. It is trying to undermine and eventually overthrow the popular revolutions in Angola and Mozambique. And it is aiming to reestablish South African imperialism's firm domination over all the countries of southern Africa.

This foreign policy of the apartheid state reveals much about its own nature. By unleashing a regional war to advance its aims, Pretoria is extending into other countries the same policy it follows at home — a policy of the bullet and the whip, designed to slap down any expression of defiance and to keep Blacks in perpetual servitude before the white "master."

O VER THE past four decades, since the rise of the new wave of anticolonial struggles in the immediate wake of World War II, every significant advance by the peoples of Africa has found an echo within South Africa itself.

The South African labor strikes, mass urban protests, and resurgence of rural unrest in the late 1940s and through the 1950s were influenced by events in the rest of the continent. New young leaders of the African National Congress (ANC), such as Nelson Mandela and Oliver Tambo, were inspired by the emerging proindependence movements in the British and French colonies of Africa, in particular by the 1952 "Mau Mau" rebellion in Kenya and the Algerian war for independence.

Before his arrest in 1962, Nelson Mandela traveled to newly independent Algeria, where he received military training and other assistance for the ANC from the government of Ahmed Ben Bella. In a December 1964 foreword to a collection of Mandela's speeches, Ben Bella, the head of the Algerian workers' and peasants' government, pointed out that in the struggle of the South African people "under the leadership of [ANC President] Albert Lutuli, Nelson Mandela, and their companions, worthy sons of Africa that they are, they know that henceforth they are not alone. Free Africa is at their sides, as are all those countries that are on the path which leads to the true liberation of mankind."

The collapse of the Portuguese colonial empire in the mid-1970s was especially encouraging to South African Blacks, who had faced setbacks and harsh repression over the previous dozen years. In September 1974, thousands of Black students rallied in South Africa to hail the freedom fighters in Mozambique, who were close to winning their country's independence under the leadership of the Mozambique Liberation Front (Frelimo).

In late 1975 and 1976, the attention of South Africa's Black townships and countryside was riveted on the war in the former Portuguese colony of Angola — a war that pitted the revolutionary People's Movement for the Liberation of Angola (MPLA), supported by Cuban internationalist fighters, against thousands of invading South African troops. The ANC and other South African political groups openly condemned the invasion and sided with the MPLA. Township youths cheered when the South African forces were driven out of Angola in March 1976. A few months later, Black urban centers across South Africa went up in massive rebellions. On June 16, the first day of the protests, youths scrawled on the walls of Orlando High School in Soweto: "Victory is certain — Orlando MPLA."

In March 1980, Zimbabwean liberation movements swept that country's preindependence elections, which the former white minority regime had been forced to agree to because of its inability to crush an expanding guerrilla struggle for liberation. Those reactionary political parties that were supported by Pretoria were trounced in the elections. Activists in Soweto quickly staged a celebration rally. One speaker asked the crowd, "If the people of Zimbabwe can be liberated, why should we not be liberated?"

As the independence war in the South African colony of Namibia mounted, so too did support within South Africa for the Namibian liberation movement. In 1984, leaders of the South West Africa People's Organisation (SWAPO) established direct contacts with South Africa's United Democratic Front, the 2-million-member anti-apartheid coalition. With the rising tally of South African casualties in the Namibian war, young South African whites have launched a campaign against military conscription.

In a similar manner, the freedom struggle of the Black South African majority has influenced the fight against colonialism beyond its own borders. Millions of Blacks from countries throughout southern Africa have worked in South Africa's gold mines or on its farms, taking political and trade union experiences back home and spurring greater political struggle and organization.

The revolutionary struggles of southern Africa are intertwined; they reinforce each other. With its economic, political, and military interests extended throughout the region, there is no way that the apartheid state can remain immune from revolutionary advances elsewhere in southern Africa. The contradictions and conflicts of the entire subcontinent are drawn into it.

## I. PRETORIA'S REGIONAL EMPIRE

**B**ESIDES STRIKING directly at the ANC, SWAPO, and those governments that aid them, Pretoria's regional aggression has another purpose as well: to defend the apartheid state's substantial economic and political interests throughout southern Africa. Victories against imperialism elsewhere in the region not only have a political impact among South African Blacks; they also undermine Pretoria's domination over southern Africa. They weaken the grip of imperialism as a whole over the continent. Thus, on its own behalf and on behalf of Washington, London, and other allied capitals, the apartheid regime acts as a regional gendarme, a guardian of reaction and imperialist oppression.

The apartheid state is itself a junior imperialist power, resting on Africa's largest industrial base. Its economy is dominated by giant monopolies and finance houses. It is driven to export capital and to seek foreign markets and sources of raw materials and labor. Southern Africa is its "hinterland," in effect a neocolonial empire to be exploited for the benefit of the South African industrialists and bankers. All the countries in the region either have South African corporations extracting their agricultural and mineral wealth, rely to some degree on South African markets and goods, have citizens working in the South African mines, or are dependent on South African–dominated rail, air, road, and communications networks.

Namibia (also known as South West Africa) is the country most directly under Pretoria's domination. It has been a South African colony since 1915. Pretoria imposed on the Namibian peoples a brutal system of colonial rule, bearing some striking similarities to apartheid itself. Africans in Namibia have to live in segregated regions and townships. Rural reserves, called Bantustans, were set up with the aim of controlling Africans and keeping them divided along language and tribal lines. Many Namibians have been deprived of their land and cattle, and thus forced onto the labor market, where they get jobs on white-owned farms and with foreign mining, fishing, and industrial companies through a contract labor system modeled on that in South Africa. Namibia's extensive mineral deposits (diamonds, uranium, zinc, copper, tungsten, manganese, and others) are exploited by South African, British, and U.S. companies, with South African firms accounting for nearly half of all foreign investments in Namibia.

From the days when it was ruled by a racist white minority regime, Zimbabwe has been economically tied to its powerful southern neighbor. By 1976, South African companies held as large a stake there as did firms from Britain, the colonial power. With the imposition of international economic sanctions against the racist Rhodesian settler regime in 1965, South Africa became its major trading partner.

Both Angola and Mozambique were penetrated by South African capital under Portuguese colonial rule. This was especially true for Mozambique, which borders directly on South Africa, not far from the industrial region around Johannesburg. South African interests financed and built Mozambique's giant Cabora Bassa hydroelectric project in order to provide electricity to South Africa. Many Mozambicans work in South African gold mines. And considerable South African trade is routed through Mozambican ports.

Botswana, Lesotho, and Swaziland are all members of the South African Customs Union, and provide South African corporations with captive markets. Lesotho, entirely surrounded by South African territory, is the most closely tied to the South African economy; about 40 percent of its entire male work force is employed in South Africa.

Even countries as far away as Zaire, Zambia, and Malawi have been drawn, to one extent or another, into South Africa's economic orbit.

With the goal of defending its political and economic stakes in the region and achieving favorable conditions for further expansion, Pretoria has for decades followed a course of military intervention beyond its borders. At first it tried to help reinforce direct European colonial rule over Africa for as long as it could. But when the rise of the massive anti-colonial struggles of the late 1950s and early 1960s no longer made that possible, the apartheid regime sought to strengthen the most proimperialist and backward political currents in the independent African states. In particular, it encouraged strife among Africans of different language and tribal backgrounds, favoring the most reactionary forces among them. In this way Pretoria attempted to obstruct efforts to forge modern, unified African nations. By doing this, the apartheid regime was simply extending into other countries the same divide-and-rule policies it follows at home.

One of Pretoria's first major interventions came in the formerly Belgian-ruled Congo. The Congo had gained its formal independence in June 1960 under the leadership of Patrice Lumumba, the most outstanding Congolese nationalist leader, whose party was the only one with a national base. Lumumba's militant denunciations of imperialism, as well as the mass mobilizations that preceded and accompanied the attainment of independence, alarmed the imperialists, including those in Pretoria. They quickly acted to bring down his government. South African mercenaries (in collaboration with the U.S. CIA and Belgian paratroopers) came to the aid of the reactionary Moïse Tshombe's short-lived secessionist state in the mineral-rich province of Katanga.

To put down this attempt at dismemberment, Lumumba appealed for international assistance, including from the United Nations. The UN did send troops, but many of the contingents, under imperialist command, actively assisted Lumumba's opponents. As Cuban journalist José M. Oriz García noted years later, the Cuban revolution was not then in a position to answer Lumumba's appeal. "At that time," he wrote, "the very young Cuban revolution was battling with arms in hand against the direct attacks of the Yankee imperialists."

Because of the Lumumba government's weakness and isolation, the imperialist assault on the Congo succeeded. Lumumba was deposed and murdered.

Several years later, in 1965, Cuban revolutionary leader Che Guevara did try to come to the Congolese peoples' aid, helping to train Lumumbaist guerrilla forces that were participating in a massive peasant rebellion against the dictatorship of Mobutu Sese Seko. On the other side, once again, were South African mercenaries who helped the regime crush this revolt. Since then, Congo, later renamed Zaire, has been ruled by one of the most corrupt, despotic, and proimperialist regimes on the entire African continent.

Although the bulk of Africa won its independence during the 1960s, the tide of liberation ebbed for a while, leaving most of southern Africa under continued colonial and racist rule. Until the early 1970s, Pretoria's main regional allies were the Portuguese colonialists ruling Angola and Mozambique and the Rhodesian settler regime. They formed a triumvirate of reaction that dominated the entire region.

Of these three powers, Pretoria was the mainstay. As the fledgling Angolan, Mozambican, and Zimbabwean liberation movements took up arms against Portuguese and Rhodesian rule in the mid-to-late 1960s, the apartheid regime came to the aid of its allies. South African paramilitary units were sent to Angola and Mozambique to assist the Portuguese army's counterinsurgency operations. In Angola this included actions against the freedom fighters of SWAPO, which had launched its armed struggle for Namibian independence in 1966 and had established some guerrilla bases in Angola's sparsely populated southern provinces.

In 1967 the ANC carried out joint campaigns in Zimbabwe with guerrillas of the Zimbabwe African People's Union. Pretoria soon dispatched South African police to help the Rhodesian regime combat this new challenge. That year and the next, a few South African attacks were also carried into Zambia, whose government provided assistance to the Zimbabwean, Namibian, and South African liberation forces.

## II. A DECADE OF REVOLUTIONARY ADVANCES

PRETORIA'S EFFORTS to hold the "front line" of independent Africa far from its own borders ultimately failed.

In the Portuguese colonies, the national liberation movements gained ground. They deepened their support among an African peasantry that had had enough of land confiscations, colonial taxes, forced labor, repression, and the lack of even the most minimal education and health facilities. The liberation organizations maintained clandestine links with urban and rural workers, who were denied any right to form unions or to strike. They more and more became the rallying points for all those who favored an end to colonial domination and the establishment of independent and sovereign states.

The movements fighting for independence also sought to advance the process of forging modern nations from the disparate language and tribal groupings that had been kept divided by centuries of Portuguese rule. They actively opposed the colonialists' division of the Black population into separate strata, such as the *indígenas* (the illiterate "natives"), the *assimilados* (the small layer of literate Africans), and the *mestiços* (those of mixed ancestry).

In Guinea-Bissau, a small Portuguese colony on the coast of West Africa, the African Party for the Independence of Guinea-Bissau and the Cape Verde Islands (PAIGC) made the earliest gains. By the beginning of the 1970s, it had won effective control of most of the countryside and had proclaimed a provisional government that won wide international recognition.

In Mozambique, Frelimo established extensive "liberated zones" in the northern provinces, benefiting from sanctuary and material support from neighboring Tanzania (which suffered from some Portuguese bombing raids as a result). By the end of the 1960s, Frelimo had clearly emerged as the vanguard liberation organization, as other currents either declined or went over to the Portuguese.

In Angola the struggle proved more difficult. The MPLA made significant gains in parts of the country during the late 1960s and early 1970s. Its progress was hampered by a number of factors, however. Most important were the relative success of the Portuguese colonial authorities in reinforcing tribal cleavages and direct imperialist support for the MPLA's chief Angolan rivals — the Angolan National Liberation Front (FNLA) and the National Union for the Total Independence of Angola (UNITA).

The FNLA, which had carried out some actions against Portuguese colonial rule in northern Angola in the early 1960s, never adopted a pan-Angolan perspective. Its base remained almost entirely among the Bakongo people of the north. It later launched attacks against MPLA fighters, received funds from the CIA, and fell increasingly under the political sponsorship of the Zairean dictatorship.

UNITA was based largely among the Ovimbundu people of the central highlands. It linked up with imperialist forces seeking to block the establishment of a united, independent Angolan nation. By the early 1970s, UNITA had concluded a tacit ceasefire arrangement with the Portuguese colonial authorities and concentrated on combating the growing activity of MPLA guerrillas in the eastern reaches of the country.

The MPLA's initial and strongest base was among the Mbundu people of the Luanda-Malange region, but it also had as members and supporters *mestiços, assimilados*, and a few revolutionary whites, and was winning new adherents among other peoples of the country. This was because the MPLA, unlike the FNLA and UNITA, sought to overcome the old tribal divisions and to lead the struggle of *all* Angolans to forge a nation and win independence from colonial rule. Also unlike the FNLA and UNITA, the MPLA actively put forward a social program for the advance of Angola's national, democratic revolution, a program that called for land reform, workers' rights, women's emancipation, economic development in the interests of Angola's toiling people, opposition to imperialist domination, and support for other southern African liberation movements.

The vanguard liberation organizations in Portugal's three main African colonies recognized that they were waging a common struggle, against the same immediate enemy. The PAIGC, Frelimo, and MPLA established close ties and influenced each other politically. They appealed for support from the international workers' movement, from the workers' states, and from liberal bourgeois forces in the capitalist countries. Most consistently they gained assistance from revolutionary Cuba. (Pedro Rodríguez Peralta, now a member of the Central Committee of the Cuban Communist Party, fought with the PAIGC; and Cuban instructors helped train some MPLA units in Congo-Brazzaville in the late 1960s.)

After more than a decade of armed struggle in Guinea-Bissau, Mozambique, and Angola, the strains and pressures of its colonial wars undermined the right-wing dictatorship within Portugal itself. It was ousted by an officers' coup in April 1974. Mass public campaigns were launched in Portugal for an end to the colonial wars. This, combined with the deteriorating morale of the Portuguese army in Africa and a new surge of proindependence mobilizations by the workers and peasants of the colonized countries, stymied the efforts of those sectors of the Portuguese ruling class that sought to maintain the African empire. One by one, through late 1974 and 1975, Portugal's African colonies gained their independence. The liberation movements came to power in Mozambique, Angola, Guinea-Bissau, the Cape Verde Islands, and the small islands of Sao Tome and Principe in the Gulf of Guinea.

THE COLLAPSE of the Portuguese colonial empire was a stunning blow to Pretoria. The front line had suddenly moved hundreds of miles southward. One of apartheid's key regional allies had been defeated. Black activists within South Africa found a new source of inspiration.

The apartheid regime went into action to try to contain the damage, and to drive the revolutionary struggle back as far as possible.

On the eve of Mozambique's independence in June 1975, sectors of the South African military and the governing National Party promoted plans to invade Mozambique and keep Frelimo from coming to power. These plans never got off the ground, though other forms of economic and military pressure were later applied to destabilize the Frelimo government.

IN ANGOLA, however, conditions were more favorable for a South African invasion. While the MPLA was the vanguard of the Angolan liberation struggle, it had not yet been able to establish its political authority in substantial regions of the country. The FNLA and UNITA — with aid from the CIA, the Zairean dictatorship, Pretoria, and right-wing sectors of the Portuguese military — launched a civil war to block the coming to power of a government led by the MPLA.

In March 1975 thousands of regular Zairean troops invaded Angola from the north, helping the FNLA secure its base in the region. In August, the first South African units crossed the border of southern Angola, from their bases in Namibia, and captured a hydroelectric dam on the Kunene River.

Encouraged by Washington to drive further, thousands of South African troops poured over the border in October and began a rapid march northward. Allied with the UNITA forces and armed with jets, tanks, artillery, and armored cars, they took city after city. On the eve of Angola's scheduled independence, November 11, enemy troops were on the outskirts of Luanda, poised to take the capital, the MPLA's main base at the time.

In many ways, the imperialist assault on Angola was similar to the one in the Congo fifteen years earlier, combining direct intervention by imperialist troops with support for local reactionary political groups that were presented as the "legitimate" representatives of the African people. The goal was also the same: to block the coming to power of the only organization with a truly national perspective; to drive back the advancing democratic revolution; and to establish a compliant regime, on the model of Mobutu's Zairean dictatorship, that would faithfully follow the dictates of Pretoria, Washington, and other imperialist capitals.

But 1975 was not 1960. Angola existed in a different Africa — and a different world.

As Cuban President Fidel Castro pointed out in a speech to a congress of the Cuban Communist Party on December 22, 1975: "Everything was ready to take over Angola before November 11. And the plan was very solid; it was a solid plan; the only thing was that the plan failed. They had not counted on international solidarity, on the support given to the heroic people of Angola by the socialist countries, in the first place, and by the revolutionary movements and progressive governments of Africa, or the support we Cubans, among the world's progressive governments, also gave Angola."

The aid that Angola received from revolutionary Cuba was the decisive factor in defeating the imperialist intervention. Without it, Angola might very well have suffered the fate of Lumumba's Congo. The liberation struggle throughout southern Africa would have been gravely set back.

Cuba not only came to Angola's aid directly, but also championed its cause internationally, stressing the importance of this battle for the entire African continent. On August 28, just a few weeks after the first South African troops crossed into southern Angola, Raúl Roa García, then Cuba's minister of foreign affairs, told a summit meeting of the Movement of Nonaligned Countries in Peru, "The process of decolonization [in Angola] has become very alarming. There is evidently a neocolonialist plot on a vast scale aimed at counteracting the liberation movements in southern Africa and setting up dependent governments in dismembered Angola so the developed capitalist world will continue to receive a constant flow of energy resources from that country, thanks to control of the transnational companies. . . . The outcome of this conflict will have a significant bearing on the upsurge or decline of the process of decolonization in Africa. The future of the oppressed and discriminated-against peoples of Namibia, Zimbabwe, and South Africa depends, to a large extent, on the outcome of the struggle in Angola."

In early October, the first Cuban military instructors arrived in Angola in response to an initial request from the MPLA government. Then, receiving a further urgent appeal, the Cuban Communist Party Central Committee decided on November 5 to send thousands of volunteer troops. This was called "Operation Carlotta," after a slave who led a rebellion in Cuba's Matanzas Province on that same date in 1843.

The first sizable Cuban troop contingents arrived in Angola several days later, just in the nick of time. The Zairean and FNLA troops in the north were pushing to capture Luanda and the oil-rich enclave of Cabinda by November 11, in order to establish an FNLA-UNITA government on the very day the country was to become officially independent. But with the MPLA's forces reinforced by the newly arrived Cuban troops, that drive was blocked. The MPLA still held Luanda on November 11.

For a while, the war was stalemated, and the Angolan revolution remained in a very precarious position. But the military situation turned in its favor as more Cuban troops poured in, as large shipments of Soviet arms began to arrive, and as new units of the MPLA's army were trained. Beginning in mid-December, the combined MPLA-Cuban forces went on the offensive, at first against the FNLA and Zairean troops in the north, and then eastward and southward against the South

African invaders and their UNITA allies.

The tide also turned internationally. The MPLA-led People's Republic of Angola won wide recognition in Africa as the country's legitimate government. Pro-MPLA demonstrations broke out in Kinshasa, the Zairean capital. With the entry of the Cuban troops into the war, the political stakes were raised for Washington, forcing it either to choose a major escalation of its intervention or to pull back. Given the international relationship of class forces at the time (just after its defeat in Vietnam), Washington chose the latter course. The U.S. Congress adopted legislation to curtail the CIA's clandestine aid to the FNLA and UNITA. This left Pretoria yet more isolated.

By March 27, 1976, the last of the South African invading troops had been pushed back across the border into Namibia.

The South African defeat in Angola was a major turning point for all of southern Africa. Fidel Castro termed it an "African Girón," recalling the Cuban revolution's victory against the U.S.-organized counterrevolutionary invasion of Cuba at Playa Girón (the Bay of Pigs) in 1961.

For the first time, the military forces of the apartheid state had been defeated in battle. For Africans throughout the region, Pretoria — despite its massive military might — was no longer the invincible power that it had seemed to be. Not only had Angola's revolution been saved, but the revolutionary struggle throughout southern Africa, including in South Africa itself, was given a tremendous boost.

ANC President Oliver Tambo visited Angola's southern border on the day that the last South African troops pulled out. He declared that the myth of Pretoria's unbeatable military strength "was destroyed by men who had been hardened in struggle over a period of fourteen years and it was a source of inspiration to know that no African country, however newly independent, need be subject to domination, harassment or bullying by a fascist regime if it is determined to defend its sovereignty and knows who its genuine friends are."

And because of the Cuban volunteers' heroic and decisive role in Angola, more and more of the oppressed and exploited — from Luanda, to the Black townships of Johannesburg, and across the African continent — counted revolutionary Cuba among those "genuine friends."

**A**LTHOUGH ANGOLA still had to live in Pretoria's shadow and suffered from continued South African aggression, the victory in 1976 gave it some room to breathe. It gained time to begin rebuilding the country from the ravages of war and to advance its anti-imperialist, democratic revolution.

But reviving economic and social life was no easy task. When the Portuguese colonialists pulled out, they left behind a country that had been pillaged for 500 years, where 85 percent of the population was illiterate and few Angolans had been trained to perform any but the most menial jobs. All but 10 percent of the 350,000 white Portuguese settlers fled, simply abandoning their positions, jobs, farms, and businesses, while taking away or destroying as much as they could. On top of that, the civil war and South African invasion had destroyed many factories, roads, and bridges, and seriously disrupted agricultural production.

In Luanda and the rest of the country, neighborhood committees, as well as other mass organizations, were formed. Angolans for the first time ever voted for a National Assembly. To supplement the regular army and help defend the country from the ongoing South African aggression, a militia, called the People's Defense Organization, was established alongside the regular army. This militia today has some 1 million members, the vast majority of them peasants and workers, out of a total population of 7.5 million. At the request of the Angolan government, Cuban troops remained in Angola to train the new army and militia and to help hold off further South African attacks.

Steps have been taken to draw the different peoples of Angola closer together. Many former supporters of the FNLA and UNITA have been reintegrated into social and political life. Literacy campaigns, health care, and other social programs have penetrated the regions where those groups originally had some influence. In addition to Portuguese, Angola's school system now uses six of the country's indigenous languages; building a united Angolan nation goes hand-in-hand with preserving and developing the country's cultural richness and diversity.

For a country where 85 percent of the population lives in rural areas, agrarian reform has been key to the entire revolutionary process. The first step was to return the lands that had been expropriated by the Portuguese to the Angolan people. About 1,500 abandoned Portuguese farms were nationalized; some were transformed into state farms and others were distributed to peasants organized into cooperatives.

But this affected only a small portion of the rural population. The vast majority still tilled their land in the most primitive material and social conditions; hand tools were the only implements for most, and private property in land had never arisen. It took the government a while to recognize the special steps needed to help them rise above a bare subsistence level. Initially officials had devoted more attention to the state farms than to providing assistance to individual peasants. "We underestimated the importance of the peasant farmer," Finance Minister Augusto Teixeira de Matos told a reporter in early 1985. Greater financial and technical support and material incentives are now being given to the small-scale producers. They have also been encouraged to organize themselves into associations, of which there are several thousand.

The weight of Portuguese colonial rule, with its taxes, forced labor, and compulsory cultivation of certain crops, kept most Angolan peasants in abysmal poverty. These conditions severely hampered the formation of a modern farming population capable of making a decent living and meeting the country's basic food needs. The end of colonialism brought an expansion of Angola's domestic market and the emergence of a more significant layer of peasants producing for the market.

The Angolan working class, which was quite small under colonial rule, has likewise been able to grow, and to organize itself for the first time along class lines. Practically no unions existed before independence. Today the overwhelming majority of Angolan workers are organized into unions, with some 600,000 belonging to the National Union of Angolan Workers.

These steps forward for Angola's peasantry and working class are part of the process through which the class forces necessary for the Angolan nation's further advance are being created and strengthened.

Independence also brought an end to Portuguese-imposed restrictions on which occupations Africans could pursue. As a result, other strata of Angolan small vendors and shopkeepers, self-employed artisans, and professionals have arisen or been strengthened. Also beginning to emerge are social layers with class interests directly in conflict with those of the toilers: large private traders and merchants, corrupt state and party officials who use their positions or family ties to amass wealth, directors of state enterprises who divert goods to their own use. These layers are most susceptible to imperialist pressures.

The weakening of direct imperialist control over the Angolan economy has aided the revolution's development. The government has nationalized all banks and insurance companies, as well as most industrial concerns. The state sector controls two-thirds of all manufacturing production and employs three-quarters of all industrial workers. The remainder of industrial production is overwhelmingly in the hands of foreign-owned companies. The government has acquired majority shares in the two biggest imperialist interests: the Gulf Oil facilities in Cabinda, and the diamond fields in the northeast. Foreign trade has also been nationalized.

Since independence, Angola's school system has been vastly expanded, and by 1980 virtually the entire school-age population had been enrolled in elementary school — extremely rare in Africa. Within five years, some 1 million Angolan adults had been taught the basics of reading and writing. Medical care was made free of charge, new health clinics were built around the country, and medical personnel visited some of the remotest towns and villages. Hundreds of Cuban volunteer teachers and doctors are playing an indispensable role in these programs.

The Angolan people, having benefited so much from international solidarity, are making their own contribution to the broader southern African struggle. Angola has opened its borders to refugees fleeing from repression: some 70,000 from Namibia, 6,500 from South Africa, and 20,000 from Zaire. The government has provided important political and military assistance to both the ANC and SWAPO.

I N MOZAMBIQUE, on South Africa's own doorstep, a democratic revolution was also opened by the victory over Portuguese colonial rule.

When they won their independence on June 25, 1975, the Mozambican masses faced many of the same problems and prospects as their Angolan brothers and sisters: near-universal illiteracy, a population ravaged by disease and hunger, an administration and economy that was at the point of collapse due to the flight of most white Portuguese settlers, and the domination of key sectors of the economy by imperialist capital (including South African). The process of building a nation from the various language and tribal groups is still in its infancy in Mozambique.

Based on the initial experiences of mass organization acquired during the period of the anticolonial struggle, mass women's and youth associations were set up soon after independence. But it was not until 1983 that Mozambique's small working class formed its first unions.

The new government nationalized all land in Mozambique. Peasants who worked the land were guaranteed the right to continue occupying their farms. Abandoned Portuguese plantations and farms became state enterprises or were distributed to peasant cooperatives. In some provinces, such as Gaza in the south, tens of thousands of acres of unused land were eventually distributed to individual peasants.

Since most Mozambican peasants live scattered throughout the countryside, in individual family encampments, the government has sought to encourage them to move into new communal villages. This makes it easier to organize the rural areas and to facilitate the provision of health care, schooling, and other social services. By the early 1980s, some 1,350 such villages had been established, encompassing 1.8 million of Mozambique's 12 million people.

Until 1983 the government had concentrated on boosting the state farms, while virtually ignoring the vast mass of near-subsistence peasants. Frelimo's Fourth Congress that year marked a shift from this policy. The congress called for more assistance to small-scale peasant producers, who account for three-quarters of all crops. Millions of hand tools were imported that year for distribution to these peasants.

Despite Mozambique's poverty, important programs have been initiated to improve social conditions. In the first five years of independence, the number of children attending primary school doubled. The overall illiteracy rate was brought down from 95 percent to 75 percent, and among Mozambicans aged ten to fourteen years it was reduced to 60 percent. Health care was significantly expanded and mass vaccination campaigns were carried out. Cuban doctors and other technical personnel have played an important role in these programs.

During the late 1970s, the government nationalized most banks, insurance companies, a shipping concern, an oil refinery, and a number of foreign-owned agricultural and industrial enterprises. Imperialist interests and a few remaining resident Portuguese businessmen continue to control sections of industry, commerce, and commercial agriculture, however. Layers of exploiting Mozambican businessmen and corrupt state and party officials have emerged since independence, as well, and are especially open to imperialist pressures and interests. Most important, South African imperialism continues to wield considerable economic leverage — and has used it to apply pressure on the Frelimo government.

Mozambique has accorded significant aid to other African liberation movements. Above all, the Mozambican government and people threw their active support behind the liberation struggle in neighboring Zimbabwe. Prior to the 1984 agreement between the governments of Mozambique and South Africa (the Nkomati accords), the ANC was allowed to establish an office in Maputo — just 40 miles from South Africa — and several hundred ANC members were given refuge in Mozambique.

ORIGINALLY PROCLAIMED as the British colony of Rhodesia in 1890 by white settlers and adventurers operating out of South Africa, Zimbabwe was ruled by a white colonial settler regime that reflected in many ways the kind of racist policies followed by its southern neighbor. The tiny minority of whites — 4 percent of the entire population of 7 million — dominated the country economically and politically.

The early white settlers seized nearly half the land in the country and an equivalent proportion of the African population's cattle. Like the Bantustans in South Africa, rural reserves were set up, to which a majority of Africans were confined in impoverished and overcrowded conditions. Many of the rest had to work on white-owned farms or for largely foreign-owned mining and industrial corporations (dominated by South African, British, and U.S. capital). Racist laws restricted African movement and Africans were denied most basic democratic rights. Only whites, and a very tiny number of Africans with sufficient property and education "qualifications," could vote.

Though influenced in part by South Africa's apartheid system, the Rhodesian state was patterned more closely after other European colonies in Africa that had had sizable white-settler populations, such as

Kenya or Algeria. It remained a direct colony of Britain — although the white-settler regime of Ian Smith proclaimed a "unilateral declaration of independence" in 1965 that received little or no international diplomatic recognition. Rhodesia was also much weaker than the apartheid state, with a significantly smaller white population to draw on and a smaller industrial base. A more recent creation, it was unable to drive Africans off the land to the same degree as in South Africa, and was not able to construct such an all-embracing system of social controls.

The armed struggle for liberation began in the 1960s, first by the Zimbabwe African People's Union (ZAPU) and later by the Zimbabwe African National Union (ZANU) as well. Their fight was for the overthrow of the racist settler regime, independence from British rule, and the recovery of the land and other wealth that had been stolen from the African majority. These liberation organizations received some direct support from the neighboring government of Zambia, and maintained bases and refugee camps in that country.

But it was the victory in Angola and the independence of neighboring Mozambique that spurred the Zimbabwean struggle into a new period of mass mobilization and insurgency. Despite their past frictions and rivalries, ZAPU and ZANU coordinated their efforts to an extent. Both stepped up their armed actions. Based mainly among Zimbabwe's majority Shona–speaking population, ZANU emerged as the larger and more influential of the two organizations. Even before Mozambique's independence, ZANU had forged close ties with Frelimo and had established guerrilla bases in Frelimo-controlled areas of Mozambique. From those bases and from others set up after Mozambican independence, ZANU sent its fighters across the border into eastern Zimbabwe. These regions, populated largely by Shona speakers, rallied on a massive scale to the insurgency and swelled ZANU's ranks. ZAPU was based mainly in the Ndebele-speaking regions in the west.

The Rhodesian regime launched a war to militarily crush the insurgency and preserve white rule "for a thousand years," as Smith boasted. More than 25,000 people, the vast majority of them African villagers, were killed during the course of the war, and more than a million were uprooted from their homes.

As the struggle intensified, Pretoria deepened its military intervention in Zimbabwe. By 1975-76 it was providing half of the Rhodesian military budget. South African pilots and technicians, military officers, jet fighters, helicopters, and arms poured into the country. South African troops set up base in southern Zimbabwe.

Following Pretoria's example of regional aggression, the Rhodesian regime took the war across its own borders. Some air strikes were directed against ZAPU bases in Zambia and Angola. But the main target was Mozambique. Rhodesian jets repeatedly flew into Mozambique, bombing and strafing Zimbabwean refugee camps, massacring thousands. The Rhodesian Central Intelligence Organisation formed a puppet army called the Mozambique National Resistance (Renamo, or MNR). It was composed largely of Mozambicans who had fought with the Portuguese against Frelimo, but also some Frelimo defectors who opposed the Mozambican revolution's course or had been expelled for corruption. These Renamo bands carried out terrorist and sabotage actions within Mozambique, causing significant economic damage and loss of life.

In 1978-79, the Frelimo government responded to these attacks by sending several hundred Mozambican troops into Zimbabwe to help fight alongside the ZANU forces. They aimed to speed the Zimbabwean victory and end the war.

Alarmed by the depth of the Zimbabwean insurgency and the growing regional support it was receiving, London, Washington, and even Pretoria eventually came to the conclusion that the Smith regime was doomed. To prevent it from being toppled militarily (with consequences that would have been difficult to control), they began applying pressure on Smith to institute some reforms that could defuse the Zimbabwean powder keg and prepare the way for the installation of a neocolonial regime.

In 1979, Bishop Abel Muzorewa and several other Blacks were brought into the government, with Muzorewa as the new prime minister. Smith, who took a different cabinet post, remained the real power in the government, however. It was later revealed that Pretoria funded Muzorewa's party to the tune of more than $1 million. But this regime failed utterly to win any degree of popular support, and the liberation war escalated further.

The U.S. and British imperialists then decided that it was necessary to try to bring ZAPU and ZANU into a negotiated, compromise settlement. Talks were held at Lancaster House, in London, and by the end of 1979 an agreement had been reached: Zimbabwe would gain its independence, following elections in which all Africans could vote for the first time, but with a constitution that entrenched continued white political privileges and property "rights" for at least the next decade.

Within this framework, the imperialists sought to keep ZAPU's and ZANU's showing in the elections as low as possible. Pretoria again threw its weight behind the parties of Muzorewa and Smith, and Rhodesian troops continued to intimidate the African population. But the Zimbabwean masses seized the opening provided by the Lancaster House accords, and made their choice felt. ZAPU and ZANU leaders, upon their return home after years in exile, were greeted with mammoth demonstrations of popular support, the largest in the country's history. Their candidates swept the elections easily. ZANU leader Robert Mugabe was slated to become the new prime minister on the day of independence.

That independence came on April 18, 1980, as the new Zimbabwean flag went up in place of Britain's Union Jack. For the Zimbabwean masses, this was a historic victory. The independence they had long fought for had been won. The hated white minority regime had been ousted. Many of the laws that restricted African rights were abrogated. Since then, African workers have won significant wage increases, and are in a better position to fight for more gains. Tens of thousands of poor rural families have gotten land. School enrollment has more than doubled since independence, and primary school is now free. Rural services, especially health care, have been expanded significantly.

Yet many problems and obstacles remain. Pretoria retains a grip on many of Zimbabwe's economic lifelines. South African President P.W. Botha has made thinly veiled threats to invade Zimbabwe if the new government does anything to undermine South African "security." The state apparatus remains infested with racist white officials (some of whom have been exposed as agents of the South African regime).

The Mugabe government has thus far abided by the Lancaster House accords. Its terms greatly hamper key democratic tasks, including enactment of a radical agrarian reform. Some 5,000 white landlords continue to own nearly half of the land, while millions of African peasants remain landless or have plots so small that they can barely survive on them. Striking African workers have had to face not only the hostile management of imperialist corporations, but at times the Zimbabwean police as well.

The process of forging a Zimbabwean nation has suffered some serious setbacks. This has been reflected in armed clashes, fostered by ZANU and ZAPU leaders, between the Shona and Ndebele supporters of the two organizations. Thousands have been killed in these conflicts.

Despite these postindependence difficulties, the downfall of the Smith regime and the attainment of Zimbabwe's independence were big blows to apartheid South Africa. Another one of its regional allies had fallen. Another bordering country is ruled by a majority Black government. Pretoria has been further isolated, and the confidence and combativity of South African Blacks have been raised yet another notch.

**W**ITH ZIMBABWE'S independence, the number of Frontline States in southern Africa increased to six: Angola, Botswana, Mozambique, Tanzania, Zambia, and Zimbabwe. These governments hold periodic meetings to discuss the prospects for the liberation of the remaining countries still under white minority rule, Namibia and South Africa. They help coordinate support for the ANC and SWAPO, which they recognize as the legitimate representatives of the South African and Namibian peoples. To counter the imperialist propaganda that economic sanctions should not be imposed on Pretoria because they would hit other countries in the region as well, the Frontline States issued an appeal in September 1985 calling for increased international pressures against Pretoria, including economic sanctions.

Since Zimbabwe is the most industrialized country in the region after South Africa itself, its independence opened up certain possibilities for greater economic cooperation among the Black-ruled states of southern Africa, and for steps to lessen their economic subordination to South African imperialism.

In April 1980, the six Frontline States were joined by Lesotho, Swaziland, and Malawi to formally launch a new regional grouping, the Southern African Development Coordination Conference (SADCC). These countries have a combined population of 60 million. The participation of the Lesotho, Swazi, and Malawian governments was an unexpected shock to the apartheid regime, since they were all viewed in Pretoria as virtual vassal states that would unquestioningly follow South African dictates. It was obvious that South Africa's control over its regional empire was diminishing.

At the time of its formation, the SADCC issued a declaration summing up the group's aspirations:

"Southern Africa is dependent on the Republic of South Africa as a focus of transport and communications, an exporter of goods and services, and as an importer of goods and cheap labour. This dependence is not a natural phenomenon nor is it simply the result of a free market economy. The nine states and one occupied territory of Southern Africa (Angola, Botswana, Lesotho, Malawi, Mozambique, Namibia, Swaziland, Tanzania, Zambia, and Zimbabwe) were, in varying degrees, deliberately incorporated — by metropolitan powers, colonial rulers, and large corporations — into the colonial and sub-colonial structures centring in general on the Republic of South Africa. The development of national economies as balanced units, let alone the welfare of the people of Southern Africa, played no part in the economic integration strategy. Not surprisingly, therefore, Southern Africa is fragmented, grossly exploited, and subject to economic manipulations by outsiders. . . .

"It is not the quest for liberation, but the entrenched racism, exploitation, and oppression which is the cause of conflict in Southern Africa. The power behind this is in large measure economic. Economic liberation is, therefore, as vital as political freedom."

The SADCC's achievements so far have been modest, but it has registered some gains. Zimbabwe sells corn to other SADCC member states, lessening their need for South African corn imports. Angola offers oil at preferential rates to fellow SADCC members. Up to the end of 1982 alone, more than fifty SADCC projects — including port improvements, road reconstruction, and railway rehabilitation — were completed or under way. As a result, Mozambican harbors and railways were handling about half of all rail traffic from Malawi and Zimbabwe, as well as daily trains from the copper mines of Zaire and Zambia. Before the SADCC was launched, these countries had to move most of their goods through South Africa.

Victory for the South African revolution could open wide the door toward economic development and cooperation for all the countries of southern Africa.

Another sign of the weakening of Pretoria's effective control over the other countries of southern Africa has been the increased political defiance that it meets. Even some of the weaker states in the region have shifted their stance toward Pretoria. During the 1970s, the government of Botswana provided sanctuary to South African and Zimbabwean refugees. The government of Leabua Jonathan in Lesotho has sharpened its condemnations of apartheid, opened diplomatic relations with some workers' states, and spoken out more forcefully in support of the ANC.

In June 1977, Pretoria received yet another blow when the pro–South African regime of James Mancham was overthrown in the Seychelles, a tiny country of more than 100 islands and 70,000 people some 1,000 miles off the coast of East Africa. The new government, headed by Albert René, shut down the South African airline's facilities on the islands. René has openly expressed his admiration for the Cuban revolution.

THE STRUGGLE in Namibia, as those elsewhere in southern Africa, received a powerful impetus from the Angolan victory over the South African invading forces in March 1976. After all, one of the aims of that invasion had been to obliterate SWAPO's presence in southern Angola.

This victory was reinforced a few months later by the massive Black youth rebellions in South Africa itself. Namibian students and teachers went on strike that year in solidarity with their South African brothers and sisters. SWAPO guerrillas, based in the northern part of Namibia and operating from regions of southern Angola, escalated their armed struggle. Since the late 1970s, the insurgency led by SWAPO has stepped up even further, particularly in the more heavily populated northern regions, but also in parts of the center and south in recent years.

Pretoria has responded by sending in some 60,000 regular South African troops. They are supplemented by tens of thousands of white and Black Namibian recruits and conscripts fighting under South African command in the South West Africa Territory Force. Entire areas of the north have been declared free-fire zones. Tens of thousands of Namibians (out of a total population of just 1.5 million) have been uprooted from their homes and forced to live in overcrowded areas under virtual military guard. South African troops have conducted periodic massacres of Namibian villagers. Suspected SWAPO supporters are routinely tortured and killed.

Despite such repression, open support for SWAPO has been increasing among other Namibian organizations, including political parties, churches, and tribal councils. Some have joined SWAPO. Taking advantage of the fact that SWAPO's internal political organization is not banned, SWAPO supporters have been able to organize public demonstrations in Windhoek and other towns from time to time, some of them involving thousands of participants. Drawing on the political example of the mammoth Black upsurge in South Africa, SWAPO issued an August 1985 appeal to the Namibian people calling for stepped-up protests, strikes, and other mass actions in Namibia as well.

SWAPO is the only organization in Namibia with a truly national base, drawing its support from Ovambos, Hereros, Damaras, and other indigenous African peoples; it also has some white members. Various attempts by the South African colonial administration to cobble together a political counterweight to SWAPO have failed abysmally. SWAPO is now widely recognized, both within Namibia and internationally, as the sole, legitimate representative of the Namibian people.

## III.  APARTHEID'S WAR AGAINST THE 'FRONT LINE'

CONFRONTED BY an entire region in revolt, Pretoria has pursued a strategy of "total war," as apartheid officials sometimes describe it. It has elevated military intervention and economic blackmail to the center of its foreign policy. No state in southern Africa has been immune. And some countries, particularly Angola and Mozambique, have not known a single day of peace over the past decade.

Washington and Pretoria each pursue their own particular imperialist interests in southern Africa, which sometimes do not coincide. Nonetheless, they share a more fundamental commitment to preserving the region as a stable arena for imperialist investment, for the extraction of raw materials, and for the superexploitation of the labor of African workers and peasants. Washington recognizes the apartheid regime as the strongest bastion for imperialist interests in sub-Saharan Africa, and Pretoria benefits from Washington's unchallenged position as the most powerful world cop for the entire imperialist system.

As one senior White House official commented shortly after the installation of the Reagan administration in 1981, the U.S. and South African governments have "shared strategic concerns in southern Africa." That is one reason why the U.S. rulers stepped up their political, military, and economic support to Pretoria, under the U.S. policy known as "constructive engagement."

While Washington refuses to recognize the Angolan government, continues to support its opponents, and seeks to impose economic embargos on the country, Pretoria has kept Angola at the top of its hit list. No sooner had the South African army been forced to pull out in 1976 than it was preparing for new attacks.

The apartheid regime's ongoing war against Angola has two interrelated goals: to punish the Angola people and obstruct their efforts to develop their country, and to strike out at the Namibian refugees and freedom fighters who have sought sanctuary and assistance there.

Many small-scale raids into Angola were conducted by South African commando units in 1976-77. The first large-scale assault following the end of the Angolan war came in May 1978, when South African jets and paratroopers attacked a Namibian refugee camp at Cassinga, massacring more than 600 Namibians, nearly half of them children. This was followed by other major invasions in subsequent years. Pretoria tried to justify these attacks as "hot pursuit" operations against SWAPO guerrillas. But they were directed primarily at Namibian — and Angolan — civilians. Thousands of Angolans have been killed and hundreds of thousands have been forced to flee their homes. Since 1975, economic damage to Angola from such South African attacks has been estimated at a staggering $10 billion.

As it did during its 1975-76 invasion, the apartheid regime also acted through local surrogates. The remnants of the reactionary UNITA bands, which had fled with the departing South African troops, were reorganized at South African bases in Namibia. Trained, armed, and financed by Pretoria, they were infiltrated back across the border into southern and central Angola to lay land mines, burn crops, sabotage economic installations, blow up bridges, massacre villagers, ambush SWAPO guerrillas, and act as scouts for South African forces. Some former troops of the FNLA, the other reactionary Angolan group, have been incorporated into a special unit of the South African army, called the Thirty-second Battalion, that also operates in southern Angola.

Often, the UNITA mercenary bands function with direct South African logistical support: air drops, radio communications, and aerial surveillance. After a massive South African invasion in August 1981, Pretoria established an occupation force of several thousand troops in southern Kunene Province, providing a secure staging area for UNITA.

In this situation, Cuban internationalist volunteers have remained, at the request of the Angola government. On average, some 25,000 Cuban volunteer fighters are stationed there at any one time (about 200,000 Cuban volunteers have served in Angola over the past decade). Occasionally, these Cubans have clashed with South African or UNITA units. But for the most part they have been held in reserve, as a backup force. Thanks to Cuban training and Soviet military equipment, the Angolan army has been significantly built up, and most of the fighting in the south has been conducted by Angolan troops and militia forces. Nevertheless, the Cuban internationalist fighters are ready to move into action should they be needed. Most are deployed along a defense line some 150-200 miles north of the Namibian border.

CUBA HAS won even more admiration throughout Africa for its firm and determined defense of Angola's sovereignty, despite more than a decade of South African attacks. This was expressed, for example, during a visit to Cuba in late September and early October 1985 by then President Julius Nyerere of Tanzania, a key figure in the grouping of Frontline States. Reflecting a view of Cuba's role that is widely held in Africa, Nyerere explained, "I have come to Cuba to say thank you to the people of Cuba, to say thank you to them for helping us in the struggle to liberate our continent. In 1975, after the freedom fighters of Mozambique and Angola had helped to liberate Portugal from fascism and to liberate their own countries, South Africa, assisted by the CIA, tried to prevent the MPLA from taking over the Government of Angola. They would have succeeded but for the support the MPLA got from Cuba. Since then, since 1975, Angola has been under constant attack. Angola would have lost its independence, even after 1975. What has saved Angola has been the commitment of our friends in Cuba to the liberation of our countries.

"So the one reason why I am here is to say thank you to Comrade Fidel, his colleagues, and people of Cuba for the help they have given us, for the help they are giving us, and I am here also to ask them to continue to give us that assistance."

Ever since 1975-76, Washington has conducted a propaganda effort aimed at denying the defensive character of the Cuban troop presence in Angola. In recent years, it has linked action on Namibia's independence from South Africa to the demand for a Cuban withdrawal from Angola. U.S. officials claim that the Cubans would "threaten" Namibia if it becomes independent while they are still in Angola.

Responding to this "linkage" demand, a joint statement was issued in February 1982 by Cuban Foreign Minister Isidoro Malmierca and Angolan Foreign Minister Paulo Jorge. "Given the hypocritical ploy of making the question of Namibia's independence conditional on the withdrawal of Cuban forces," the statement declared, "the Angola and Cuban governments reiterate that the presence of those forces, which results from the aggression of the South African racist and fascist troops, in close alliance with the United States of America, constitutes an absolutely sovereign and legitimate act by the two countries and thus has no bearing whatsoever on the Namibian problem."

The Angola government has repeatedly stated that any departure of Cuban troops would have to be predicated on a complete withdrawal of all South African troops from Angola, an end to all aggression against Angola by Washington, Pretoria, and their allies, and concrete moves toward Namibia's independence.

In February 1984, representatives of the Angolan, South African, and U.S. governments signed an agreement providing for a one-month phased South African withdrawal from the areas of southern Angola then occupied by South African troops.

Nonetheless, Pretoria took more than a year to complete its pullout. And then, as if to make the point that nothing had really changed, it quickly launched new acts of aggression. In May 1985 a South African commando unit attempted to blow up Angola's Cabinda oil facilities, which are partially owned by Gulf Oil of the United States. One South African officer was captured in the abortive raid. The Angolan government responded by breaking off talks with Pretoria. Then in September 1985 South African troops again invaded southern Angola, both to strike at SWAPO forces and to help UNITA counter a major Angolan government offensive. General Malan for the first time publicly admitted that Pretoria was aiding UNITA, and warned of yet further invasions. "South Africa's security interests in the south of Angola are of the greatest importance," he declared, "and its security forces will respond appropriately to any threat there."

Parallel to these ongoing South African attacks, U.S. imperialism has turned up its own pressures and threats against Angola. In early June 1985 — less than two weeks after the South African commando raid in Cabinda — Lewis Lehrman, a millionaire friend of Reagan's, flew Nicaraguan, Afghan, and Laotian counterrevolutionary representatives into southern Angola to meet UNITA's Jonas Savimbi. This *contra* confederacy formed a new alliance called the "Democratic International." A letter from Reagan gave the venture the U.S. president's blessing.

This was followed the next month by the bipartisan decision in the U.S. Congress to lift the so-called Clark amendment, adopted in late 1975, which had formally barred the U.S. government from funding UNITA and other opponents of the Angola government. By October, Congress was moving toward approval of both open and covert U.S. financial support to UNITA.

The Angolan government, which had pursued discussions with Washington around Namibia and other southern Africa questions, angrily suspended all such contacts for several months after the Clark amendment was repealed. An Angola Foreign Ministry statement declared, "The repeal of the Clark amendment will leave the U.S. administration and international imperialism free to openly and directly intervene in Angola and exercise military and political pressures on the Angolan state." Coming at a time "when the forces of the racist Pretoria regime and its UNITA puppets are desperately attempting to destabilize the economy of the People's Republic of Angola," the statement went on, the amendment's repeal "is further evidence of the complicity which has always existed between the U.S. Administration and the reactionary and racist Pretoria regime."

**M**OZAMBIQUE IS the other main target of South African aggression. Though Pretoria has not so far launched massive invasion forces against Mozambique, it has nevertheless waged a relentless war of mercenary intervention, economic blackmail, and destabilization designed to destroy the Mozambican revolution.

The apartheid regime's first move was to wield its economic club. South African trade through the harbor of Maputo, the capital, was cut back, reducing Mozambique's income from customs duties. The number of Mozambicans working as contract laborers in South Africa was cut by the South African authorities from 118,000 to about 40,000, leading to reduced earnings for Mozambique and a rise in the country's unemployment level. Other imperialist powers have also applied economic pressure, refusing to grant export credits or cutting off food assistance (as the Reagan adminstration did for a time). According to President Samora Machel, there is an "undeclared economic blockade against our country."

When these economic measures failed to wring concessions from the Mozambican government, Pretoria added military aggression. Near the end of the Zimbabwean war, South African pilots flew some of the Rhodesian bombing missions over Mozambique. Later, on several occasions, South African jets and paratroop commandos struck briefly into Maputo to attack ANC refugee houses and Mozambican factories.

So far, such direct incursions have been rare. The apartheid authorities have instead relied on the Renamo mercenary army. Pretoria took over direction of this counterrevolutionary outfit from the Rhodesian regime after the latter's downfall. After some setbacks at the hands of Mozambican troops, Renamo was reorganized and put back into action — on a massive scale. Its base was shifted to Zoabostad, in South Africa's Transvaal Province.

By 1984 Renamo had thousands of fighters operating within Mozambique, in nine out of Mozambique's ten provinces. They live by pillaging the countryside and terrorizing villagers, thus earning their popular designation as "bandits." They routinely torture, mutilate, and kill teachers, doctors, Frelimo members, and anyone who shows the slightest support for the revolution. They burn down schools and health clinics. By late 1983 they had destroyed 1,000 rural shops; 20 sawmills, cotton gins, and tea factories; and more than 200 communal villages. Special targets have been the railway and oil pipeline linking Mozambique and Zimbabwe, which have been cut several times. Renamo burned grain stores and ambushed relief convoys during the massive drought and famine of the early 1980s, in which more than 100,000 Mozambicans starved to death.

Despite the scope of Renamo's activities, it has no real social base in the country. Without direct South African support, it could not survive. It benefits from regular South African air drops and reconnaissance information on the location of Mozambican troops. Weapons captured from Renamo often bear distinct South African markings, and some supposed Renamo sabotage actions have in fact been carried out by South African commandos.

By early 1984, Mozambique was in a desperate position. Renamo was operating in larger areas of the country than Frelimo did during the last days of Portuguese rule. The countryside had been devastated by drought and famine and by the destruction wrought by the Renamo bands. In the cities, unemployment and food shortages increased. Mozambique's economic difficulties were worsening. Its debts to imperialist banks and governments climbed to $1.4 billion. These imperialist financial institutions made it clear that any renegotiation of debt repayment schedules was contingent on a "peace" agreement with Pretoria. And the apartheid regime, for its part, indicated that support for Renamo would continue until Frelimo made some political concessions.

Under this pressure, direct negotiations were opened between the Mozambican and South African governments. On March 16, 1984, Machel traveled to the Nkomati River along the border between the two countries to meet South African President Botha and sign a formal nonaggression treaty. The accord committed both sides to prevent their territory, waters, or air space from being "used as a base, thoroughfare or in any other way by another state, government, foreign military forces, organizations or individuals which plan or prepare acts of violence, terrorism or aggression" against the other.

On Pretoria's part, this meant promising to halt its aid to Renamo. In return, Frelimo agreed to cut back on the facilities it provided to the ANC. Although the ANC had no guerrilla bases in Mozambique (as Pretoria charged), it did have several hundred members there and used Mozambique as a thoroughfare for its fighters traveling from other countries into South Africa. Within weeks, most ANC members in Mozambique had been expelled, and the liberation organization was reduced to a ten-person diplomatic mission.

The Nkomati accord was a blow to the struggle against the apartheid regime. The ANC National Executive Committee, in a statement issued the day the accord was signed, said: "Such accords, concluded as they are with a regime which has no moral or legal right to govern our country, cannot but help to perpetuate the illegitimate rule of the South African white settler minority. It is exactly for this reason that this minority has over the years sought to bind independent Africa to such agreements."

While the Mozambican government lived up to its part of the accord, Pretoria had no intention of doing likewise.

Even as President Botha was signing the Nkomati accord, yet more arms and funds were being funneled to Renamo. In the months that followed, terrorist activities stepped up and even spread to new parts of the country. Renamo forces opened new bases in neighboring Malawi (where South African personnel function freely) and struck into Mozambique's northern provinces. In the south, they carried out attacks ever closer to Maputo itself. By 1985, Frelimo officials were estimating the costs of the South African destabilization over the previous ten years at $4.5 billion — or about twice Mozambique's annual gross national product. Under conditions of widespread economic dislocation, corruption and blackmarketeering spread yet further.

As the extent of this counterrevolutionary war hit home, the Mozambican government stepped up its efforts to form a new popular militia and appealed to its allies for more aid. Several hundred Tanzanian troops arrived to train the militia, and several thousand Zimbabwean troops came to help guard the railways and pipeline and assist in the military drive against Renamo. ANC leaders have found a somewhat warmer reception in Maputo. Mozambique's Foreign Minister Joaquim Chissano declared, "If international measures are not taken to stop South Africa from escalating its aggression, Mozambique may require more and more assistance from countries belonging to the Warsaw Pact. We know that only the socialist countries are supporting us against South African aggression."

In late August 1985, airborne Mozambican and Zimbabwean troops overran Renamo's main base at Gorongoza Mountain in central Mozambique. Hundreds of mercenaries were killed and considerable quantities of arms were captured. Mozambican forces also found a diary detailing regular contacts with South African military personnel.

Confronted with this evidence of its violations of the Nkomati accord, the South African government finally admitted as much. According to Foreign Minister Roelof Botha, these "technical" violations, as he termed them, included regular radio communications between Renamo and the South African military, air drops to the guerrillas, assistance in building an airstrip, transportation of Renamo field officers in and out of Mozambique by submarine, and three clandestine visits to Renamo's Gorongoza base by South Africa's deputy minister of foreign affairs.

The pressures on Mozambique have been reflected in other foreign policy moves as well. Parallel to the opening of the negotiations between Maputo and Pretoria that paved the way for the Nkomati accord, the Mozambican government launched new diplomatic initiatives designed to smooth its relations with the West European imperialist powers. This was highlighted by President Samora Machel's tour of Portugal, France, Britain, Belgium, the Netherlands, and other countries in October 1983. Various economic assistance agreements were concluded, and the British government sent some military advisers to Mozambique. Such ties have expanded further in the wake of the signing of the Nkomati accord and with the Mozambican government's decision to liberalize its conditions for foreign investment in Mozambique and to join the World Bank and International Monetary Fund.

Contacts with Washington have also become more cordial, reflected in a shift in the U.S. government's formal stance toward Mozambique. The U.S. food shipments that had been suspended in 1981 were resumed, and in 1984 Washington provided Mozambique with $43 million in food aid making Mozambique the largest such recipient of U.S. emergency food assistance. In September-October 1985, during a visit to the United States, President Machel met with various corporations to seek greater U.S. investment in Mozambique; he also held talks with Reagan.

JUST TWO weeks after the signing of the Nkomati accord, the monarchy of tiny Swaziland, sandwiched between South Africa and Mozambique, announced that it too had signed a security pact with Pretoria. Long under South African political domination, the Swazi government set out with particular relish to detain and expel South African refugees in Swaziland who were known or suspected to be ANC supporters. A few were killed or handed over to the South African authorities. Prime Minister Bhekimpi Dlamini accused ANC members of being a "scourge of foreign criminals." Swazi citizens who had expressed sympathy for the ANC were also hit by this crackdown.

Lesotho, the other tiny state in the region, has come under more concerted pressure and attack, due to the government's declared support for the ANC. In December 1982, South African paratroopers attacked several ANC refugee houses in the Lesotho capital, Maseru, massacring thirty South Africans and twelve Lesotho citizens. A group called the Lesotho Liberation Army has carried out numerous sabotage actions and some assassinations. It operates out of South Africa, with the apartheid regime's full approval and assistance. From time to time, Pretoria has held up imports to Lesotho, all of which must pass through South African territory. Speaking before the United Nations in October 1985,

Lesotho's King Moshoeshoe II stated, "Lesotho, as an enclave surrounded by South Africa, has found herself in an almost helpless position in the face of acts of political blackmail, disinvestment, and destabilization, master-minded from South Africa." Because of such pressure, some 100 ANC refugees have left Lesotho for other African countries.

Botswana, bordering South Africa on the north, has repeatedly accused South African planes of violating its airspace from bases in Namibia. South African agents have entered Botswana to spy on ANC members and other refugees. Some South African exiles have been assassinated, including during a June 1985 South African commando raid on Botswana's capital, Gaborone.

After Zimbabwe's independence, many former members of the elite Selous Scouts, a Rhodesian counterinsurgency force of white and Black troops, were integrated into the South African army, some for possible future use against Zimbabwe. Their continued connections in Zimbabwe and their knowledge of the country have been invaluable to Pretoria's military planners. ANC leaders in Zimbabwe have been assassinated, and some economic facilities have been destroyed. Taking advantage of the rift between ZAPU and ZANU, Pretoria has recruited some former ZAPU troops and sent them back into the Ndebele areas of Zimbabwe to carry out attacks against government forces and further fuel the frictions between the Ndebeles and Shonas. In August 1982, Zimbabwean troops killed three white South African soldiers discovered twenty miles inside the country. Their apparent goal had been to sabotage the railway line that runs through Zimbabwe to Maputo.

For Zambia, the end of the Zimbabwean war brought a halt to the Rhodesian air strikes into that country. But there have continued to be occasional small-scale South African attacks along the Zambian border with Namibia. In 1980 Pretoria was accused of involvement in a failed coup attempt against the Zambian government. A group of South African–trained terrorists carried out a low-level guerrilla campaign in northwestern Zambia until their leader was killed in late 1982. ANC leaders and offices in the Zambian capital have been attacked several times by South African agents.

Even the faraway Seychelles has not been safe. In late 1981, white mercenaries and South African military and intelligence personnel flew to the Seychelles Islands in a bid to overthrow the government of Albert René. They were discovered at the airport and the attempt was aborted. The leader of this mercenary band was Mike Hoare, well known for his involvement in the earlier South African mercenary ventures in the Congo. Hoare later revealed that the South African cabinet had approved of the coup plan, as had the U.S. CIA. Then in August 1982, figures within the Seychelles army tried to overthrow the government; during the course of their action they appealed to Pretoria for "support." This coup attempt was put down with the assistance of Tanzanian troops, who were in the Seychelles at the request of the René government.

IN WAGING its war against southern Africa, the apartheid regime has pursued several overall goals. All of them are interrelated and aim at preserving its racist rule within South Africa and its continued oppression and exploitation of the entire subcontinent, in league with the other imperialist powers.

• The first goal is to deny sanctuary and support to the ANC and SWAPO anywhere in southern Africa. This includes training facilities, refugee camps, medical clinics, public headquarters, propaganda centers, diplomatic offices, transit for ANC and SWAPO guerrillas through neighboring countries, and even expressions of political support for the liberation organizations by the governments of the region.

As a justification for its attacks against ANC and SWAPO members and supporters abroad, Pretoria claims that it is striking only at military targets, at guerrilla bases. Yet the ANC has repeatedly stressed that it does not maintain guerrilla bases in neighboring countries because of the vulnerability of those states to direct South African attack. It has pointed out that its own military strategy must thus be different from that of other liberation movements in southern Africa, most of which were able to have defensible rear bases in neighboring states.

The ANC has emphasized time and again that it *does* have bases, however — inside South Africa. Speaking to Frelimo's Fourth Congress in April 1983, Oliver Tambo stated, "We are going to reveal a secret that is no secret at all, we are going to reveal where our military bases really are. Gentlemen of the Press may take note: our bases are in a country not far from here, where members of Umkhonto we Sizwe, military wing of our organisation, and spearhead of the struggle against apartheid, can be found. Our bases are in South Africa itself, our bases are among the people of our country, our bases are everywhere, in the cities, in the mountains. . . . The regime cannot find these bases. Therefore it invents mythical bases in neighboring countries. For, it is easier to massacre refugees in their beds or to send bandits to murder teachers and health workers in Juham [Mozambique] than it is to stop the revolutionary process inside South Africa itself."

The best confirmation of where the ANC is based came a little more than a year later — and just a few months after the signing of the Nkomati accord, which Pretoria had boasted would be a crippling blow to the ANC. In August and September 1984 the recent wave of popular outpourings against the apartheid system began. And in greater numbers than ever before, the oppressed of South Africa have rallied to the banner of the ANC. That was their answer to Nkomati.

• Another key goal of Pretoria is to destabilize the governments of Angola and Mozambique. The tenacity and combativity of the Angolan and Mozambican liberation fighters in their struggle for independence set an example for all the peoples of southern Africa of how to struggle against imperialist oppression and of how to inflict defeats on the powerful apartheid state. The MPLA- and Frelimo-led governments that came to power in 1975 openly solidarized with the ANC and SWAPO and with the fight for independence and majority rule in Zimbabwe.

The apartheid regime is determined to erode and eventually reverse these gains. Through its own actions and those of its mercenary surrogates, Pretoria has sought to wear down the spirits of the Angolan and Mozambican people, to force those governments to concentrate more of their scarce resources on military defense, and to obstruct efforts to develop their economies and bring improvements in the lives of their peoples.

This has already taken a serious toll in lives and economic destruction in both countries. It has forced a halt to some social programs and postponed others. It has made it more difficult to combat the persistent problems of profiteering and corruption, and has emboldened those emerging social layers that are hostile to the interests of the toiling masses. The South African aggression has also taken a political toll, especially in Mozambique, with the Nkomati accord. Nevertheless, the apartheid regime is still far from its aim of wiping out the gains of the Mozambican and Angolan revolutions and imposing servile regimes that will bow to its will.

• A no-less-important goal, from Pretoria's perspective, is the expulsion of the Cuban internationalist volunteers from Angola. Their very presence there is an obstacle to the South African drive to bring down the Angolan revolution and helps the Angolan government stand up to the tremendous South African and U.S. pressures to break its solidarity with the ANC and SWAPO. It is also a key factor in the politics of the entire region, making it more difficult for Pretoria — and Washington — to move forcefully against other independent states.

• Finally, Pretoria aims to keep the entire southern African region under the domination of South African imperialism. Its attacks against neighboring states reveal a determination to punish any manifestation of political or economic independence. Some of the South African–sponsored sabotage actions in Lesotho, Mozambique, Zimbabwe, and Angola, such as the destruction of railways and oil pipelines, have clearly been directed at disrupting the efforts at regional cooperation among the member states of the SADCC.

THE FREEDOM struggle in southern Africa is the battle of an entire region. It is a struggle against imperialist oppression, reflected most immediately and directly in the fight against the apartheid state, imperialism's strongest bastion on the African continent.

The survival of the apartheid state — supported by a broad alliance of North American, West European, and Pacific imperialist powers — is the main obstacle to southern Africa's further social advance. Its overthrow by the South African masses will open up new avenues and possibilities for the whole region — for the revolutions in Angola and Mozambique and for the peoples of Zimbabwe, Namibia, Lesotho, and countries far from South Africa's own borders.

"Indeed," Oliver Tambo said in a March 1984 statement, "the peoples of southern Africa are perfectly aware that the only guarantee of lasting peace and security for their countries is the liberation of South Africa and Namibia. Our inevitable victory will serve also the fundamental and permanent interests of all the peoples in our region, Africa, and the rest of the world."

Besides ending apartheid's regional aggression, the liberation of South Africa will also make that country's vast economic and human resources available, for the first time, to benefit the less-developed states of southern Africa. Rather than feeding off the rest of the subcontinent, South Africa will become an equal partner, contributing to the development and progress of the region as a whole.

A free South Africa will open the doors to genuine freedom for all the peoples of southern Africa.

---

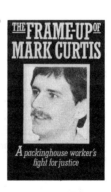

# "South Africa's racists broke their teeth at Cuito Cuanavale."

—Fidel Castro, December 1988

**IN DEFENSE OF SOCIALISM**
*Four Speeches on the 30th Anniversary of the Cuban Revolution*
by Fidel Castro

# CUBA'S INTERNATIONALIST VOLUNTEERS IN ANGOLA

by Fidel Castro

# 'An African Girón': May 1976

*The following is an excerpt from an April 19, 1976, speech commemorating the fifteenth anniversary of the Cuban victory at the Bay of Pigs (Playa Girón). Originally published in the May 2, 1976,* Granma Weekly Review, *it is © 1981 and reprinted here from* Fidel Castro Speeches: Cuba's Internationalist Foreign Policy 1975-80 *by permission of Pathfinder Press.*

**I**N COMMEMORATING this, the fifteenth anniversary of the heroic, glorious victory at Girón, our people have an additional reason to be proud, which constitutes their finest expression of internationalism and transcends the boundaries of this continent: the historical victory of the people of Angola, [*Prolonged applause*] to whom we offered the generous and unlimited solidarity of our revolution.

At Girón, African blood was shed, that of the selfless descendants of a people who were slaves before they became workers, and who were exploited workers before they became masters of their homeland. And in Africa, together with the blood of the heroic fighters of Angola, Cuban blood, that of the sons of Martí, Maceo, and Agramonte, that of the heirs to the internationalist tradition set by Máximo Gómez[1] and Che Guevara, [*Prolonged applause*] also flowed. Those who once enslaved man and sent him to America perhaps never imagined that one of those peoples who received the slaves would one day send their fighters to struggle for freedom in Africa.

The victory in Angola was the twin sister of the victory at Girón. [*Applause*] For the Yankee imperialists, Angola represents an African

Girón. At one time we said that imperialism had suffered its great defeats in the month of April: Girón, Vietnam, Cambodia,[2] etc. This time the defeat came in March. On the twenty-seventh of that month, when the last South African soldiers crossed the Namibian border, after a retreat of more than 700 kilometers, one of the most brilliant pages in the liberation of Black Africa was written.

[President Gerald] Ford and [Secretary of State Henry] Kissinger are irritated by the defeat. And like two little thundering Jupiters, they have made terrible threats against Cuba.

Ford, in an electoral campaign rally in Miami, competing for the votes of the Cuban counterrevolutionary colony with his rival Reagan, who, to be sure, is much more reactionary, called the prime minister of Cuba an international outlaw because of the aid our people gave to Angola. Even some United States press columnists were surprised to hear such epithets emerge from the illustrious mouth of Mr. Ford. Moreover, perhaps as one indication of Ford's low level of development, which is becoming proverbial, he declared on one occasion that Cuba's action in Angola was similar to what happened in Ethiopia in Mussolini's time. And later on, not satisfied with that most original historical simile, he compared the events in Angola to Hitler's dismemberment of Czechoslovakia after Munich.

The war in Angola was really Kissinger's war. Against the advice of some of his closest collaborators, he insisted on carrying out covert operations to liquidate the MPLA through the counterrevolutionary FNLA and UNITA groups, with the support of white mercenaries, Zaire, and South Africa. It is said that the CIA actually warned him that such clandestine operations could not be kept secret. Aside from the fact that from the time it was founded the FNLA was supported by the CIA, a fact now publicly acknowledged, the United States invested tens of millions of dollars from the spring of 1975 on to supply arms and instructors to the counterrevolutionary, secessionist Angolan groups. Instigated by the United States, regular troops from Zaire entered Angolan territory in the summer of that same year, while South African military forces occupied the Kunene area in the month of August and sent arms and instructors to UNITA bands.

At that time there wasn't a single Cuban instructor in Angola. The first material aid and the first Cuban instructors reached Angola at the beginning of October, at the request of the MPLA, when Angola was being openly invaded by foreign forces. However, no Cuban military unit had been sent to Angola to participate directly in the fight, nor was that projected.

On October 23, [1975,] also instigated by the United States, South African regular army troops, supported by tanks and artillery, invaded Angolan territory across the Namibian border and penetrated deeply into the country, advancing between 60 and 70 kilometers a day. On November 3, they had penetrated more than 500 kilometers into Angola, meeting their first resistance on the outskirts of Benguela, from the personnel of a recently organized school for Angolan recruits and from their Cuban instructors, who had virtually no means for halting the attack by South African tanks, infantry, and artillery.

On November 5, 1975, at the request of the MPLA, the leadership of our party decided to send with great urgency a battalion of regular troops with antitank weapons [*Applause*] to help the Angolan patriots resist the invasion of the South African racists. This was the first Cuban troop unit sent to Angola. When it arrived in the country, the foreign interventionists in the north were 25 kilometers from Luanda, their 140-millimeter artillery was bombing the suburbs of the capital, and the South African fascists had already penetrated more than 700 kilometers into the south from the Namibian border, while Cabinda was heroically defended by MPLA fighters and a handful of Cuban instructors.

I do not mean to relate the events of the Angolan war, the later development of which is generally known to everyone, but rather to point out the occasion, the form, and the circumstances in which our aid began. These facts now form part of history.[3]

The enemy has talked about the number of Cubans in Angola. It is sufficient to say that once the struggle began, Cuba sent the men and the weapons necessary to win that struggle. [*Applause*] To give due honor to our people, we must say that hundreds of thousands of fighters from our regular troops and reserves were ready to fight alongside their Angolan brothers. [*Applause*]

Our losses were minimal. In spite of the fact that the war was fought on four fronts and that our fighters fought alongside the heroic MPLA soldiers in the liberation of almost a million square kilometers [*Applause*] that had been occupied by the interventionists and their accomplices, fewer Cuban soldiers were killed in action in over four months of fighting in Angola than in the three days of fighting at Girón. [*Applause*]

CUBA ALONE bears the responsibility for taking that decision. The USSR had always helped the peoples of the Portuguese colonies in their struggle for independence, provided besieged Angola with basic aid in military equipment, and collaborated with us when imperialism had cut off practically all our air routes to Africa, but it never requested that a single Cuban be sent to that country. The USSR is extraordinarily respectful and careful in its relations with Cuba. A decision of that nature could only be made by our own party. [*Applause*]

Ford and Kissinger lie to the people of the United States and to world public opinion when they try to place the responsibility for Cuba's action in solidarity with Angola on the Soviet Union.

Ford and Kissinger lie when they seek to blame the Congress of the United States for the defeat of the interventionists in Angola because Congress failed to authorize new funds for the FNLA and UNITA counterrevolutionary groups. Congress made those decisions on December 16, 18, and 19. By that time, the CIA had already supplied large amounts in arms. Zairean troops had been repulsed in Luanda, Cabinda had been saved, the South Africans were contained and demoralized on the banks of the Queve River, and no shipment of arms from the CIA would have changed the already inexorable course of events. Today the arms would be in the hands of the revolutionary forces, like many of those the CIA supplied earlier.

Ford and Kissinger lie to the people of the United States, and especially to the Black population of that country, when they hide the fact that the fascist and racist troops of South Africa criminally invaded Angolan territory long before Cuba sent any regular units of soldiers there.

There are some other lies on the part of Ford and Kissinger in relation to Angola which need not be analyzed now. Ford and Kissinger know perfectly well that everything I say is true.

In this solemn commemoration ceremony, I am not going to say what I think of the insolent epithets Ford has used in his political campaign through the South of the United States and of other cynical aspects of his imperial policy; I will confine myself, for now, to replying that he is a common liar. [*Applause*]

True, events in Angola resemble those of Ethiopia,[4] but in reverse. In Angola, the imperialists, the racists, the aggressors symbolized by the CIA, the South African troops, and the white mercenaries did not win victory nor did they occupy the country; victory was won by those who were attacked, by the revolutionaries, by the heroic Black people of Angola. [*Applause*]

True, events in Angola resemble those of Czechoslovakia after Munich,[5] but also in reverse: the people who were attacked received the solidarity of the revolutionary movement, and the imperialists and racists could not dismember the country or divide up its wealth or assassinate its finest sons and daughters. Angola is united, its territory is unified, and today it is a bulwark of liberty and dignity in Africa. The swastika of the South African racists does not fly over the palace of Luanda. [*Applause*]

We advise Mr. Ford to study a bit of true history and draw the correct conclusions from its lessons.

With the imperialist defeat in Angola, Mr. Kissinger scarcely has time enough to run from place to place whipping up fear of the Cuban revolution. Some days ago he traveled through half a dozen Latin American countries and now he has announced a new trip to several countries in Africa, a continent he never deigned to look at before his African Girón.

NO LATIN American country, whatever its social system, will have anything to fear from the armed forces of Cuba. It is our deepest conviction that each people must be free to build their own destiny; that each people and only the people of each country must and will make their own revolution. The government of Cuba has never thought of taking revolution to any nation of this hemisphere with the arms of its military units. Such an idea would be absurd and ridiculous. Nor is it Cuba who stole the major part of its territory from Mexico, landed 40,000 marines to crush the revolution in Santo Domingo, occupies part of Panamanian territory, oppresses a Latin people in Puerto Rico, plans assassinations of foreign leaders, or exploits the wealth and natural resources of any people in this hemisphere.

No country of Black Africa has anything to fear from Cuban military personnel. We are a Latin-African people — enemies of colonialism, neocolonialism, racism, and apartheid, which Yankee imperialism aids and protects.

They say that Kissinger wants to meet in Africa with the representatives of the liberation movements of that continent. Anything is possible in Black Africa after the Girón of Angola. [*Applause*] But what kind of hypocritical, cynical, and pharisaical words can Kissinger speak to the African liberation movements, to the representatives of the oppressed peoples of Rhodesia, Namibia, and South Africa — he who represents the empire that unscrupulously supported Portuguese colonialism and today aids, protects, and supports with economic and political means the South African and Rhodesian racists, in brazen violation of United Nations agreements and resolutions?

Ford and Kissinger have the inveterate habit of using blackmail and threat as a tool of foreign policy. Not long ago they threatened the oil-producing countries with military measures. Now they are using the same cynical and shameless language against Cuba. They are not the first Yankee rulers who have used, to no avail, these intimidating tactics against our homeland. Eisenhower, Kennedy, Johnson, and Nixon all tried to intimidate Cuba. All, without exception, underestimated the Cuban revolution; all were mistaken. [*Applause*] Cuba cannot be intimidated by bellicose threats. It is possible to know when and how a war on Cuba can be started; four madmen could decide that at any time; but what is impossible to know is when and how it would end. [*Prolonged applause*]

Only peoples who have no dignity can be intimidated. We have already lived through the October Crisis of 1962, and scores of atomic weapons pointed at Cuba did not make our people — not even the children — hesitate. [*Applause*] The people of Cuba can answer Kissinger's threats with the verses of a classical Spanish poem:

And if I fall,
What is life?
I already
Gave it up for lost
When,
Fearlessly,
I tore off the yoke
Of the slave. [*Applause*]

The Yankee imperialists have hundreds of thousands of soldiers abroad; they have military bases on all continents and in all seas. In Korea, Japan, the Philippines, Turkey, Western Europe, Panama, and many other places, their military installations can be counted by the dozens and the hundreds. In Cuba itself they occupy by force a piece of our territory.

What moral and legal right do they have to protest that Cuba provides instructors and assistance for the technical preparation of the armies of African countries and of other parts of the underdeveloped world that request them?

What right do they have to criticize the aid and solidarity we give to a sister people of Africa such as Angola, who have been criminally attacked?

The imperialists are pained that Cuba, the attacked and blockaded country they tried to destroy fifteen years ago by a mercenary invasion, is today a solid and indestructible bulwark of the world revolutionary movement, whose example of bravery, dignity, and determination gives encouragement to peoples in their struggle for liberation. [*Applause*]

On the other hand, our revolutionary action is in keeping with the world balance of forces and the interest of world peace. We are not enemies of détente or of peaceful coexistence between states with different social systems based on strict respect for the norms of international law. We would even be willing to maintain normal relations with the United States on the basis of mutual respect and sovereign equality, without renouncing any of our principles and without giving up the struggle on an international level to ensure that the norms of peaceful coexistence and respect for the rights of each nation are applied to all the peoples of the world, without exception.

The United States occupies a piece of our territory in Guantánamo; the United States has maintained a criminal blockade against our country for more than fifteen years. Cuba will never bow before this imperialist policy of hostility and force and will struggle against it tirelessly. We have said that there can be no negotiations while there is a blockade. No one can negotiate with a dagger at his chest. It doesn't matter if we spend a further twenty years without relations with the United States. [*Applause*] We have learned to live without them, and by basing ourselves on our solid and indestructible friendship with the USSR we have advanced more in these years [*Applause*] than any other country in Latin America. While trade with the United States might perhaps mean certain advantages and a faster rate of development, we prefer to move less rapidly but with our heads held high and the flag of dignity fully unfurled. [*Prolonged applause*] We will not exchange the revolutionary birthright we hold as the first socialist revolution in the Western Hemisphere for a plate of lentils. [*Applause*]

# 'We Will Stay As Long As Necessary': January 1985

*The following is excerpted from an interview with Fidel Castro conducted by* Washington Post *correspondents Karen DeYoung, Jim Hoagland, and Leonard Downie on January 30, 1985. The entire transcript of the interview was published in the February 24, 1985,* Granma Weekly Review *and this excerpt is © 1985 and reprinted here from* War and Crisis in the Americas: Fidel Castro Speeches 1984-85, *by permission of Pathfinder Press.*

*Karen De Young:* Can I ask you a question about Angola?

Do you see any chance, if there is an agreement between South Africa and Angola facilitated by the United States leading to the withdrawal of Cuban forces from Angola, of this perhaps reducing tension between the United States and Cuba, which would in turn reduce tension in other areas?

*Fidel Castro:* I think that wherever solutions are obtained this helps diminish tension everywhere. I think an isolated agreement in one place not only helps relations between the countries of the area but exerts a positive influence on the whole international scene. Well, were there to be an agreement there, an agreement acceptable to the Angolans — the Angolans are the ones who must decide — with real guarantees for Angolan security, that is possible. We feel those guarantees should include: implementation of [United Nations] Resolution 435,[6] the independence of Namibia, a halt to aid for UNITA — that is, the South African FDN [Nicaraguan Democratic Force] — with verification, of course, by means of an international agreement signed by the various sides at the

Security Council. In a period of time it would be possible to withdraw —
the Angolans have said three years — the Southern Troops Grouping,
which constitutes the bulk of the [Cuban] forces stationed there, leaving
others in the central and northern parts of the country whose withdrawal
would be discussed and agreed upon by Cubans and Angolans, depending
on the prevailing climate of security. That is the idea.

The South Africans have been organizing subversive groups and using
them in Angola for eight years now. Angola is a very big country with extensive communications, large bridges, and those groups can do a lot of
damage. The Angolans would need time to replace our troops with their
forces; they can't do it all of a sudden.

They are working in good faith to find a solution. The countries of
southern Africa, of Black Africa, have a very firm position on this. They
oppose linking Resolution 435 to the withdrawal of Cuban troops.

I will tell you the truth, the frontline states of Black Africa in general
are not happy with the idea of the withdrawal of Cuban troops; they feel
very threatened by South Africa. That is a fact and you can go and speak
to them; the countries of Black Africa are the ones best able to explain
their positions. We know that all the independent countries of southern
Africa are not happy with the withdrawal idea, because the Cuban forces
are the only outside forces that have helped them against South Africa.
They feel that when those forces leave they might be at the mercy of South
Africa, because South Africa has been very aggressive, and they are very
distrustful.

There is something else: even though the South African forces pull
back to their border, they can be at the Angolan border in twenty-four
hours, while we are 10,000 kilometers away. These are the realities and
they totally distrust South Africa. Neither Angola nor the other countries
of Black Africa are happy at the prospect.

I don't want to speak for them, you can talk to them; you can ask Nyerere for his views, Zambia and Zimbabwe for their views, the Congo and
Mozambique. They of course want an overall solution, with peace for
Mozambique and Angola, with guarantees; but they are very distrustful
of South Africa, because it has been very aggressive and has created
counterrevolutionary bands in Angola and Mozambique.

In Mozambique there was peace, there was no civil war, there were no
problems. The South Africans organized former Portuguese colonialists,
soldiers who served with Rhodesia's Ian Smith, and Blacks who had been
with the Portuguese. They organized and trained them and they supplied
weapons, planes, and helicopters. The war in Mozambique was created
by South Africa.

South Africa also sponsors subversion in the small nation of Lesotho.

None of these countries feels protected against South African activity,
not one of them. They also have strong feelings of rejection for apartheid.

All African states, all nations of Black Africa, states ruled by both leftist and rightist movements, are united by their hatred of apartheid, their revulsion of apartheid. They are not resigned to it; there is not one that isn't against apartheid. We have supported those who have fought apartheid, and fought the aggressors.

*Jim Hoagland:* I understand that right now the Cuban troops in the south are stationed along a static defense line, for protection in the event of South African attack.

*Castro:* Of course, they are in a strategic line, because the South Africans have certain advantages near the border, near their air and logistical bases; that is the area they move in. Our forces defend a strategic line further back to cope with any large-scale South African attack. Their positions and defense and counterattack mission are determined by rigorous military and technical considerations.

*Hoagland:* Do they participate in the fighting against UNITA?

*Castro:* No, they do not participate directly in the fighting against UNITA. That is a task for the Angolan units, although we give them troop combat advice and support with technical means if required. We have trained many of their command cadres, selected from among the best fighters.

*Hoagland:* In the event of withdrawal, would it always be to the center and north?

*Castro:* No, those forces would be brought back to Cuba.

*Hoagland:* But after the withdrawal of the troops from the south would there still be 10,000 Cuban soldiers north of the thirteenth parallel?

*Castro:* Yes, about 10,000, because the problem is that figures have been given on the number of troops in the south, but not on those in the center or north, only approximate ones. They are reserves in the event of a complicated situation arising. If an agreement is reached, we will strictly fulfill our obligations. There are 20,000 in the Southern Troops Grouping, and they are the bulk of the Cuban forces.

Angola has many strategic points. It is a very large country, nearly a million and a half square kilometers. It is fourteen times the size of Cuba, with thousands of kilometers of roads, large rivers, bridges, many vital strategic points, hydroelectric power plants, etc.

Our forces occupy a number of strategic communications links and airports.

Cabinda is a very important spot for Angola. Everybody wanted to take Cabinda, and it is vital for Angola's economy. In 1975, Zaire attacked Cabinda to take over the oil. Gulf Oil is working there and I think they are satisfied. They have worked and turned out their oil, they have their business and nobody has obstructed them, and it has been well defended. We are not trying to defend the interests of Gulf Oil, we are defending the interests of Angola and that oil benefits both Angola and Gulf. We defend the interests of Angola and indirectly those of Gulf. Those forces are not covered by the negotiations taking place.

The positions occupied by the forces in the south can't be vacated in a few weeks, because the Angolan army must take over, and it needs time and cadres, new units and means, because it must also fight the UNITA mercenary bands. They need some time, as we see it, not less than three years to be able to take on this task; that is reasonable, perfectly reasonable. If they did otherwise, they would face some very serious problems. They need more time to replace the other troops, since it is a huge country with a series of strategic spots: airports, bridges, industries, and hydroelectric plants. We are currently defending many of those points.

They have a strong army, which is gaining in experience, cadres, and fighting spirit. They have increased their forces and, in time, in the future they will be able to defend their country against foreign attack while also opposing subversion and fighting UNITA.

UNITA exists because of foreign aid. UNITA struck a deal with South Africa. For Black Africa this is treason, a deal with the South African racists is treason. We are the ones who benefit most from a settlement. I tell you frankly, we benefit most; we have been there for nine years, more than 200,000 Cubans have been to Angola. This is a real effort and we have no economic interest in Angola at all. But if a solution acceptable to Angola does not materialize, we will firmly continue with our support to that country as long as is necessary.

It has often been reported, perhaps even by the *Washington Post*, that the Angolans pay for the Cuban troops stationed there. I want to say that no life of any Cuban has its price. It cannot be paid for with $1 trillion or $100 billion. Our military cooperation has never been paid for in any country of the world where we have given it, never! Neither in Angola nor anywhere else. Some countries with the means have paid for civilian cooperation: doctors, engineers. In the great majority of countries, that cooperation is also free.

Often the United States does not understand how we can do this, all that it costs, if Cuba doesn't have the hard currency. That doesn't cost us hard currency. We pay salary here in Cuba for all those rendering internationalist cooperation; civilians, military, officers, all have their salary paid here. Many are from the reserves, workers from the reserves who are in military units. Their salary is paid in Cuba. The country where they go provides housing and food and we pay their salary. We have thousands of people working in those conditions now, without involving hard-currency expenditure. Nor does their return mean unemployment, because we are paying them here. Nor does it mean a cut in spending because they would do other work in Cuba. It doesn't create unemployment or any other problems.

We can do this for a basic reason which is not economic: we have the people to do it with. That is the secret, and that is what the revolution has created. That is what I was telling you about. I talked about the 2,000 teachers, when we had 2,000 teachers in Nicaragua, it is because we could do it; but we could send 30,000 or 100,000 because they have been educated with that idea. These are motivations and moral values that the revolution has sown in them all. In this, we have an overwhelming advantage over all nations of Latin America and the Third World. I don't think any other country with a relatively small population has such top-quality human potential.

Sometimes the country we are helping is very poor and we also pay part of the expenses of our personnel. But the general rule is: housing and food are provided by the country and we pay the salaries. We send eight doctors to one apartment; it proves easier for the host nation to have eight doctors in small lodgings. If they seek a doctor in Europe, they must provide a home for the family, pay his vacations, and spend about $40,000 or $50,000 a year. Meanwhile, eight of our doctors live in one apartment, they are provided for, and are not paid for their work. Those are the bases of our cooperation in all countries.

A few countries with the means to do so pay for civilian cooperation, a few countries, for the doctors, teachers, engineers, construction workers. There are two or three countries, which I won't go into. About 90 percent of the countries are very poor and we don't charge for our help.

We also have 22,000 scholarship students in Cuba from more than eighty countries; many doctors, engineers, and technicians from these countries have been trained in Cuba. We are sincerely concerned about the situation in Third World nations. It is not simply diplomatic and political activity, it is a reality which we feel and have experienced and which we raise at all international forums: at the UN, before the socialist countries, in the Movement of Nonaligned Countries, everywhere. We have become very aware of the social, sanitary, educational, and other problems. It is not a case of seeking relations; although of course there has been a quest for relations because, in response to the efforts to isolate us, we tried to extend our relations. I truly say we are deeply concerned about the tragedy of the Third World. I personally involved myself in these problems of cooperation, doctors, teachers, cooperation in agriculture, etc.

I think a major effort of international cooperation and large-scale investment is required in Africa if we are to come up with a strategic solution to its food problems and prevent a natural holocaust there. And I will tell you the truth: rather than spend money on space weapons and star wars, I think the world and even God — for those who are believers — would be much more grateful if the money were used to prevent the disaster which is threatening Africa and hundreds of millions of people, since the desert is moving south or north at increasing speed. Television programs broadcast images of widespread famine all over the world and people find out what is happening.

In social terms, the situation in Africa is different from that of Latin America: tens of millions, hundreds of millions of people live in hamlets as they did hundreds or thousands of years ago. They live there with their rudimentary farming. They are very stoic and resigned. They are killed by disease, hunger, and drought, but there is no explosion; it is not like in Latin America. In Latin America, there are many millions of blue- and white-collar workers, intermediate sectors, intellectuals, educated people. What I am trying to say is that the class structure in Latin America is different from that of Africa. You can't say Africa is exploding in social terms; you can say Africa is dying. Latin America is exploding; it has a different social structure.

*Hoagland:* Regarding Angola, why do you think the United States is playing a positive role?

*Castro:* Well, I say it would be positive if results were to be obtained. I would even venture to say it is positive that they try to seek political solutions to regional problems. If they are truly seeking a solution I think several factors are involved: there is antipathy for South Africa all over the world; there is a lot of antipathy for apartheid even in the United States.

In the United States, there is a current opposed to apartheid and cooperation with South Africa. I think the United States is interested in its relations with Black Africa, and it really doesn't want to appear as being linked to the policy of apartheid. I think the United States has an obsessive desire to get Cuban troops out of Angola, perhaps because of their special mentality. It seems that the only country in the world that can have troops everywhere is the United States, and the fact that a small country such as Cuba has some troops in a few places would seem to violate a tradition, established norms. It would seem to be truly inconceivable. I really don't know why they have magnified it so much, but it could be summed up as appearing to them as irreverence and disrespect. We really didn't send those forces there to offend or irritate the United States in all truth; we would rather send doctors and teachers than soldiers. We only hope that one day none of these countries will require military cooperation.

I think it is forgotten that we have had links with the MPLA [People's Movement for the Liberation of Angola] since they started their war of independence, for almost twenty years. When the MPLA was on the brink of winning independence, those other groups were created. UNITA was really set up by the Portuguese as a counter organization to the MPLA, and UNITA joined forces with South Africa to crush the

MPLA. We didn't send troops initially; at the request of the Angolan patriots, we sent instructors and weapons for the MPLA. They were in the south, in various places, a few dozen instructors.

When the invasion, the frontal South African attack took place, allied to UNITA, in their advance they attacked the military training school and the Cubans with their students resisted the South African advance. The first Cubans were killed there. Afterwards, the aggressors continued their advance toward Luanda, and Zaire attacked from the north. As the South Africans rapidly advanced from the south, we sent the first unit by air, a battalion of special troops, which occupied positions south of Luanda, along various strategic routes. In those days, bridges had to be blown up over the Queve River as they approached Luanda. That unit helped hold back the South Africans. A complex situation had been created and it had to be solved; we weren't going to leave that unit there alone. That was what decided the dispatch of other units.

That was how events unfurled. We had never thought of sending troops, but neither had we thought of the likelihood of such a situation, a blatant South African attack in which Cubans would be killed and the lives of other instructors jeopardized, along with Angolan independence itself. We had to send the units, and then the others. Then we sent all that were necessary to get them out.

They were about 1,000 kilometers inside Angola and we put the pressure on. When they realized that the battle was for real, they started to pull back toward the Namibian border and at the end held talks with our officers on the border. Then there was a period of calm, a certain period of calm and then they started up again. They started their raids on Angola, on the pretext of the struggle against SWAPO.

We know the South Africans very well, their psychology; we don't underestimate them at all. They have spent a lot of money on weapons in the last ten years. But neither do we overestimate them. We are aware of their problems, their limitations, their psychology, and their way of doing things.

I think the South Africans right now are obstructing U.S. efforts in the area. The greatest problems faced by the United States are not with Cuba or Angola; they are with South Africa. That is the truth as we see it.

*Hoagland:* Can I ask you about a couple of details which normally you would not discuss? But since there are things of which I think you can be proud, in the context in which we have been talking, allow me to ask them.

How many Cuban lives have been lost in Angola since 1975?

*Castro:* We have had our casualties but have not given out any information. We didn't feel it was convenient to do so. Our policy has been not to give casualty information; that has been the policy right from the start. The enemy must not have that information. We will know how to honor in a fitting manner those killed in revolutionary struggles, here and elsewhere.

# 'No Future for Bantustans in Namibia': May 1985

*The following is excerpted from a May 29, 1985, speech to Namibian students studying in Cuba. The English text is from the June 9 issue of* Granma Weekly Review.

**W**HILE THERE is tragedy in Namibia, there is even greater tragedy in South Africa, where 24 million Africans are totally deprived of their rights by a small and arrogant white minority. This year in particular has been characterized by the apartheid regime's ferocious repression of the African population of South Africa; they have murdered hundreds of people in a few months and the killing continues.

As you know, the United Nations has been making a major effort to speed up the independence of Namibia. The secretary-general of the UN has expressed here the hope that you will constitute the 160th member state of the UN.

But what are they doing? While they confer with Angola and there are contacts and negotiations in which the United States claims to be an intermediary or mediator acting in good faith — in spite of the fact that it organized and supports [Jonas] Savimbi, in addition to the South Africans — in a treacherous attack they try to destroy in one blow the vital and fundamental economic resources of Angola.[7] What can you expect from fascists? What can you expect from racists and oppressors?

With our support and cooperation, Angola has advocated the search for a peace formula, which should be preceded by implementation of UN Resolution 435 and the independence of Namibia. What are the South Africans doing now? Trying to organize Bantustans in Namibia. I ask, is there any future for Bantustans in Namibia? [*Shouts of "No!"*] Will the Namibian people permit the organization of Bantustans? [*Shouts of "Never!"*] They will not permit it, nor will the people of South Africa.

Angola proposed a formula, and with their characteristic insolence and arrogance the racists and their U.S. allies said "No" and posed the absurd demand for the withdrawal of the Cuban internationalist fighters in Angola in a few months. They turned down the Angolan formula contemptuously. The Angolans had proposed the withdrawal of Cuban forces from southern Angola over a thirty-six month period. The withdrawal of Cuban personnel in central and northern Angola or in Cabinda was not subject to negotiation.

Perhaps in their fantasy-ridden dreams the U.S. government and the South African racists thought we were eager to get out of Angola and leave it at the mercy of imperialist perfidy and treason. No, no, 200,000 Cubans have passed through Angola, but if another 200,000 must pass through Angola then they will, because we are not impatient or rushed in any way. [*Applause*]

And, of course, Angola is a sovereign and independent country which has firmly maintained its loyalty and solidarity with the liberation movement and people of Namibia, and as long as Angola says that Resolution 435 must be implemented and the independence of Namibia is necessary, we will be there alongside the Angolans, without discussion or doubt of any kind.

There have been negotiations, but we have a firm and unshakable position. If you don't have a firm position, you can't negotiate, much less with arrogant, cynical, and shameless governments that always take the wrong path. We Cubans will fulfill our internationalist duty there as long as necessary. [*Applause*]

I really don't think it will take too long because the fascist regime in South Africa won't hold out much longer, the hateful apartheid system won't last much longer. It is really in dire straits now because of the struggle of the Namibian people and the struggle of the South African people, whose heroic resistance grows by the day.

South Africa is going through the worst crisis in its history, since the price of gold per ounce is no longer $700; it's just barely $300. It doesn't have the money to finance its adventures and is faced with economic, social, and political problems of all kinds, in spite of the U.S. investments and those of the Western countries in South Africa and Namibia. It is bogged down in the worst economic crisis and especially the worst political crisis in its history. [*Applause and shouts*] It can't ask for handouts at gunpoint.

I think this is an excellent opportunity, here in the presence of the UN delegation, to state our position. There will be no solution in southern Africa without Resolution 435 and the independence of Namibia! [*Applause*] And as long as Angola agrees — and we have no doubt that this is the Angolan position — as long as UN Resolution 435 is not implemented and as long as Namibia is not independent, or at least as long as there are no concrete and necessary steps taken to implement the resolution and achieve real and meaningful independence, not a single Cuban soldier will leave Angola! [*Prolonged applause*]

And if more soldiers are needed, we will send more soldiers, [*Applause*] because in the face of every attack by imperialism and the racists, we have always reacted by reinforcing Angola and there are still a number of Cubans there, always prepared, alert, and ready to fight in the face of any enemy escalation. We have always been Angola's reinforcements.

You know very well what our people are like, you know that we are millions of men and women ready to struggle. Moreover, when we send our fighters to Angola we don't weaken ourselves, because we have many more fighters than weapons in Cuba. [*Applause*] So we could have 100,000 soldiers abroad if necessary and we wouldn't weaken ourselves in the least, because there are hundreds of thousands of young men and women here that are trained and for whom there are not enough weapons, and we have a lot of weapons. [*Applause and shouts of "Viva Cuba! Viva Commander-in-chief Fidel Castro Ruz! Patria o Muerte! Venceremos!"*]

When our men and women fulfill internationalist missions, be they civilian or military, they always return to our country with more revolutionary, patriotic, and internationalist spirit.

If one day the imperialists dare attack our country, they'll see what they will encounter in Cuba. [*Applause*] They'll see what it's like to fight against an entire people, men, women, young people, old people, and even children! They'll see that a country of ten million people ready to struggle can never be defeated.

WE ARE ready for everything, our country is organized from one end to the other and prepared for all combat conditions, even for total occupation of the country. They would suffer more deaths in our country than they did in World War II and in the end they would bite the dust of defeat, because we have created the conditions which enable us to feel that we are invincible. [*Applause*]

You know that even this little island which is separated from the bulk of our territory will be defended, and how! From the orange groves, forests, towns, homes, streams, fortifications, and stones. And in that case, the African youth would fight at our sides. [*Applause*] That is internationalism, that is reciprocity.

And I want you to tell me how they could manage to occupy even this little island, because even under a flower there may be a soldier and when they think there is just a garden nearby they encounter a platoon of soldiers with all their weapons. [*Laughter and applause*]

We have studied all the techniques and experiences of all the countries that have struggled for liberation in the last few decades. We have collected and developed the techniques and used them to instruct our people. Just as the Namibian people can be absolutely sure and confident that the UN, in the first place, will continue pushing for implementation of Resolution 435 and the independence of your country, you can be sure that we will be in Angola as long as necessary. [*Shouts*]

We will be there until Namibia is independent, and the friends of Africa and of Namibia will support you until you are free.

Nobody can give assurances if it will be the 160th member of the UN. I don't know if there is some small island held by the colonialists somewhere in the world that will become independent and be number 160. I wouldn't dare to say which one it will be, perhaps 162, 163, or 164. But I do say with complete assurance that you will be free!

Patria o Muerte!

Venceremos!

[*Ovation*]

## Notes

1. José Martí, Antonio Maceo, Ignacio Agramonte, and Máximo Gómez were all leaders and outstanding fighters in the Cuban wars for independence during the second half of the nineteenth century.

2. The U.S. was defeated at Playa Girón (the Bay of Pigs) on April 19, 1961. The defeat of the U.S.-backed dictatorships in South Vietnam and Cambodia both occurred in April 1975.

3. For a complete account of the war and the Cuban role in it, see "Cuba in Angola: Operation Carlotta" by Gabriel García Márquez in *Fidel Castro Speeches: Cuba's Internationalist Foreign Policy 1975-80* (New York: Pathfinder Press, 1981) pp. 339-357.

4. This refers to the 1935 Italian invasion and occupation of Ethiopia.

5. This refers to the March 1939 German occupation of Czechoslovakia following the Munich Pact.

6. Resolution 435 was adopted by the United Nations Security Council on September 29, 1978. It calls for the repeal of all repressive laws in Namibia, the holding of free elections there under UN supervision and control, and the convoking of a Namibian constituent assembly to frame an independence constitution.

7. Earlier in this speech Castro spoke about an attack by a South African commando squad in May 1985 on oil installations in Angola's Cabinda province. The squad was defeated by Angolan troops shortly after it landed; the commander was captured and two members of the squad were killed.

The Communist International in Lenin's Time

LENIN'S STRUGGLE FOR A REVOLUTIONARY INTERNATIONAL

Documents 1907-1916
The Preparatory Years

## Lenin's Struggle for a Revolutionary International

*Documents 1907-1916*
*The Preparatory Years*

The struggle led by Lenin in the years before the October 1917 Russian revolution to forge a revolutionary leadership to counter the growing influence in the Socialist movement of leaders who had made their peace with capitalist rule. 624 pp., $25.95

## Bolshevism and the Russian Revolution: A Debate

edited by Steve Clark

Assessments of lessons from the Russian revolution, especially the political contributions of V.I. Lenin and the Bolshevik Party, by Doug Jenness and Ernest Mandel. $3.75

## Two Tactics of Social Democracy in the Democratic Revolution

by V.I. Lenin

Written in 1905, this pamphlet presents the Bolshevik strategy to mobilize the working class in the leadership of the peasantry to make the revolution in Russia. 160 pp., $.95

## The Challenge of the Left Opposition

by Leon Trotsky

Three volumes of speeches and writings from the years 1923-29. These documents record the efforts of communists in the Soviet Union to maintain the revolutionary and internationalist course charted by Lenin under assault by a privileged bureaucratic layer. Each volume $24.95.

## Two Study Guides on Lenin's Writings

by Steve Clark and John Riddell

Study guides to Lenin's political strategy in making the Russian revolution and his writings on the role of Soviet power and the Communist International following the October 1917 revolution. 19 pp., $1.00

*Available from Pathfinder.*

# Leon Trotsky: "What Were My Disagreements with Lenin on the Character of the Russian Revolution?"

## Introduction

### by Steve Clark

PUBLISHED BELOW, for the first time in English, is a 1927 manuscript by Leon Trotsky. The English translation, from a typed Russian-language manuscript in the Trotsky Papers at Harvard University's Houghton Library, is by Pathfinder Press. The manuscript appears to have been drafted by Trotsky as part of a larger document; its opening passage, for example, refers to matters that were "presented above." The fragment printed here was never published by Trotsky in Russian or any other language.

Nothing in the Houghton Library archives indicates whether the manuscript was drafted as part of a planned article, a speech, or for some other purpose. It is not dated. Evidence from the contents of the manuscript itself, however, indicates that it was drafted in the summer of 1927, following the bloody defeat of the Chinese revolution in April and May of that year.

A decisive factor in bringing about the defeat in China had been Joseph Stalin's abandonment of the revolutionary internationalist strategy that had guided the Soviet Communist Party and Communist International under V.I. Lenin's leadership. Under Stalin's direction, the Comintern's Executive Committee had advocated a strategy in China that ceded the leadership of the democratic, anti-imperialist revolution to the bourgeois nationalist forces of Gen. Chiang Kai-shek. Chiang's Kuomintang (KMT — Nationalist Party) represented the interests of the Chinese capitalists and landlords. It was an obstacle to the struggle by the peasant majority and the working class to free China from imperialist domination, establish a democratic republic, carry through a thoroughgoing agrarian reform, and institute labor rights.

Nonetheless, the Comintern majority ordered the Chinese CP to accept Chiang's leadership and to refrain from criticism of the KMT's course. This policy was adopted and implemented by the CP leadership, although not without hesitation and resistance. The interests of the Chinese workers and peasants were subordinated to maintaining a bloc with Chiang Kai-shek, whom the Comintern majority hailed as a great revolutionary. The fruit of this class-collaborationist course was the massacre of thousands of Communists and other workers in Shanghai at the hands of Chiang's army in April 1927, followed by further defeats the next month.

To deflect attention from this disastrous outcome and other defeats flowing from their foreign and domestic policies, Stalin and his supporters sought to shift the debate in the leading bodies of the Soviet CP and Comintern onto Trotsky's political differences with Lenin prior to 1917 — especially Trotsky's theory of permanent revolution (which Trotsky had counterposed to the Bolsheviks' advocacy of the revolutionary democratic dictatorship of the proletariat and peasantry in Russia). In this way, they sought to cloud the issues under debate and to discredit the revolutionary current within the leadership of the party and the International, in which Trotsky was playing the central role.

This had been a favorite method of Stalin and his allies ever since 1923-24, when they had begun to scuttle Leninist policies. The specter of "permanent revolution" began to be introduced into every political debate that arose in the Soviet CP and the Comintern. Trotsky had consistently spoken out against such efforts by Stalin to obfuscate the debate over current political matters by diverting attention to this and other political and programmatic differences between Trotsky and the Bolsheviks prior to 1917.

"I have no intention, comrades, of raising the question of the theory of permanent revolution," Trotsky stated at the Fifteenth Soviet CP Congress in November 1926. "This theory — in respect both to what has been right in it and to what has been incomplete and wrong — has nothing whatever to do with our present contentions."[1] Nonetheless, Stalin and his supporters continued to harp on Trotsky's pre-1917 differences with Lenin during the debates in the Soviet Communist leadership.

In the 1927 manuscript published below, Trotsky sought to clarify what the differences had actually been between himself and Lenin on the class character and strategy of the Russian revolution. Trotsky wrote:

I argued that the victory of the revolution would mean the dictatorship of the proletariat. Lenin objected that the dictatorship of the proletariat was one of the possibilities at one of the later stages of the revolution, but that we had yet to pass through the democratic stage, in which the proletariat could be in power only through a coalition with the petty bourgeoisie. To that I replied that our immediate tasks were unquestionably bourgeois-democratic in character and that there could be various stages along the way to the realization of those tasks. . . . In order to carry out even the democratic tasks, a dictatorship of the proletariat would be necessary.

T HE BOLSHEVIKS' strategy was based on a double understanding: (1) that a bourgeois democratic revolution against landlordism and tsarism was on the agenda in Russia; and (2) that to advance the triumph of this revolution, the working class had to lead the fight for a revolutionary democratic dictatorship of the proletariat and peasantry.

The liberal bourgeoisie in Russia was incapable of leading the bourgeois democratic revolution and carrying out its tasks in a thoroughgoing manner, the Bolsheviks explained. Only an alliance of the working class and peasant majority could topple the tsarist state and bring to power a government that could carry through the democratic revolution and open the road to the transition to the socialist revolution. This Bolshevik strategy was at the very heart of the debate among Russian revolutionists over the tasks of the proletariat in the bourgeois democratic revolution.[2]

Lenin always clearly differentiated between the bourgeois democratic and the socialist revolutions in Russia.[3] Trotsky did not. As Lenin wrote in 1910, "Trotsky's major mistake is that he ignores the bourgeois character of the [Russian] revolution and has no clear conception of the transition from this revolution to the socialist revolution."[4]

Lenin did not alter his views on this decisive strategic question subsequent to the Bolshevik-led revolution in October 1917. To the contrary. "It was the Bolsheviks," Lenin emphasized in 1918, "who strictly differentiated between the bourgeois-democratic revolution and socialist revolution: by carrying through the former, they opened the door for the transition to the latter. This was the only policy that was revolutionary and Marxist."[5]

By the beginning of 1928, shortly after completing the manuscript published below, Trotsky had been expelled from the Soviet CP by the Stalin-led majority and banished to internal exile in Alma Ata in Soviet Central Asia. In early 1929 he was deported from the Soviet Union. While in forced exile he came to the conclusion that he had been too willing earlier in the 1920s, in writings and speeches such as that printed here, to acknowledge errors in his pre-1917 theory of permanent revolution.[6]

Following his expulsion from the Soviet Union, Trotsky increasingly linked the disastrous Stalinist course in China with what he considered to be ambiguities in Lenin's pre-1917 strategy for the Russian revolution. He began to trace the political continuity of revolutionary Marxism back to his own theory of permanent revolution, *as opposed to* the Bol-sheviks' political strategy.

This shift introduced a leftist bias into Trotsky's political struggle in the 1930s to apply the communist program and strategy of Lenin, and to defend it against the Stalinist second wave of Menshevism. The article "Their Trotsky and Ours: Communist Continuity Today" by Jack Barnes, published in the Fall 1983 issue of *New International*, discusses the political consequences of this for the Fourth International and its parties in countries around the world. Trotsky's 1927 manuscript is pre-sented as part of the discussion that has been carried on in these pages and elsewhere on the revolutionary continuity of communism.

This translation is published by permission of the Houghton Library and Pathfinder Press.

October 1985

# What Were My Disagreements With Lenin On the Character of the Russian Revolution?

## by Leon Trotsky

IN OPPOSITION to falsely interpreted quotations torn out of context, we have presented, above, a more or less coherent, though far from com-plete, picture of the real development of the views on the character of our revolution and the tendencies of its development. A great deal that is ac-cidental, secondary, and irrelevant got stuck onto this important ques-tion, as always happens in a factional struggle, especially an emigré fac-tional struggle, and this tended to cover over and push into the back-ground what is essential and important. All that is inevitable in any strug-gle. But now, when the dispute has long since receded into the past, we can and must discard the shell in order to get at the kernel of the question.

There was no difference in principle in our assessment of the basic forces of the revolution. This was shown with ample clarity by 1905 and especially by 1917. But there was a difference of political approach. Re-duced to its essence, this difference could be formulated as follows:

I argued that the victory of the revolution would mean the dictatorship of the proletariat. Lenin objected that the dictatorship of the proletariat was one of the possibilities at one of the later stages of the revolution, but that we had yet to pass through the democratic stage, in which the proletariat could be in power only through a coalition with the petty bourgeoisie.

To that I replied that our immediate tasks were unquestionably bourgeois-democratic in character and that there could be various stages along the way to the realization of those tasks, with one or another transitional type of power — I didn't deny that — but that these transitional forms could only have an episodic character. In order to carry out even the democratic tasks, a dictatorship of the proletariat would be necessary. Without at all trying to leap over the democratic stage, or the natural stages of the class struggle in general, I argued that we should immediately take as our main aim the conquest of power by the proletarian vanguard.

Lenin answered: that is something that we would never disavow; we will see how the situation develops, the international situation in particular, and so on. For now, however, we have to put the "three whales" in the forefront.[7] These "three whales" will provide a solid foundation for the revolutionary coalition of the proletariat and peasantry.

Between these two ways of posing the question there is a difference, but there is nothing approximating a contradiction. This difference in approach led on occasion to polemics, but they were always incidental and episodic. Lenin's position placed the politically active aspects in the forefront. My position accented or emphasized the broad revolutionary-historical perspective. Here there was a difference of approach, but not a contradiction. This was best seen when the two lines intersected in action. That is what happened in 1905 and 1917.[8]

Today — after the making of the October Revolution — one would have to be either extremely narrow-minded or extremely unscrupulous to portray these two points of view as irreconcilable. October 1917 reconciled them very well. That Lenin put the democratic stage of the revolution and the program of the "three whales" in the forefront, that he emphasized them in every way and made a polemical point of them, was undeniably correct and indispensable politically and tactically.

And when I spoke of incompleteness and gaps in the so-called theory of "permanent revolution,"[9] I had in mind precisely the fact that I simply accepted the democratic stage as something taken for granted, accepted it not only in words but in deeds, as the experience of 1905 shows well enough. But in my theoretical prognoses I was far from always maintaining a clear, distinct, and fully-rounded perspective of the possible successive stages of the revolution. In particular statements and articles, I may have given the impression, at the time when those articles were written, that I was "ignoring" the objective democratic tasks and the elemental democratic forces of the revolution, when in fact I simply considered them self-evident and took them as given. This is proven completely by other works I wrote from other angles or for other purposes. A certain one-sidedness in one or another article on this question over a period of a dozen years (1905-1917) amounts to the kind of "bending the stick too far" — to use Lenin's expression — which is absolutely inevitable in any ideological struggle over big questions.[10] This is also the explanation for a polemical response by Lenin here or there, prompted by one or another formulation in a particular article of mine. But in no case were these addressed to my overall assessment of the revolution or to the nature of my participation in it.

ONE OF my critics,[11] in a vulgarizing way, once attributed to me the thought that not all of Lenin's polemical judgments should be taken at face value but that certain political and pedagogical corrections of no small importance should be made in them. My critic put it this way: [The manuscript contains here the notation, "Quotation about mountain and molehill."]

In these words there is a grain of truth, as anyone who knows Lenin from his writings will see. But the idea is expressed with exceptional psychological rudeness and crudity. "Lenin made a mountain out of a molehill." The same author in another place uses the expression that Lenin defended an idea, "foaming at the mouth." Neither foaming at the mouth nor making a mountain out of a molehill is in any way in keeping with the real image of Lenin. Not by any means. On the other hand, these two expressions could not be more in keeping with the image of the person who wrote them. It was said long ago, the style is the man.

In any case, the truth is that since I did not belong to the Bolshevik faction, or, later to the Bolshevik Party, Lenin was not at all inclined to search for opportunities to express agreement with one or another of my views. And if he had to do so on the most important questions, as I have shown above, that means that our agreement was so obvious that it demanded to be recognized. On the other hand, on the occasions when Lenin polemicized against me, he was not at all attempting to give a "fair assessment" of my views. Rather, he was pursuing the fighting tasks of the moment — and more often than not these did not have to do with me at all but with one or another group of Bolsheviks, at whom he needed to fire a warning shot on a disputed question.

But however things stood concerning Lenin's old polemics against me on the questions of the character of the revolution; and whatever the case on whether I understood Lenin correctly on this question in the past or even whether I understand him correctly now — let us even grant for the moment that I was unable to grasp what is readily comprehensible to Martynov, Slepkov, Rafes, Skvortsov-Stepanov, Kuusinen, and in general to all the Lyadovs,[12] regardless of age or gender — there still remains before us one quite minor, but very thorny, little question: How did it happen that those who never disagreed with Lenin on the basic question of the character of the Russian revolution, those who shared his view in full, etc., etc., took such a shamefully opportunist position [in 1917]? To be sure some only took that position as long as they were left to their own resources, but others persisted in it even after Lenin's return to Russia. How could they have taken such a position on the very question on which the ideological life of the party had centered for the preceding twelve years?[13]

But the question that must be answered is not whether I leaped over the agrarian-democratic stage. Solid historical facts and my whole earlier exposition on this question show that to be untrue. Rather the question is, how was it that my bitterly remorseless critics failed at the most important juncture to leap far enough? Was it only because nobody has the capacity to grasp beyond their reach?

Such an explanation would be perfectly valid in individual cases. But in this instance we are dealing with a whole layer of the party, educated from 1905 on according to a certain orientation. Is it not possible, as a way of softening the political blame, to accept the explanation that Lenin took for granted the possibility of the bourgeois revolution growing over into the socialist revolution and that in the course of the polemic he pushed that historical variant too far into the background and did not go into it sufficiently, did not explain it enough — not only the theoretical possibility but the profound political probability that the proletariat in Russia would find itself in power earlier than in the advanced capitalist countries?

If his sealed coach had not passed through Germany in March 1917,[14] if Lenin with his group of comrades and, above all, his authority and dynamism, had not arrived in Petrograd at the beginning of April, the October revolution — not in general, as some among us love to speculate, but the particular revolution that happened on October 25, Old Style[15] — that revolution might never have come to pass. As the March Conference (the minutes of which have not been published to this day) testifies irrefutably,[16] an authoritative group of leading Bolsheviks, or more exactly, a whole layer of the party would have saddled the party, in place of Lenin's policy of an unremitting offensive, with a policy of sitting on the fence, a policy of division of labor with the Provisional Government, a policy of not frightening off the bourgeoisie, a policy of semiacceptance of the imperialist war hidden under the pacifist manifestos to the peoples of the whole world.

Lenin, after proposing his theses of April 4,[17] ran into accusations of nothing more nor less than Trotskyism! What, I ask you, would have happened if to the great misfortune of the Russian revolution, Lenin had been cut off from Russia or killed on the way, and the orientation toward an armed uprising and the dictatorship of the proletariat had been proclaimed to be — something else? What would have happened then?

After everything we have gone through in the last few years it is not

at all hard to imagine. The initiators of a change of orientation and slo
gans, that is, the advocates of a course aimed at seizing power, woul
have become the object of a furious denunciation as ultralefts, a
Trotskyists, as violators of the traditions of Bolshevism, and — wh
knows? — as counterrevolutionaries. All the Lyadovs would hav
plunged into this polemic as ducks take to water.

To be sure, the proletariat would have exerted powerful pressure from
below and might have broken through the democratic front, but deprive
of a united, far-sighted, and audacious leadership, it would have eventu
ally, a month sooner or later, run up against a victorious Kornilovist,[1]
Chiang Kai-shekist coup. After that a seven-mile-long resolution woul
have been written, that everything had gone strictly according to th
laws of Marx, since the bourgeoisie inherently betrays the proletaria
and Bonapartist generals inherently make coups serving th
bourgeoisie's interests. Moreover, "we foresaw this all along."[19]

Any attempt to point out to the complacent philistines that their fore
sight was not worth a tin kopek, since the task is not to foresee the vic
tory of the bourgeoisie but to ensure the victory of the proletariat, suc
an attempt would have inspired an additional resolution, to the effec
that everything had happened on the basis of the relationship of forces
that the proletariat of backward Russia, especially in the context of th
imperialist slaughter, could not leap over historical stages, and that suc
a program could only be put forward by supporters of permanent revolu
tion, against which Lenin had fought to the last day of his life.

That is how history is now written. And it is made just as badly as
is written.

## Notes

1. Leon Trotsky, *The Challenge of the Left Opposition (1926-27)* (New York
Pathfinder Press, 1980), p. 145.
2. This introduction will not attempt to review the differences between th
strategic perspectives of the Mensheviks and Bolsheviks in the Russian revolu
tion, and where Trotsky stood in relation to these conflicting political courses
For this, readers are referred to the following sources:

•The works of Lenin and Trotsky on this question. The best know
presentation of the Bolshevik position is Lenin's 1905 book, *Two Tactic
of Social-Democracy in the Democratic Revolution* (Lenin, *Collected Work*
[hereinafter *CW*] [Moscow: Foreign Languages Publishing House, 1962]
vol. 9, pp. 15-140). Trotsky's view is summarized in his 1906 work, *Results an
Prospects* in Trotsky, *The Permanent Revolution* (New York: Pathfinde
Press, 1969).

A reading list of Lenin's main writings on this question — before, during, an
after the 1917 revolutions in Russia — has been prepared by the National Edu

cation Department of the Socialist Workers Party and can be obtained by sending $1.50 to: SWP National Education Department, 14 Charles Lane, New York, N.Y. 10014.

In addition, see the 1915 articles by Lenin, Trotsky, and Gregory Zinoviev in Chapter 9 on "Russia: Toward Revolution" in the book, *Lenin's Struggle for a Revolutionary International: Documents 1907-1916, The Preparatory Years.* (New York: Monad Press, 1984).

For Trotsky's other major discussions of this question earlier in the political struggle with the Stalin-led faction, see the 1924 works, "The Lessons of October" and "Our Differences," in *The Challenge of the Left Opposition (1923-25),* (New York: Pathfinder Press, 1975).

•The article "Their Trotsky and Ours: Communist Continuity Today" by Jack Barnes, published in the Fall 1983 issue of *New International;* and "The Workers' and Farmers' Government: A Popular Revolutionary Dictatorship" by Mary-Alice Waters, published in the Spring-Summer 1984 issue of *New International.*

•The Education for Socialists publication *Bolshevism and the Russian Revolution: A Debate,* which includes articles by Doug Jenness and Ernest Mandel, as well as Lenin's 1921 article, "On the Fourth Anniversary of the Russian Revolution."

3. In a June 1905 polemic with Georgi Plekhanov, Lenin wrote: "Marx and Engels in 1850 did not differentiate between democratic dictatorship and socialist dictatorship [in the 1848-49 revolution in Germany], or, rather, they did not mention the former at all, since they considered capitalism to be in a state of senile decay and socialism near." (Lenin, "On the Provisional Revolutionary Government," *CW*, vol. 8, p. 471) This was Lenin's primary criticism of Marx and Engels's writings in 1850 summing up the lessons of the revolution in Germany.

4. Lenin, "The Aim of the Proletarian Struggle in Our Revolution," *CW*, vol. 5, p. 371.

5. Lenin, "The Proletarian Revolution and the Renegade Kautsky," *CW*, vol. 28, p. 311.

6. Trotsky wrote the following in his 1929 introduction to his book, *The Permanent Revolution*: "Not having re-read my old works for a long time, I was ready in advance to admit defects in them more serious and important than really were there. I became convinced of this in 1928, when the political leisure imposed upon me by exile in Alma-Ata gave me the opportunity to re-read, pencil in hand, my old writings on the problems of the permanent revolution." (*Permanent Revolution*, p. 130)

Trotsky's main writings following his expulsion from the Soviet CP on the question of his pre-1917 differences with Lenin can be found in the above work, as well as in *Leon Trotsky on China* (New York: Monad Press, 1976), especially pp. 276-90, 291-341, and 578-91; and "Three Conceptions of the Russian Revolution," in *Writings of Leon Trotsky* [1939-1940] (New York: Pathfinder Press, 1969), pp. 55-73.

7. The Bolsheviks focused their propaganda around three revolutionary democratic demands: a democratic republic, confiscation of the big estates, and an eight-hour day. These became known as the "three whales of Bolshevism."

8. In the Russian manuscript at Harvard's Houghton Library, this paragraph appeared on a separate sheet of paper with a handwritten page number placing it at the end of the fragment published here. In the opinion of the editors, this was the result of an erroneous transposition of sheets at some point in the filing process. This passage makes no sense as the last paragraph of the manuscript and seems to fit at the point in the manuscript where it has been placed in this translation.

9. This seems to be a reference to Trotsky's speech to the Fifteenth Congress of the Soviet Communist Party, held in 1926, cited in the above introduction.

10. A short while later, Trotsky made a similar point in his book, *The Permanent Revolution,* written in October 1928 during his forced internal exile in Alma-Ata. There Trotsky was more concrete about the political questions on which he had expressed "a certain one-sidedness." He wrote:

"In the 12 years (1905-17) of my revolutionary journalistic activity, there are also articles in which the episodic circumstances and even the episodic polemical exaggerations inevitable in struggle protrude into the foreground in violation of the strategic line. Thus, for example, articles can be found in which I expressed doubts about the future revolutionary role of the peasantry *as a whole, as an estate,* and in connection with this refused to designate, especially during the imperialist war, the future Russian revolution as 'national,' for I felt this designation to be ambiguous." (*The Permanent Revolution* [New York: Pathfinder Press, 1969], pp. 171-72.)

11. There is no indication in the manuscript about whether Trotsky is referring to Stalin or someone else in the Stalin faction.

12. All six of these individuals were prominent spokespersons for the Stalinist faction of the Soviet Communist Party in the mid-1920s. A. S. Martynov (1865-1935) was a leading writer and spokesperson for the Mensheviks and an opponent of the October revolution. He joined the Communist Party in 1923 and achieved prominence as a "theoretician" of its Stalinist faction. M. N. Lyadov (1872- 1947) was a leading Bolshevik in 1903-1908 who became a Menshevik; he rejoined the Soviet Communist Party in 1920 and became a prominent party historian.

13. Stalin, Kamenev, and some other Bolshevik leaders initially opposed Lenin's revolutionary position of uncompromising political opposition to the capitalist Provisional Government that came to power in Russia following the February 1917 overthrow of the tsar. They adapted to the Provisional Government's course toward continuing participation in the interimperialist war, and began to seek greater common ground with the Mensheviks. They opposed Lenin's orientation toward a fight for all power to the soviets of workers', peasants', and soldiers' representatives. By the time of the All-Russian Bolshevik Party conference in late April 1917, held three weeks after Lenin's return to Russia, Kamenev was alone among the most prominent party leaders in retaining these positions, and Lenin's positions were overwhelmingly adopted.

For Trotsky's account of these events, see the first volume of his *History of the Russian Revolution,* especially Chapter XVI on "Rearming the Party" and the chapters just before and after it (New York: Monad Press, 1980), pp. 285-357.

For a different view of these events, see "Our Political Continuity with Bolshevism" by Doug Jenness, particularly the section on, "Were the Bolsheviks Disarmed?" in *Bolshevism and the Russian Revolution: A Debate* (New York: Pathfinder Press, 1985), pp. 32-34.

14. When the Russian revolution broke out in early 1917, Lenin and other prominent Russian socialists living in forced exile in Switzerland were refused passage to Russia by the Allied powers (Britain, France, Italy, Russia, etc.). They then received permission from the German government to cross Germany on their way to Russia. Lenin and his companions were confined to a sealed coach while in transit and could not leave the train until it left German territory. Lenin arrived in Petrograd on April 3.

15. Old Style refers to the Julian calendar used by Russia and a few other countries at the time. Its dates were thirteen days earlier than the Gregorian calendar, which was then used by most other countries of western Europe and America and was introduced in Russia following the October revolution.

16. Trotsky is referring to the March 27-April 4, 1917, Bolshevik Party conference, at which Stalin defended his policy of critical support to the Provisional Government and convergence with the Mensheviks. Stalin subsequently suppressed the minutes of this conference. Trotsky published them in his 1931 work *The Stalin School of Falsification* (New York: Pathfinder Press, 1972), pp. 231-301.

17. See Lenin, "Tasks of the Proletariat in the Present Revolution," *CW* vol. 24, pp. 21-26. This article is usually referred to as the April Theses.

18. General Lavr G. Kornilov (1870-1918) became the Provisional Government's commander-in-chief in July 1917 and led a counterrevolutionary putsch in September 1917.

19. Following the defeat of the Chinese revolution of 1925-27, Stalin, in his article "Questions of the Chinese Revolution," implied that the line of the Comintern leadership had foreseen the betrayal of the revolution by the Chinese bourgeoisie. Despite the disastrous consequences of the class-collaborationist course that the Stalin-led Comintern Executive Committee had imposed on the Chinese Communist Party, Stalin wrote a few weeks after the Shanghai massacre that these events had "fully confirmed the correctness of this line." (Joseph Stalin, "The Question of the Chinese Revolution," *Collected Works*, [Moscow: Foreign Languages Publishing House, 1954], vol. 9, pp. 227, 228).

### Socialism: Utopian and Scientific
by Frederick Engels

Explains the origins of the materialist world outlook of the modern communist workers movement. A classic of Marxism. 63 pp., $2.50

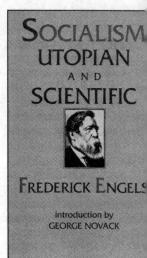

### The Communist Manifesto
by Karl Marx and Frederick Engels

First published in 1848, this is the founding program of the revolutionary working-class movement and its fight for socialism. 48 pp., $2.50

### Imperialism, The Highest Stage of Capitalism
by V.I. Lenin

Written during World War I, this pamphlet presents Lenin's explanation of how capitalism is transformed into imperialism — with colonial oppression, interimperialist wars, and revolutions the result. 128 pp., $2.95

### State and Revolution
by V.I. Lenin

Written on the eve of the October 1917 Russian revolution to counter the political misleadership of the Mensheviks and others falsely speaking in the name of Marxism. Lenin reasserts the true views of Marx and Engels and the real lessons of the 1905 and February 1917 revolutions in Russia on the relationship of the state and revolution. 103 pp., $2.00

### The Revolution Betrayed
*What Is the Soviet Union and Where is it Going?*

by Leon Trotsky

The classic work laying out the communist viewpoint on the social character of the Soviet Union and political tasks of the working class following the rise of the Stalin-led bureaucratic caste. 314 pp., $17.95

### The History of the Russian Revolution
by Leon Trotsky

Complete and unabridged. 1336 pp., $26.95

*Available from Pathfinder.*

# Semicolonial Countries and Semi-Industrialized Dependent Countries

## by Ernest Mandel

### The Inventory

IN THE course of the last twenty years, a series of semicolonial countries have experienced a genuine industrial "takeoff." Their social and economic stucture has been profoundly modified. The relationship of forces between different social classes and segments of classes has been shaken up. The way in which they fit into the international capitalist economy is no longer the same. By the same token, their political relations with the imperialist powers have undergone a change.

Even though these are quantitative and not qualitative changes, they are sufficiently important to merit being registered and codified as such. They entail, in particular, changes in the weight of the different tactical components in revolutionary strategy as a whole, which, itself, remains the same — i.e., determined by the logic of the law of uneven and combined development in the imperialist epoch: the strategy of permanent revolution. This is why it is high time that Marxists generalized the use of new and more precise categories in their analyses.

From the beginning of the imperialist epoch up to the beginning of the 1950s, the underdeveloped countries were generally subdivided into colonial countries properly so-called and semicolonial countries. However, the difference between the two concerned less the socioeconomic structure than the *political* form of imperialist domination. In the colonial countries, there was direct political domination (direct exercise of state power) by the imperialist powers themselves. In the semicolonial countries, there was *indirect* political domination by the imperialist powers, the day-to-day exercise of power remaining in the hands of the indigenous ruling classes (not necessarily bourgeois classes: one thinks of Haile Selassie's Ethiopia, Saudi Arabia under Ibn Saud, Iran, and Afghanistan). In these latter countries imperialism ruled but did not gov-

149

ern. The indigenous ruling classes were associated as junior partners in
the exercise of power.

At the time when the movement for national liberation in the colonial
and semicolonial countries experienced a near universal rise in the aftermath of the Second World War — due to the weakening of the colonial
powers in the course of that war but above all as a result of the victory of
the Chinese revolution — the transformation of direct imperialist domination into indirect imperialist domination was generalized. Almost all
the old colonies gained their formal political independence.

By about 1963 the totality of underdeveloped countries, with a few
exceptions, were classed in the category of semicolonial countries.
Some of these were, moreover, emancipated from imperialist domination thanks to a victorious socialist revolution: China, North Korea,
North Vietnam, Cuba (and the majority of countries in Eastern Europe,
which also had a semicolonial status before the Second World War).

Today, a new, major distinction imposes itself among the underdeveloped countries. Whatever one's judgment may be as regards their political, financial, and economic relations with imperialism, it is undeniable that some of them have undergone a change in their internal political situation, which today is incomparable with the situation in 1910,
1920, 1930, 1940, or 1950. They have gone beyond a first phase of prolonged industrialization, which now places them in a situation of semi-
industrialization, more advanced than that known — to give a historical
reference — in Russia in 1917 or Spain in 1936.

The great majority of semicolonial countries have not undergone this
process of rapid and prolonged semi-industrialization, with all the consequences that follow from it. To continue to classify all the underdeveloped countries together in a jumble in one and the same category, that
of semicolonial countries, is hence a growing source of confusion. It
does not permit one to take into account the fundamental distinctions
vital for the understanding of reality and for the elaboration of correct
revolutionary tactics. That is why a new subdivision of underdeveloped
countries is necessary: between semicolonial countries properly so-
called on the one hand, and semi-industrialized dependent countries on
the other (some small colonial countries persist, notably in the Antilles,
some islands in the Pacific and the Indian Ocean; Hong Kong from a for-
mal-political point of view.)

One can also express this subdivision in another way: in the *genera*
category of countries dominated by imperialism, a subdivision should be
made between semi-industrialized countries and semicolonial countries
in the traditional sense of the word.

The statistics provided below permit an instant grasp of the sound
basis for this distinction:

Table 1

| | Share of Gross National Product | | | | Employment | | | |
|---|---|---|---|---|---|---|---|---|
| | Agriculture | | Manufacturing Industry | | Agriculture | | Industry | |
| | 1960 | 1981 | 1960 | 1981 | 1960 | 1981 | 1960 | 1981 |
| Chad | 52% | — | 4% | 4% | 95% | 85% | 2% | 7% |
| Bangladesh | 58% | 54% | 5% | 8% | 87% | 74% | 3% | 11% |
| Ethiopia | 65% | 50% | 26% | 16% | 88% | 80% | 7% | 13% |
| Nepal | — | — | — | — | 95% | 93% | 2% | 2% |
| Burma | 33% | 47% | 12% | 10% | — | 67% | — | 10% |
| Afghanistan | — | — | — | — | 85% | 76% | 6% | 8% |
| Mali | 55% | 42% | 15% | 16% | 94% | 73% | 3% | 12% |
| Malawi | 58% | 43% | 16% | 13% | 92% | 86% | 3% | 5% |
| Zaïre | 30% | 32% | 13% | 3% | 83% | 75% | 9% | 13% |
| Uganda | 52% | 75% | 9% | 4% | 89% | 83% | 4% | 6% |
| Burundi | — | 56% | — | 9% | 93% | 84% | 3% | 5% |
| Upper Volta | 55% | 41% | 9% | 13% | 92% | 82% | 5% | 13% |
| Rwanda | 80% | 46% | 1% | 16% | 95% | 91% | 1% | 2% |
| India | 50% | 37% | 14% | 18% | 74% | 69% | 11% | 13% |
| Tanzania | 57% | 52% | 5% | 9% | 89% | 83% | 4% | 6% |
| Haiti | — | — | — | — | 80% | 74% | 6% | 7% |
| Sri Lanka | 32% | 28% | 15% | 16% | 56% | 54% | 14% | 14% |
| Pakistan | 46% | 30% | 12% | 17% | 61% | 57% | 18% | 20% |
| Kenya | 38% | 32% | 9% | 13% | 86% | 78% | 5% | 10% |
| Indonesia | 50% | 24% | — | 12% | 75% | 55% | 8% | 15% |
| Bolivia | 26% | 18% | 15% | 14% | 61% | 50% | 18% | 24% |
| Honduras | 27% | 32% | 13% | 17% | 70% | 63% | 11% | 15% |
| Zambia | 11% | 18% | 4% | 18% | 79% | 67% | 7% | 11% |
| Egypt | 30% | 21% | 20% | 32% | 58% | 50% | 12% | 30% |
| El Salvador | 32% | 26% | 15% | 15% | 62% | 50% | 17% | 22% |
| Thailand | 40% | 24% | 13% | 20% | 84% | 76% | 4% | 9% |
| Philippines | 26% | 23% | 20% | 25% | 61% | 46% | 15% | 17% |
| South Korea | 37% | 17% | 14% | 28% | 66% | 34% | 9% | 29% |
| Algeria | 16% | 6% | 8% | 11% | 67% | 25% | 12% | 25% |
| Brazil | 16% | 13% | 26% | 27% | 52% | 30% | 15% | 24% |
| Argentina | 16% | 9% | 33% | 25% | 20% | 13% | 36% | 28% |
| Mexico | 16% | 8% | 19% | 22% | 55% | 36% | 20% | 26% |
| South Africa | 12% | 7% | 21% | 23% | 32% | 30% | 30% | 29% |
| Taiwan | — | 7% | 22% | 40% | — | 35% | — | 38% |
| Hong Kong | 4% | 1% | 27% | 28% | 8% | 3% | 52% | 57% |
| Singapore | 4% | 1% | 12% | 30% | 8% | 2% | 23% | 39% |

(Source: United Nations statistics, except for Taiwan: *Statistical Yearbook of the Republic of China*, 1982.)

## Table 1A

| | Per Capita Gross National Product (1981, in current U.S. dollars) | Life Expectancy at Birth (1981) | Percent Adult Illiteracy (1981) |
|---|---|---|---|
| Chad | 110 | 43 | 85% |
| Bangladesh | 140 | 48 | 74% |
| Ethiopia | 140 | 46 | 85% |
| Nepal | 150 | 45 | 81% |
| Burma | 190 | 54 | 34% |
| Afghanistan | 190? | 37 | 80% |
| Mali | 190 | 45 | 90% |
| Malawi | 200 | 44 | 75% |
| Zaire | 210 | 50 | 45% |
| Uganda | 220 | 48 | 48% |
| Burundi | 230 | 45 | 75% |
| Upper Volta | 240 | 44 | 95% |
| Rwanda | 250 | 46 | 50% |
| India | 260 | 52 | 64% |
| Tanzania | 280 | 52 | 21% |
| Haiti | 300 | 54 | 77% |
| Sri Lanka | 400 | 69 | 15% |
| Pakistan | 350 | 50 | 76% |
| Kenya | 420 | 56 | 53% |
| Indonesia | 530 | 54 | 38% |
| Bolivia | 600 | 51 | 37% |
| Honduras | 600 | 59 | 40% |
| Zambia | 600 | 51 | 56% |
| Egypt | 650 | 57 | 56% |
| El Salvador | 650 | 63 | 38% |
| Thailand | 770 | 63 | 14% |
| Philippines | 790 | 63 | 25% |
| South Korea | 1,700 | 66 | 7% |
| Taiwan | 1,770 | — | 10% |
| Algeria | 2,140 | 56 | 65% |
| Brazil | 2,220 | 64 | 24% |
| Mexico | 2,250 | 66 | 17% |
| Argentina | 2,560 | 71 | 7% |
| South Africa | 2,770 | 63 | — |
| Hong Kong | 5,100 | 75 | 10% |
| Singapore | 5,240 | 72 | 17% |

(Source: *Ibid.*)

To interpret this table correctly, one should bear in mind that the category "industry" includes at one and the same time manufacturing industry and mining. The small weight of manufacturing industry in the Gross National Product and the much greater weight of industrial employment, can therefore reflect the rise of a mining sector. That is the case notably in Algeria, in Indonesia, and in Bolivia. The spectacular decline of the peasantry, without a corresponding rise in industrial employment, reflects the rural exodus that is crystallized in an underemployed urban population, marginalized or lumpenized (in the bourgeois statistics this is called "expansion of the tertiary sector"). This is the case particularly in Indonesia, Thailand, the Philippines, El Salvador, Brazil, and Mexico. Correlatively, there appears a disproportion between agricultural employment and the contribution of agriculture in the Gross National Product, a disproportion that manifests itself above all in the countries of Black Africa like Zaïre, Kenya, Zambia, and Nigeria (in the latter country peasants represented 50 percent of the active population in 1981 but produced only 23 percent of the GNP), in the countries of Central America, in Bolivia, in Peru (peasants there represent 39 percent of the active population but produced only 9 percent of the GNP), in Mexico (peasants there represented 36 percent of the active population and produced only 8 percent of the GNP), just as in South and Southeast Asia (in Thailand peasants represented 76 percent of the active population but produced only 24 percent of the value of the GNP). Let us also note the case of Egypt, where the peasantry still represents 50 percent of the active population but produces only 21 percent of the GNP, and that of Morocco: 50 percent of the active population, 14 percent of the GNP . . .

This crying disproportion reflects the low productivity of traditional agriculture, certainly, but one that is reinforced by the superexploitation and poverty of the peasantry provoked by the pricing and export policies (of commercialization) that have been decided on.

---

Table 2

**Structure of Production in
Manufacturing Industry, 1978**

|              | Capital Goods* | Consumer Goods |
|--------------|----------------|----------------|
| Bangladesh   | 4.3%           | 72.3%          |
| Nigeria      | 6.2%           | 64.2%          |
| Venezuela    | 7.5%           | 51.7%          |
| Hong Kong    | 7.9%           | 80.5%          |
| Colombia     | 8.4%           | 68.3%          |
| Philippines  | 9.4%           | 74.5%          |
| Indonesia    | 9.3%           | 75.8%          |

|  | Capital Goods* | Consumer Goods |
|---|---|---|
| Mexico | 11.6%** | 59.8% |
| South Korea | 14.3%** | 64.3% |
| India | 22.3% | 48.7% |
| Singapore | 24.1% | 51.3% |

(Source: *Ibid.*)

*"Capital goods" includes machinery, as well as electrical machinery apart from consumer durables and means of transportation. There is a third category of industrial manufactured goods called "intermediary goods," which includes steel, refined petroleum, petrochemical products, and so forth. Consumer durables such as radios, televisions, and other household appliances are included in the category of consumer goods.

**The percentages for these two countries rose significantly in 1980, 1981, and 1982. The *Economist* (August 14, 1982) gives the figure of 18 percent for South Korea in 1981. The percentage of consumer goods fell to 47 percent.

In 1980, the products of manufacturing industry represented 21.4 percent of exports in Argentina; 44.9 percent of the exports of Brazil (as against 15.2 percent in 1970); 43.4 percent of the exports of Singapore and 86.5 percent of the exports of Taiwan (in 1981); 93.8 percent of the exports of Hong Kong; and 90.5 percent of the exports of South Korea (as against 14 percent in 1960!).

Capital goods represent, in the total of exports:

### Table 3

|  | 1962 | 1977 |
|---|---|---|
| Hong Kong | 4.9% | 16.2% |
| South Korea | 2.6% | 17.4% |
| Taiwan | 1.7% | 21.0% |
| Singapore | 9.8% | 24.5% |

(Source: Patrick Tissier, "L'industrialisation dans huit pays asiatiques depuis la Seconde Guerre Mondiale" [Industrialization in eight Asian countries since the Second World War] in *Critiques de l'économie politique,* no. 14, January-March, 1981. The whole of this issue is a valuable source of data for the subject treated in the present article, as are the books of Pierre Salama).

## What has changed

THE PICTURE that emerges from this tableau is that of an impressive correlation of various indices. A series of countries have emerged that are clearly situated on the borderline between industrialized countries and underdeveloped countries. Included are Mexico, Argentina, Brazil, South Korea, Taiwan, Singapore, Hong Kong (South Africa, Egypt,

Algeria, India, as well as the oil-exporting countries with a low population density occupy a separate place).

For the seven countries first mentioned, there exists a correlation between the following factors:

• the now preponderant weight of industry in economic activity;

• the preponderant weight of wage labor, the proletariat, of the towns and the countryside in the economically active population;

• the preponderant weight of industrial products in exports;

• a per capita income that is on average ten times as large as that of the poorer countries and which approaches that of the weakest imperialist countries (the per capita GNP in Brazil, Argentina, and Mexico is practically equal to that of Portugal; that of Hong Kong and Singapore to that of Spain).

The transitory and limiting cases in which this correlation is no longer complete, all have specific characteristics. South Africa remains essentially an exporting country of mineral raw materials (gold, diamonds, etc.) and not of manufactured products. The per capita "averages" for employment and income in that country are further distorted if a subdivision is not made between the white population and the Black/Coloured population; the gap between the two remains huge, fluctuating around a ratio of 1/10 or 1/8. India remains essentially a country with a "dualist" economy, characterized by a mass of poor village and "marginalized" urban population that has not felt any consequence of the industrial "takeoff." The same remark applies in large measure to Egypt and Algeria, where industrialization has decisively "taken off" but has not succeeded in neutralizing demographic pressure, i.e., it has not had sufficient cumulative effects on the whole of society.

As regards the petroleum-exporting countries with a low population density, the income per inhabitant there has sometimes risen strongly, reflecting the windfall of petrodollars (here too the average cannot betaken to mean very much, in view of the tremendous social inequalities that continue to prevail in some of these countries), without eliminating many of the other indices of underdevelopment:

Table 3A

|  | Per Capita Income | Life Expectancy at Birth | Manufacturing Industry as % of GNP | Adult Illiterates as % of Total Adults |
|---|---|---|---|---|
| Libya | $8,450 | 57 | 3% | *** |
| Saudi Arabia | $12,600 | 55 | 4% | 75% |
| Arab Emirates | $24,660 | 63 | 4% | 40% |
| Kuwait | $20,900 | 70 | 4% | 44% |

(Source: United Nations statistics.)

The following conclusion thus emerges: to take account of world reality today, Marxists should introduce a new differentiation in the characterization of capitalist countries — that of semi-industrialized dependent countries, countries that preserve only some of the classical characteristics of semicolonial countries but no longer all of them, and should not be called so any more.

They are no longer characterized by a fundamental economic stagnation. They are no longer countries with a preponderantly agricultural structure. They are no longer confined to the production and export of agricultural and mineral raw materials, nor to production of a single crop or product.

These traditional characteristics of semicolonial countries are, in the last analysis, the consequences and not the causes of two structural characteristics emphasized by Lenin: their domination by imperialist finance capital and their political domination (Lenin used above all the term "diplomatic") by imperialism. What has become of these two characteristics?

From a financial point of view, the most important change that has taken place in these countries over the last decades consists in the appearance of an *autonomous finance capital,* independent of those of the imperialist countries.[1] In all the countries mentioned above, as well as in a series of others (notably Syria, Iraq, and Iran), it is no longer true that the majority of the banks and the bulk of large-scale industry and mining are imperialist property, as was the case in the first half of the century. The share of *imperialist property* has dramatically declined in those countries in favor of:

- either national-monopolist capitalist ownership (banking groups, financial groups, and "national" industrial groups, whether state owned, privately owned, or of mixed state-private ownership);

- or ownership of the *joint-venture* type: imperialist multinationals associated with groups of national-monopolist capitalists.

One can waste a lot of time in disputes about the *magnitude* of the change. But that there is change, that one would need to be blind to deny. There is a fundamental difference between Iran dominated by the Anglo-Iranian Oil Company, Brazil dominated by the big U.S. trusts, Argentina dominated by the big British and U.S. trusts, India completely dominated by British finance capital, let us say around 1930, 1940, or 1950 — typical situations to which the formula "semicolonial" applies (without talking about Egypt dominated by the Suez Canal Company) — on the one hand, and the situation of those countries today on the other.[2]

The same remark applies at the level of political structures. Because foreign finance capital completely dominated the economy of these countries, the state was in its turn essentially the instrument of that capital. The essential function of the government was to assure the valorization and accumulation of foreign capital and not "national" capitalist accumulation. These governments were the puppets of imperialism. To claim that the same can be said of Nasser, Mossadegh, or Khomeini, of Perón or of the military dictatorship in Brazil, of Nehru and Mrs. Gandhi, the successors of President Alemán in Mexico, and of the governments of Singapore and South Korea is to utter plain nonsense.

It suffices to observe the phenomenon of the bloc of so-called nonaligned countries to see the observable "diplomatic" change, however great the limits of the phenomenon in other respects and however much its practical results may be confined to pure rhetoric. One can hardly imagine King Farouk, General Chiang Kai-shek, Emperor Haile Selassie, Reza Shah, Colonel Batista, and President Varga, King Carol of Romania, and King Boris of Bulgaria getting together with President Cárdenas to form a "bloc of nonaligned countries" and holding their own, let us say in 1934 or in 1938, be it only in the sphere of rhetoric, against London, Paris, Washington, Berlin, and Tokyo put together, in the diplomatic arena — for example, during successive sessions of the League of Nations. Now, back then those were the typical representatives of the semicolonial countries in the classical sense of the word.

One can tighten up the issue even further by completing the financial and political analysis with a more nuanced analysis of the structure of social power. The semicolonies were (and are) dominated traditionally by an oligarchy of which the essential elements are hegemonic foreign capital, the traditional ruling classes (generally, though not always, big landowners) and an "extended" comprador bourgeoisie, which André Gunder Frank has appropriately called "lumpen-bourgeoisie." But that does not have a great deal in common with the reality of today in São Paulo, Mexico City, Buenos Aires, Seoul, Hong Kong, Singapore, Taipei, Bombay, or indeed Cairo, Algiers, and Johannesburg.

A new "oligarchy" has grown up in those countries, of which the essential elements are the "national" monopolist groups, the apex of the state bureaucracy (often, but not always, military functionaries) and the representatives of the imperialist multinationals. This is not the case in the great majority of underdeveloped countries where, by and large, the old oligarchy rules. But it is the case in a dozen countries occupying an "intermediate" position on the capitalist world market.

To EMPHASIZE once more the necessity of this reclassification, we submit in evidence three phenomena:

• Heavy industry, including the production of capital goods by certain semi-industrialized dependent countries, today occupies an important place on the world market. Thus, South Korea is the third largest shipbuilder in the world. It builds two times more tonnage per year than the United States, more than Great Britain, France, and West Germany put together! Can one seriously claim that we are dealing with a situation "typical" of semicolonial countries, such as Lenin and Marxists understood it in 1910, 1920, 1930, 1940, or even 1950? One of the results of this situation is that certain semi-industrialized dependent countries are becoming producers and exporters of arms (above all Brazil with the Xingu plane, but also India and other countries).[3]

• The most powerful banks in the semi-industrialized dependent countries have, in the world rating of the biggest banks, outstripped those of a series of less important imperialist countries. Thus, the Banco do Brasil is placed, both in terms of its own capital and of the mass of the sum of deposits, ahead of the biggest bank of Sweden, Australia, Spain, Denmark, Norway, Austria, and Portugal. One will say that Brazil is much bigger than Australia, Sweden, Denmark, Norway, Austria, and Spain. That is true. But so it was already in 1930, 1940, 1950. Why, if it is simply a question of population size, did its biggest bank not occupy a similar place on the world capital market back in those days?

• The appearance of an autonomous finance capital and of a real banking power has culminated in an initial — to be sure still modest — export of capital by some of the semi-industrialized countries, above all Brazil, Hong Kong, Singapore, Mexico, South Korea, and also the richer OPEC countries.

Thus, one of the richest Chinese shipowners of Hong Kong, C.Y. Tung, bought the powerful British group Furness Whity (*Le Monde,* April 19, 1982). The shipowners of Hong Kong moreover rank first in the world, having surpassed, and by a long way, their Greek counterparts. The richest group among them, that of Sir Yung Pao, possesses a fleet equal to the entire fleet of all the shipowners of the USA put together, which is twice the size of the entire French commercial fleet (*Le Monde,* August 21-22, 1983).

Is it "revisionism" to introduce this new classification? Not at all. Following Bukharin, Lenin himself introduced new categories, those precisely of imperialist countries and semicolonial countries, which Marx and Engels never used.[4] The Fourth International introduced a new category, that of "bureaucratized workers' states," which the Third International in the epoch of Lenin and Trotsky did not use. To acknowledge a new phenomenon — inasmuch as it really involves a *lasting* phenomenon and not merely a temporary and conjunctural change — to give it a name and a definition, i.e., to formulate new concepts as tools of analysis, to integrate them in a coherent manner into the totality of Marxist instruments of analysis, that is, not "revising" Marxism but to the contrary enriching it, making it better able to understand reality in order to change it in the interests of the emancipation of the workers and all the oppressed, i.e., in the interest of the world socialist revolution.

Far from being a safeguard of "orthodoxy," the refusal to register and explain important observable changes in the real world generally leads, after a certain interval, to a frenetic and liquidationist revisionism, the new facts being in the long run more stubborn and more convincing than the best preserved dogmas in the refrigerator.

## What has not changed

To ACKNOWLEDGE the existence in the capitalist world today of a series of semi-industrialized dependent countries — largely distinct from the semicolonial countries in the classical sense of the word — is this to put in question the theory or the strategy of permanent revolution? Not at all.

The theory of permanent revolution has as premise the law of uneven and combined *development* of backward countries in the imperialist epoch, not some "law" of permanent or absolute stagnation in these countries. In no way whatsoever does it claim that *none* of the historical tasks of the national bourgeois (or national-democratic) revolution can be realized under bourgeois or petty-bourgeois nationalist leaderships. Otherwise it would already have been rendered null and void in the 1950s and 1960s, given the near universal conquest of formal political independence by the old colonies.

It affirms rather the inability, on the part of the bourgeoisie and the nationalist petty-bourgeoisie in the backward countries, to realize the *totality* of the historical tasks of the national-bourgeois revolution in the imperialist epoch. The reason is that under a capitalist regime, with the maintenance of the bourgeois state and in the framework of the world capitalist market, an integral modernization, a *cumulative* process of development, is no longer possible anywhere. In other words: the Russian, Brazilian, Mexican, Argentine, Korean, and Chinese bourgeoisie no longer could and no longer can create a new Italy, a new France, a new Germany, or a new Japan, not to speak about a new United States. Because of this those countries have suffered, are suffering, and continue to suffer a thousand pangs of underdevelopment or of lopsided and deformed development — combining the evils of the precapitalist past with those of capitalism. For the same reason, socialist revolution, the seizure of power by the proletariat supported by the poor peasantry, was, is, and remains indispensable in these countries. But that does not imply that an initial genuine industrial takeoff would be impossible there within the framework of capitalism, quite the contrary.

Let us add that the historic justification of the socialist revolution in the semi-industrialized dependent countries does not lean exclusively on the nonrealization of the *sum total* of the classical tasks of the national-democratic revolution. It is also supported — we would even say that it is supported *more and more* — by the growing acuteness of the tasks of the proletarian revolution in these countries. As is known, neither the Dutch bourgeois revolution nor the English revolution, nor the American revolution, nor the Great French Revolution were confronted with the problem of structural and conjunctural unemployment provoked by fluctuation in the *capitalist* rate of profit (the unemployment which they experienced resulted from the decomposition of *precapitalist* relations of production). At the center of these revolutions one does not find the problem of underdeveloped social services in the urban environment (housing, health, education, water, gas and electricity, road networks, public transport, etc.), i.e., the acuteness of the *new needs of the masses created by capitalist development itself* but which the bourgeoisie of those countries is incapable of satisfying.

Now, these problems are found at the heart of the aspirations and the struggles of the masses today in the countries mentioned above. If one adds to this the problems of superexploitation suffered by the proletariat in these countries precisely within the framework of a successful "industrial takeoff" (inflation, periodic decline in real wages, speedups, despotism on the shop floor, etc.), it is plain that the tasks with which the revolution is confronted in those countries represent a *combination* of the historic tasks of the national-democratic revolution and the historic tasks of the proletarian revolution, a combination within which the weight of the "specifically" proletarian tasks is increased precisely in function of the successful industrial "takeoff." The definition of "semicolonial countries" does not allow us to take account adequately of this combination. The concept of "semi-industrialized dependent countries" permits it much better.

Some comrades have expressed the objection that the abandonment of the definition of a dozen countries as "semicolonial countries" could encourage grave political errors (essentially of a sectarian type). For this reason, they think it is necessary to stick to traditional language. This line of reasoning contains a double error.

In the first place there is an error of method. There are no "dangerous" or "untimely" ideas within the framework of *scientific* socialism. There are true or false ideas, more exactly theses confirmed or falsified by empirical data, working hypotheses confirmed or rendered invalid by historical experience. One can be opposed to the subdivision of underdeveloped countries into semicolonial countries and semi-industrialized dependent countries if one demonstrates that it does not take account of social, economic, and political reality considered as a whole, that it does not correspond to the facts, that it constitutes an improper generalization of purely conjunctural phenomena, etc. If one succeeds in *demonstrating* this (which no one has done up till now), one would only have proved that the idea is false, and by no means that it is "dangerous." If, on the contrary, the facts confirm that we are dealing with a lasting structural distinction that is indispensable for understanding the way in which these societies are evolving, then the new concept, far from being "untimely," is an indispensable tool of analysis and for formulating political tasks.

Next, there is an error of deduction. From the definition of some (a small number) of underdeveloped countries as semi-industrialized dependent countries one can in no way whatsoever deduce the "fatalist" conclusion that we are modifying the conception of the *totality* of international capitalist economy and society as based on imperialist domination. The relations between imperialism and semi-industrialized countries remain relations of rulers and ruled, of exploiters and exploited, of oppressors and oppressed. *The anti-imperialist tasks hence remain in force in the semi-industrialized dependent countries.*

We reject all hypotheses that some of these countries are being transformed into "subimperialist" countries or into "minor imperialist powers," or that there is no structural difference anymore between them and the "weakest" imperialist countries. It follows that for us, a war between a semi-industrialized dependent country and an imperialist country remains a just war on the part of the former, whatever be its political regime. The strengthening of imperialism that results from the victory of the second would have adverse consequences for the world socialist revolution throughout the world as a whole.[5]

That is the criterion that we used in opposing the aggression of British imperialism against Argentina at the time of the Malvinas War, without pretending that this irreducible opposition in itself resolved all the tactical questions with which the Argentinian proletariat was confronted, in particular the task of continuing its relentless struggle without interruption, not even for a single day, against the dictatorial military *junta*.

T HE FACT is that the new definition of a certain number of backward countries does not imply a modification of revolutionary strategy, has nothing to do with an excessive "tacticism" with pedagogic needs in relation to the masses "led astray by nationalist verbiage," nor any other subjective criteria of the same nature. It follows from a overall view (and not at all from a narrow and one-sided one) of *the total social reality of these countries. Some of their structural traits have changed but others have not.* Herein lies all the complexity of the problem that lays the foundation for maintaining the strategy of *permanent* revolution, i.e., the upholding of the tasks, mobilizations, and tactics arising from the unresolved historical problems of the national-democratic revolution:

1. Foreign capital, even if it is no longer predominant from a property point of view, remains present and powerful in numerous branches in the

country. The *specific* demand for its expropriation therefore retains all of its value (and can even become the key demand at certain moments in the political conjuncture).

2. Financial domination by imperialism remains real, even if it no longer primarily takes the form of foreign *ownership* but of indebtedness. The demand for the cancellation of this foreign debt and for halting debt-service payments therefore retains all of its value.

3. Technological dependence in relation to the imperialist centers is almost total. It is, moreover, accompanied by a current transfer of outdated technologies and indeed used equipment (read on this subject the article by Pierre Salama, "Spécificités de l'internationalisation du capital en Amérique latine" [Specific aspects of the internationalization of capital in Latin America], in *Revue Tiers Monde*, vol. XIX, no. 74, April-June, 1978). Services now play a very important role in the dependence of these countries.

4. Dependence on the world capitalist market remains fundamental and implies the *transfer of value* created within the country in favor of imperialist capital (in particular by means of unequal exchange), i.e., the *survival of colonial superprofits*. The demands for a break with the international capitalist economy, for autonomous development particularly of technology, for a closer economic collaboration with the workers' states, for an attempt to break the stranglehold of the law of value in particular through the massive use of barter-trade and by the creation of a world pool of raw materials, retain all of their value.

5. Military and diplomatic dependence in relation to imperialism, even if it no longer has the near total aspect that it has for the semicolonial countries properly so-called, continue to be enormous. It entails as a consequence that demands such as those for the removal of imperialist military bases, the break with the military alliances imposed by imperialism, the refusal to send army officers to imperialist training centers, and the active support to all national liberation movements elsewhere in the world, ought to be part of the action program of the revolutionaries in those countries. These demands periodically gain a good response beyond the proletarian masses themselves. They can and should serve as a platform for anti-imperialist fronts with diverse social and political forces, conceived as united fronts *in action and for action* to achieve clearly defined objectives.

6. The agrarian question remains a burning one. Its weight in the revolutionary program is qualitatively superior to that which it takes up in the imperialist countries, even the weaker ones. If the weight of the peasantry has declined everywhere in the semi-industrialized countries in relative terms — and dramatically so — it remains high in absolute terms. Peasant masses, peasants' demands, peasants' organizations, and peasant struggles continue therefore to occupy a key place in the class

struggle dynamics and should occupy a key place in revolutionary strategy — as they did in tsarist Russia, which was however not considered by Lenin as a semicolonial country.

One will know even better what has changed and what has not in the countries at issue after having closely examined the question of financial dependence of these countries in relation to imperialist countries. In the classical semicolonial countries, financial domination was exercised in the first half of the twentieth century *by the appropriation* of natural resources (mines, plantations) and the creation of enterprises *owned by foreign imperialists* (banks, factories, public service enterprises, etc.).

This appropriation of the means of production and exchange, to be sure, has often been prepared by indebtedness (witness the classic case of Egypt in the period of building the Suez Canal). But it has likewise been a characteristic of the imperialist epoch that the indebtedness of colonial and semicolonial countries to foreign countries *has been transformed* into the appropriation of the big means of production by foreign capital. The parallel with what happened inside the advanced (imperialist) countries themselves is, moreover, striking. There, too, bank credit to industrial and commercial capital, and hence growing indebtedness to the banks, is as old as capitalism itself. The imperialist epoch signifies the tendency of these credits to be transformed into shares, i.e., the subordination of industrial capital to banking capital by *the acquisition of ownership*. It is this direct control, through appropriation and not by means of credit that, moreover, remains the standard definition of finance capital since Hilferding, a definition wholly accepted by Lenin.

In the semi-industrialized dependent countries the evolution has been in the other direction. Formerly dominated *directly* by the fact that the ownership of their key enterprises was in the hands of imperialist capital, these countries are no longer so other than *indirectly* by means of credit. This domination remains oppressive, harsh, burdensome, explosive. From the underdeveloped countries more than $70 billion return every year to the imperialist centers in the form of interest (above all) and of dividends (less than in the past). But it has visibly changed in form. And this change in form implies also a change in content.

**W**HEN IMPERIALIST capital is the owner of the principal enterprises, and in particular of the principal banks and financial groups of an underdeveloped country, *it dominates the capital market, lays down the principal avenues of capital accumulation, and determines the principal fields for productive investment*. It is moreover for this fundamental reason (and not in function of some kind of "conspiracy" or essentially political or ideological factors) that the colonial and semicolonial economy has known a form of development complementary to that of the imperialist countries, that it has been obliged to limit itself to the production of raw materials or a single major product.

When the ownership of the principal enterprises escapes from imperialist capital, it is the big monopolies and financial groups of the underdeveloped countries themselves,[6] often represented, reinforced, or supported by the bourgeois state, that determine the principal fields for investment. They are able to do this because they are the ones who dominate the capital market (whether "fed" by inflation or not; that is another story). Whether they do it in close association with *certain* imperialist multinationals or in order to start a conflict with others, is a conjunctural question that must be examined concretely, case by case and step by step. But that they have acquired financial autonomy to be able to do it *thanks to the fact that the ownership of banks and industry has escaped up to a certain point from imperialist capital,* that is what is decisive from the point of view of Marxism for the changes that have occurred over the last twenty, twenty-five years.

*This autonomy nevertheless remains quite relative and hence limited.* The underdeveloped countries remain the poor relations of the capitalist world. All proportions guarded, their ruling classes (with the exception of some of the OPEC countries), remain by the same token the poor relations of the international bourgeoisie. The needs for capital to sustain the industrialization process in the long term go far beyond the available assets of the local bourgeoisies. The contribution of foreign capital remains enormous and can even increase. In some cases one can even see a return in force of imperialist ownership in one or another branch. Technological dependence remains nearly total. Backwardness persists, be it under a new and specific form. Hence, the flow of international loans toward these countries, and the parallel outflow of interest payments abroad. Dependence and financial domination continue. That is what has not changed.

This analysis can only be contested if it is shown that the bigger banks and financial groups of the countries mentioned are, in reality, controlled by "secret" imperialist shareholders, that behind the credits there is a "hidden" ownership concealed by straw men. Such a demonstration, which has been attempted in the case of South Korea in relation to Japan (and to a lesser extent in the case of Mexico in relation the United States) has failed. It implies moreover a misapprehension of one important aspect of the industrial "takeoff." This process *occurs not at all in a complementary manner but rather in direct competition with the imperialist power formerly dominant in the country:* on this score see the development of the steel industry, shipbuilding, and electronics assembly in South Korea. To suggest that these developments are "controlled behind the scenes" by Japanese capital is absurd. The South Korean groups Hyundai, Daewoo, Samsung, etc., are financial groups *competing* with

Mitsubishi, Mitsui, Dai Ichi, etc., and not controlled by the latter.

In addition, opponents of the thesis of the autonomy of finance capital in the semi-industrialized dependent countries are led to affirm in one place what they deny in another. They insist strongly on the fact that in the course of the last two years — i.e., at a time when the economic crisis hit the semi-industrialized countries head-on — foreign capital has tried to reappropriate *direct ownership* of an entire series of large enterprises inside these countries. That is correct, although one should not exaggerate the magnitude of the phenomenon. But if this is so, doesn't it prove that direct ownership is something much more advantageous for the imperialist trusts and banks than mere indirect control through credit?

### The international economic crisis, revealer of the change and of its limits

THE LONG economic depression that for over ten years has plagued the international capitalist economy allows us to gauge precisely both the reality and the limits of the structural changes that the semi-industrialized dependent countries have experienced. It allows us to refute, even more clearly than the period of growth that preceded it, a whole series of myths and mystifications about the economic expansion in these countries.

The crisis has ended up by hitting — even if not all at once — each of the semi-industrialized countries. Their development continues to be determined fundamentally by the capitalist world market. They continue to be ruled by the law of value. Their *capitalist* nature is hence totally confirmed, without any reservation.

One might think — today! — that we are stating a commonplace. However, those of us who did not cease for a moment to defend this "commonplace" in the past are able to recall that the official program of the Communist Party of the Soviet Union, adopted at its Twenty-Second Congress, expressed a high opinion of the "noncapitalist road of development" in which countries like India, Egypt, and Algeria were presumably engaged. We can see today what fate history reserved for that false thesis.

The same goes for the thesis defended by the Brazilian theoretician Bresser Pereira who, inspired by the views of Castoriadis on the "bureaucratic class" and of Bettelheim on the "state bourgeoisie," saw in the importance of the state sector in the semi-industrialized countries and in the preponderant role of the state as stimulator of industrialization, the proof that the "private" bourgeoisie was no longer the ruling class in countries like Brazil and Egypt. The mistake is a big one. Its nature is revealed by the current crisis. Capitalist is any economy *dominated* by the capitalist world market — that is, by the law of value — whatever might be the sociopolitical mediations by which it is imposed. Noncapitalist is any economy that escapes the *domination* of the world market — that is, of the law of value — even if it does not escape from its influence.

In the latter case, the "state bureaucracy" of the USSR, etc., limits its privileges, by and large, to the sphere of consumption. If it accumulates money and draws interest on it, this remains fundamentally for the purpose of immediate or deferred consumption. Private accumulation of entrepreneurial capital occurs only in the interstices of such an economy, and occupies the space left free by the planned economy. It is carried on by social actors different from those of the *nomenklatura* [high state and party functionaries], even if it can be realized only with the complicity, i.e., through the corruption, of the latter.

By contrast, in the underdeveloped capitalist countries, including the semi-industrialized countries, the state sector, even if it is preponderant, in the long term plays the role of stimulating the private sector. The top functionaries of the state bureaucracy, including the military hierarchy, plunder the state budget and the budget of the nationalized enterprises, by no means essentially for the purpose of consumption, but for the purpose of accumulating private capital, with a view to becoming private entrepreneurs. Given the size of their plunder, they are getting there one after the other. Let us remember that at the dawn of industrial capitalism in Europe and North America, the pillage of public finance also played a very important role in the private accumulation of capital, i.e., of the first great bourgeois fortunes. See in this regard section six of chapter twenty-four of the first volume of *Capital*. See likewise the role of the robber barons in the constitution of the big capitalist monopolies in the USA. In Japan, it was precisely the state that created the first heavy industries, which were subsequently privatized.

The capitalist crisis, which always affects the weak in a sharper way than the strong, has ended up by dislocating the economies of the semi-industrialized countries much more sharply than those of the imperialist countries. In the former countries, it has provoked above all a much more profound social crisis. Declines in the purchasing power of money wages to the order of 20-25 percent have been registered. In the case of Bolivia we are talking about a reduction of more that 50 percent.

In the poorest semicolonial countries, this drop in the standard of living takes the stunning form of crises of undernourishment and immediate famine for significant layers of the population. This is explained by the fact of the low starting level of these countries. Jacques Chonchol has published the following figures concerning the average daily intake of calories and proteins in a series of Latin American countries in 1970:

Table 4

| | Calories | Total Protein (Grams) | Animal Proteins (Grams) |
|---|---|---|---|
| Argentina | 3,036 | 98 | 60 |
| Mexico | 2,660 | 67 | 16 |
| Brazil | 2,613 | 65 | 22 |
| Bolivia | 1,902 | 49 | 14 |
| El Salvador | 1,873 | 46 | 14 |
| Haiti | 1,896 | 47 | 5 |

Averages:
For Latin America: 2,600 calories
For low-income earners: 1,700 - 2,300 calories
For low-income wage earners in El Salvador: 1,200 - 1,300 calories

(Source: Jacques Chonchol, "Problèmes alimentaires en Amérique latine: malnuitrition et dependance" [Food problems in Latin America: malnutrition and dependency], in *Amérique Latine*, no. 4).

When one considers that the 50 percent of the population with the lowest incomes in Bolivia are hardly more "prosperous" than those of El Salvador, and that their daily food ration has fallen again by 20 to 25 percent after 1970 as a result of the crisis, one obtains a level of nutrition on the order of 1,100 to 1,200 calories per day per person, i.e., the equivalent of that in a Nazi concentration camp in 1940 (we are talking about a "normal" concentration camp in 1940, and not the extermination camps like Auschwitz in 1942-44).

Undernourishment and famine are reinforced by a systematic policy of replacing the production of foodstuffs with commercial farming for the export market. Thus, in Brazil, despite famine in the northeast of the country, the harvest of beans dropped by 45 percent and that of rice by 20 percent in 1983, while the coffee harvest went up by 79 percent and that of soybeans by 13 percent.

But even if Argentina, Mexico, Brazil, or the semi-industrialized countries of Asia have by no means experienced as catastrophic a deterioration in workers' conditions, the decline there is no less spectacular. It is estimated that in Mexico the crisis and austerity have had the effect of cancelling out most of workers' gains in purchasing power over the last twenty, if not thirty years. In South Korea, real wages in 1982 dropped below their 1978 level. Social explosions are inevitable under these conditions.

The crisis has nevertheless also confirmed that the semi-industrialization of these countries is irreversible. All of these countries have retained, throughout and despite the crisis, their modern industry. In none of these countries has the industrial sector collapsed. In fact, the declines in industrial production have not been as steep as those in Great Britain, or indeed Spain or Portugal. None of these countries has been subjected to a process of de-industrialization, so typical for the colonial and semicolonial countries during the 1930s.[7] This goes to show that semi-industrialization does represent a lasting structural change, not an unwarranted extrapolation of purely conjunctural trends.

At the same time, the crisis has clearly shown that semi-industrialization remains what it is, i.e., a *partial* industrialization, and that it cannot carry on without limits in time, any more than it can extend to an ever-increasing number of countries.[8] It is not cumulative precisely because it is dependent, i.e., *overdetermined by what happens on the capitalist world market, above all in the imperialist countries, which continue to represent the major part of that market.*

The idea of a continuous takeoff of growth and prosperity in the Pacific region (which is supposed to gradually replace the Atlantic as the center of the international capitalist economy) is contradicted by the facts. The same goes for the idea of an alleged "new model of accumulation" originating in Japan and spreading to the international capitalist economy by concentric circles.[9] This "restructuring" will not make it possible to overcome the crisis. It is, to the contrary, the crisis that is undermining the process of restructuring.

I N AN interesting article entitled "Le fordisme periphérique étranglé par le monétarisme central" [Peripheral fordism strangled by central monetarism] in *Amérique latine,* no. 16, October-December, 1983, Alain Lipietz arrives at a similar conclusion. It is a step forward for this author, who doesn't seem to support any more the theories of "regulation," i.e., of an effective restructuring of international capitalism through the current crisis. But the very title of his article implies a new error.

It is not "central monetarism," i.e., the scarcity of credits and the rising level of interest rates in the metropolitan countries, that renders a continuous takeoff of industrialization impossible in the semi-industrialized countries. The fundamental obstacle lies in the stagnation of the world market resulting from the crisis. Monetarism is not the cause but simply an aggravating factor, in the same way that monetarism is not the cause of the crisis in the imperialist countries but a factor that has accentuated it.

The crisis arose from the internal contradictions of the capitalist system, notably the long-term fall in the rate of profit caused by the rising organic composition of capital, which could no longer be neutralized by increases in the rate of surplus value under conditions of full employment. It arose from the slackening expansion of the demand of "final consumers," i.e., the growth of excess capacity in one sector after another among those that "carried" the expansion.[10] This meant that more and more inflation (of paper money and of credit, i.e., bank money) was necessary to avoid the crisis. Once it had passed a certain limit, the rate of inflation began to strangle the expansion instead of sustain it; it would have done so quite irrespective of subjective options or specific economic policies. Monetarism has been one response to this material evolution, not its cause.

What slows down the industrialization drive of the countries mentioned earlier is not mainly their indebtedness. It is the fact that their principal exports today (or planned for tomorrow) — oil, petrochemical products, steel, shipping vessels; tomorrow automobiles and electronics — run up against a stagnant or declining demand on the world market. All massive transfers of production from the imperialist countries to the semi-industrialized countries in these sectors *reduce* world demand even more, instead of raise it, notably because the wages of workers in these industries are much lower in Brazil and South Korea (even if they will go up there in the long term) than in France, West Germany, Japan, or in the USA. Such transfers hence amplify overproduction, the slump in sales and the global crisis in the long run. It is because of this that the bank credits accorded to these countries are reduced and not in the first instance because of fears of insolvency, even though such fears are obviously real and do play a role in the motivation of the international bankers.

## Table 5

### Hourly Wage Costs in 1979 (in current U.S. dollars)

| | | | |
|---|---|---|---|
| United States | 9.09 | Mexico | 2.31 |
| West Germany | 11.33 | Brazil | 1.80 |
| France | 8.17 | Hong Kong | 1.25 |
| Italy | 7.38 | South Korea | 1.14 (0.37 in 1975) |
| Spain | 5.82 | Taiwan | 1.01 |
| Japan | 5.58 | | |

Source: J.R. Chaponnière, "La République de Corée, un nouveau pays industriel" [The Republic of Korea: a new industrial country], Notes et Études Documentaires, *La Documentation française*, pp. 4667-68, May 19, 1982.)[11]

One should never forget that the international capitalist economy forms a whole. There are not two sectors separated and insulated from each other: the imperialist countries on the one hand and the underdeveloped countries on the other. The stimulus for the takeoff of credits to the semi-industrialized countries came from the imperialist banks and not from the governments of these countries. Those credits have not been offered for altruistic reasons nor basically because the Western banks had at their disposal an overabundance of money capital (the latter factor, fed by the petrodollars after 1973, however, has played a significant role in the motivation of the banks). The principal reason for this strenuous expansion of international credit was precisely the crisis itself, which was marked by a freeze of productive investment and of the internal expansion of credit in the imperialist countries themselves, i.e., the profit needs (and competition) of the banks.

THE INTERNATIONAL capitalist system has in addition been confronted with the fact that, for various reasons that we cannot enter into here, the flow of *direct* imperialist investments to the underdeveloped countries has not ceased to fall relatively in the course of the last twenty years:

---

Table 6

**Investment in developing countries as a percentage of the
total direct investment of major imperialist countries**

|  | **1960** | **1980** |
|---|---|---|
| USA | 40% | 25% |
| West Germany | 36% | 20% |
| Great Britain | 36% | 20% |
| Japan | 60% | 47% |

(Source: Dominique de Laubier, "Les investissements internationaux: Quels changements pour les années quatre-vingt" [Foreign investments: what changes in the 1980s], in *Economie prospective internationale*, Fourth Quarter, 1982.)

---

Under these conditions, the increased resort to bank credit by the semi-industrialized countries constitutes an attempt to parry a blow from the system in the face of insufficient growth of direct investment. *The expansion of credit to semi-industrialized countries represents nothing but an attempt to open an additional market to exporting industries of the imperialist countries,* an attempt that is risky from a "technical" point of view, and sheer folly from the standpoint of the "conservative banker," but that makes a lot of sense from the point of view of certain big monopolies in the imperialist countries.

Moreover, if there is a stiff price to be paid, it will not be the cashiers who will foot the bill. The profits will have been pocketed by the big banks and monopolies, and the cost will undoubtedly be paid by the public treasury, i.e., by the taxpayers (and by consumers in the form of additional inflation). For the same reason, it is very unlikely that banking (finance) capital will really strangle the economy of the semi-industrialized and OPEC countries. It would thereby strangle 25 percent of its own clients (that is the share of the "Third World" in world imports). It will no doubt be content with "nationalizing" the losses in part at the expense of its "own" nation, and in part at the expense of the "underdeveloped nations."

If the United States today suffers from a huge trade deficit, this is not only due to the overvaluation of the dollar. It is also due to the drop in its exports to the "Third World" in function of international credit restrictions. In 1983, U.S. exports to Latin America alone dropped by $20 billion!

This global perspective on the international capitalist economy enables us to do away with another myth that has often polarized the debates between Marxist theoreticians of the "Third World." *It is false to suppose that the initial industrialization or the semi-industrialization of the underdeveloped countries* (at least of some among them) *can only be carried out in absolute, fierce, permanent opposition to "imperialism" as a whole, that is to the sum total of all the big monopolies, all the big banks of the imperialist centers and all the multinationals.* It is false to suppose that this semi-industrialization passes necessarily through an "anti-imperialist struggle" or constitutes in itself a "stage in the struggle against imperialism."

Wᴇ ʜᴀᴠᴇ argued along these lines for twenty years: from the time when the predominant monopolist sectors of the imperialist countries became exporters of capital goods and no longer exporters of consumer goods, including durable consumer goods, it was inevitable that at least some of the multinationals and imperialist banks would be interested in a partial industrialization of some underdeveloped countries. Assisted by inter-imperialist competition, this trend could only be amplified.

It follows from this that the "new oligarchy," which in the semi-industrialized countries links the "state bureaucracy" and the "national" monopolies to the multinationals, in no way implies a halt to industrialization. It could even stimulate it, but under particular forms and within given limits.

It follows likewise that the advances of industrialization in themselves do not at all guarantee the gradual elimination of these multinationals from the "power bloc." Such advances could even reinforce their weight.

The "limits" of "industrialization models" — first by "import substitution of consumer durables"; then by the boosting of exports; tomorrow without doubt by the relative and modest expansion of the "national" production of capital goods — have therefore never been an *absolute limit*. It has simply been limited in space and time by the fact of its articulation with the particular conjunctures — with new time-limits — on the capitalist world market. To fight against these successive models as such is to fight against windmills. It is the totality of the capitalist "project" *of cumulative and continuous industrialization* (of modernization) that ought to be attacked as utopian and bankrupt in the context of contemporary international capitalism, not its particular and conjunctural forms that are gradually substituted for one another.

THE BOURGEOISIE of the semi-industrialized countries is not the lackey of imperialism (as was the case and undoubtedly still is for the ruling classes of the semicolonial countries). If it acts as it does in association (sometimes close, at other times conflicting) with imperialism, this is neither due to inertia or lack of autonomous power. Much to the contrary, it already disposes of not inconsiderable economic power. It is conversely in function of its own, well-understood economic, social, and political *class interests* that it acts in the way that it does. It would be ridiculous for a Marxist to try to convince capitalists that he understands their interests much better than they do themselves!

In today's world, a world in which the capitalist system is a system historically in decline, quite irrespective of its periodic phases of economic growth, the fate of the bourgeoisie of the semi-industrialized dependent countries is inextricably bound up with that of the system as a whole, and in the first instance with its principal mainstays, which are the imperialist powers. To undermine these powers is, for the bourgeoisie of the semi-industrialized countries, to saw through the branch on which it is perched and to precipitate its own fall. It suffices to see the panicky response of the powerful Chinese bourgeoisie of Hong Kong to the idea that British imperialism could be forced to withdraw from that country; it suffices to understand the motive that inspires the countries of the so-called Contadora group,[12] to wit the fear that the revolution will knock on the door of Mexico if it triumphs in Guatemala, to understand in what sense the ruling classes of the semi-industrialized countries are inextricably tied to imperialism, not only by financial and technological dependence but above all by social, political, and therefore military reasons.

In today's world the fundamental contradiction is between capital and labor, between the counterrevolution and the *social* revolution, not between "imperialism" and "anti-imperialist forces," confounding all social classes.[13]

In the framework of global bourgeois forces, the bourgeoisie of the "Third World," above all in the semi-industrialized countries (and the OPEC countries), strives to redistribute in its own favor the surplus value extracted around the world from proletarians (and this at the expense of the imperialist bourgeoisie's share). It periodically seeks to cash in on anti-imperialist sentiments or indeed anti-imperialist actions of the masses. That is nothing new. It will continue tomorrow. It is the fundamental law of capitalist competition. That struggle for redistribution may be fierce at certain conjunctural moments. It may be accompanied by a rhetoric even more virulent than the material struggle. But it will not break out of the narrow parameters to which it remains confined in our historical epoch: the indispensable solidarity of all those who appropriate surplus value, in the face of recurrent efforts of wage labor to put a stop to the appropriation and the production of surplus value itself.

The sooner revolutionaries and workers in the so-called "Third World" countries understand this, the sooner their debates will regain the strategic clarity necessary for victories on a grand scale, and the sooner the era of false debates, false dilemmas, and strategic errors will be left behind.[14]

February 1, 1984

## Notes

1. Some time ago we drew attention to this phenomenon of capital accumulation that took place in certain OPEC countries in the aftermath of the "explosion" of oil prices in 1973. See Ernest Mandel, "An Arab and Iranian Finance Capital Emerges," in *Intercontinental Press,* vol. 12, no. 39, November 4, 1974, pp. 1437-41. And: "Encore une fois sur l'emergence d'un capital financier autonome dans plusieurs pays semi-coloniaux" [Once again on the emergence of autonomous finance capital in a number of semicolonial countries], in *Critiques d'économie politique,* no. 22, October-December, 1975. See also N. Jafar, "La nature de la période" [The nature of the period], published in four parts in *Inprecor* (Paris), February 15 (no. 45), March 1 (no. 46), March 15 (no. 47), and March 30, 1979 (no. 48/49).

2. One could quote numerous sources on the traditional Marxist characterization of semicolonial countries. We limit ourselves to mentioning the program of the Comintern, adopted at its sixth congress, which emphasizes industrial underdevelopment and the fact that the decisive industrial, commercial, and banking firms are, just as in the area of transport, in the hands of foreign imperialist groups. This definition is not criticized in Trotsky's critique of the Comintern program. (See Leon Trotsky, "The Draft Program of the Communist International — A Criticism of Fundamentals," in *The Third International After Lenin,* third edition [New York: Pathfinder Press, 1970]. See Jane Degras, ed., *The Communist International: 1919-1943 Documents* vol. II [London: Frank Cass, 1971] pp. 472ff.)

3. On the partial foothold gained by semi-industrialized countries in the field of advanced technology see, for India, *Croissance des jeunes nations* (May 1983); for South Korea, *Far Eastern Economic Review,* April 7, 1983; for Brazil, *Amérique latine,* no. 13, January-March, 1983.

4. Note furthermore that Lenin, at the time of editing his pamphlet on imperialism, expressed himself with great prudence as to the possibility of the appearance of intermediate categories. See in particular his classification of underdeveloped countries into colonies, semicolonies, and financially dependent countries (V.I. Lenin, *Notebooks on Imperialism* in *Collected Works* [Moscow: Progress Publishers, 1968], vol. 39, p. 235). See also likewise in that pamphlet itself the following passage: "We have already referred to one form of dependence — the semi-colony. An example of another is provided by Argentina" (V.I. Lenin, *Imperialism, the Highest Stage of Capitalism* in *Selected Works* [Moscow: Progress Publishers, 1963], vol. 1, p. 697).

5. Should one by the same token label South Africa an "imperialist" country to justify our support to Angola, to Namibia, to Mozambique, or no matter what other semicolonial country in Africa engaged in a military conflict with Pretoria? No, because it suffices to characterize the state of South Africa as a semi-industrialized *settlers' colony and as such a military arm of imperialism,* to define as reactionary all wars that it wages against a semicolonial country.

6. The Marxist economist Samuel Lichtenczteyn, a former lecturer at the University of Montevideo, has devoted an interesting study to autonomous finance capital in Latin America. He stresses in particular the preponderant role that banking capital is starting to play in Uruguay under the military dictatorship in that country.

7. The exception to this rule appears to be Argentina. But the de facto "de-industrialization" which this country has known preceded the international economic crisis for some time, being determined essentially by modification in the relationship of forces within the possessing classes. It will become a thing of the past after the downfall of the military dictatorship.

8. The semi-industrialization of *some* underdeveloped countries has undoubtedly created ten or twelve million new industrial jobs, perhaps as many as twenty million. But André Gunder Frank has estimated at 400 million the number of unemployed and semi-employed in the Third World as a whole. One can see why there will not be many new Taiwans and South Koreas, never mind new Brazils.

9. It is false to claim that the relocation of certain industrial branches, notably in Asia, took place at the expense of the industry of the imperialist countries. An OECD study shows that such "relocation" created more jobs in the imperialist centers (notably in the capital goods industry) than it eliminated in the "old" branches (see *L'incidence des nouveaux pays industriels sur la production et les échanges des produits manufactures.* [The impact of new industrial countries on the production and exchange of manufactured products], Paris, Organization for Economic Cooperation and Development [OECD], 1979). Herein lies the rational basis of the "Brandt report" and other appeals by important imperialist sectors (above all European, Canadian, and Japanese, but not only in these countries) in favor of increasing the extent of "North-South collaboration." Obviously, certain branches like the textile industry and shipbuilding have lost many

bs in Europe, but others have gained many.

10. The whole of this analysis has been developed by us for more than ten ears. See our books *The Second Slump,* second edition (London: Verso, 1980) nd *La crise 1974-1982* (Paris: Flammarion, 1982).

11. These averages do not mean a great deal. In the South Korean clothing in-ustry, the first to go one better than Japanese and European competitors, wages vere *one-third* of what they were in the construction industry, and half of what ney were in the steel industry. In the small South Korean firms, men earned $3 day in 1979 and women $2 a day for working days that easily span nine to ten ours (J.R. Chaponnière, op. cit., pp. 72, 75).

12. A group composed of Mexico, Venezuela, Colombia, and Panama that is rying to end the civil war in El Salvador and Nicaragua by means of negotiated ompromise, with the aim of safeguarding the capitalist mode of production in Central America with the possible exception of Nicaragua.

13. Trotsky wrote in the *Emergency Manifesto of the Fourth International* May 1940) that "The Fourth International does not draw watertight distinctions etween the backward and the advanced countries, the democratic and the ocialist revolutions. It combines them and subordinates them to the world strug-le of the oppressed against the oppressors. Just as the only genuinely revolu-onary force of our era is the international proletariat, so the only real program liquidate all oppression, social and national, is the program of the permanent volution" (*Writings of Leon Trotsky 1939-1940,* second edition [New York: athfinder Press, 1973], p. 203).

14. We shall try to analyze the main theoretical debates surrounding the prob-ms of "dependence" and "models of development" in a subsequent article.

# Once Again On the Workers' and Peasants' Government and the Workers' State: A Self-Criticism

## By Livio Maitan

THE ARTICLE by Comrade Salah Jaber on "Proletarian Revolution and Dictatorship of the Proletariat," published in the last issue of our magazine, [*Quatrième Internationale*, vol.3, no.15] raises a number of major problems. Over the last several months, other revolutionary Marxist publications have discussed similar subjects.[1] We would like to contribute to this debate in three areas: (1) verifying the points of agreement with Jaber and clarifying some of the questions he raises; (2) reviewing the errors of analysis and method that the Fourth International made and trying to grasp their origin; (3) outlining some thoughts on the general problem of the workers' and peasants' government of the workers' state.

## A FEW SUMMARY POINTS

One might claim that, after all, Jaber merely summarizes basic concepts and refers us to classical passages that everyone ought to know. Unfortunately, certain concepts were either forgotten or applied in a false or distorted manner. *It is to Jaber's credit that he restored them and applied them in a fundamentally correct way in his analysis of the revolutionary experiences of the last forty years.*

Let us underline the three points that follow:

a. It is especially important that the Marxist and Leninist theory of the state be repeated and reaffirmed, since it is rejected or entirely falsified by the overwhelming majority of parties or currents claiming to be part of the workers' movement. The state is a political-military apparatus whose aim is to maintain existing relationships of production and property relations and the rule of the social classes that profit from them.

176

The military apparatus is the ultimate guarantee that the state, in the broad sense, can fulfill its function and not be challenged by the exploited classes.

If that is the case, it is correct to conclude that the critical moment of a revolutionary breakthrough, the qualitative leap, occurs in the political realm, i.e., it takes place when the bourgeois state apparatus is smashed and the new, proletarian power is established (regardless of the specific institutional forms it may take).

Jaber feels, correctly, that a well-known passage in *The Revolution Betrayed* concerning the social character of the U.S.S.R. and its leadership is not relevant in this light. Indeed, in the passage in question,[2] Trotsky does not aim to determine by what criterion we may state that a workers' state has been created; he describes the elements making up an already consolidated workers' state. From the standpoint of characterizing a ruling layer, moreover, the decisive criterion is precisely its attitude toward the relations of production: does it act in such a way as to preserve them, or not?

This does not imply — as Trotsky himself explained — that the qualitative leap in reverse will take place only when the socioeconomic gains of the revolution are lost. It will take place when the class nature of the political power has changed.

b. The notion of dual power — as it was set forth by Lenin and Trotsky — is a precise, eminently political notion. It must not be diluted by being applied to situations where the proletariat holds political power and bourgeois layers still hold economic power. Such situations should be analyzed and characterized from the standpoint of the general problem of transitional societies, and not from the standpoint of the revolutionary process before the qualitative leap. One of the errors of the resolution on Nicaragua adopted by the Eleventh World Congress of the Fourth International was precisely in this area: political power was counterposed to economic power, and the conclusion was drawn that a dual-power situation still existed and that the qualitative change in the nature of the state had not yet occurred.[3]

c. It is necessary to reject any interpretation of the workers' and peasants' government that might imply the existence of a separate, autonomous phase of the revolutionary process, in which the governmental power could have changed hands without the dictatorship of the proletariat being established. We will come back to this question later. But if we accept the above mentioned hypothesis, the result is either that it is possible to imagine a workers' and peasants' government operating during an entire period through revolutionary anticapitalist measures in the context of a state that remains bourgeois (this is the paradoxical thesis defended by the leadership of the U.S. Socialist Workers Party and other currents of the Fourth International), or — as Jaber correctly indicates

— that we end up with the idea, an old idea strongly rejected by our movement, of a workers' and peasants' state, or, in other terms, a "dictatorship of the proletariat and peasantry."

When Jaber wrote his article, he did not know that a few months later Socialist Workers Party leader Jack Barnes would come to the conclusion that the workers' and peasants' government is a necessary phase of the revolutionary process in all countries, separate from the dictatorship of the proletariat, and that we ought to speak not of one, but of two "qualitative leaps" — namely, from dual power to the workers' and peasants' government, and from the workers' and peasants' government to the workers' state. The least one can say is that those who adopt such a perspective do not take the theory of permanent revolution too seriously!

## A NECESSARY BALANCE SHEET

IN THE historical part of his document Comrade Jaber summarizes the series of positions taken by the Fourth International on the revolutions after World War II. *The errors he condemns were in fact made*. That is why we cannot spare ourselves an explicit self-criticism, but at the same time we must ask ourselves why we went wrong — sometimes so badly! — while starting from the correct theoretical premises of Marxism and Leninism that we defended, usually against the stream, for decades.

We are going to take up the points raised by Jaber with our own clarifications and comments. At the outset, we will draw attention to the following: *our errors usually take the form of a wrong application of the concept of the workers' and peasants' government. In reality, what is involved are delays, hesitations, errors in understanding revolutionary processes in their totality*.

### The Yugoslav revolution

The question of whether bourgeois power had been destroyed and a workers' state established in Yugoslavia was raised in our ranks only after the Yugoslav leadership's break with the Soviet bureaucracy and the Cominform in June 1948.[4] This fact is significant in itself.

In the resolution on the Yugoslav revolution adopted by the Third World Congress (1951), we applied — for the first time in our history — the concept of a workers' and peasants' government, referring to the period from November 1943 to October 1945. We said, in particular: "the CPY [Yugoslav Communist Party] having in fact conquered power in the liberated territories, this part of Yugoslavia ceased to be a bourgeois state; under a workers' and peasants' government it advanced toward the final accomplishment of the proletarian revolution."[5]

In retrospect, the document expresses no uncertainty as to the dynamic of the process, or the proletarian – although bureaucratic – character of the leadership. In fact, in the words of the Transitional Program, it views the workers' and peasants' government as merely a "short episode" on the road to the dictatorship of the proletariat.

We should add that the criterion invoked to indicate the "first decisive stage" of the revolution is the replacement of the old bourgeois state apparatus — of which only fragments remained — by a "new centralized state apparatus, based on the people's committees." The bourgeoisie as a class — the document explains — had lost power, and the departure of the two bourgeois ministers after the coalition government interlude was merely the "final expression" of that fact. It explains, moreover, that in 1945-46 "the conquests of the Yugoslav proletarian revolution were generalized and legally consolidated."

But if that is true, why date the birth of the workers' state from the departure of the two bourgeois ministers — who were incapable of preventing the fact that "all the remnants of bourgeois political power *were* eliminated" precisely during their term in government — and not date it from the end of 1943?

In fact, our understanding of the Yugoslav revolution was hampered by two premises, which weighed heavily, even if they were not explicitly formulated: the Yugoslav Communist Party was a Stalinist party like the others; and such a party was incapable of leading a victorious revolution. We began to correct our approach from the moment when the specifics of the Yugoslav Communist Party appeared in broad daylight, forcing us to reexamine our previous analyses and estimates in a critical spirit. But we retained a somewhat simplistic idea of coalition governments and their role, which prevented us from admitting that there may be a coalition government and a workers' state at the same time.

## Workers' and peasants' government in China?

We cannot try here to take up the problem of our movement's overall record on China, including Trotsky's positions at the end of the 1920s. It is unquestionable that very serious errors were made on several occasions, and that this had negative long-term consequences on building the Fourth International in China and in a whole number of Asian countries. For our part, we indicated on other occasions that Trotsky, the Chinese revolutionary Marxists, and our entire movement had made a false analysis of the Chinese situation, which had led them to state at the founding congress in 1938 that "the Chinese Stalinists have formally liquidated 'Soviet China,' handed over to Chiang Kai-shek the remnants of the peasant Red Armies, openly renounced the agrarian struggle, explicitly abandoned the class interests of the workers. . . . They have proclaimed themselves the gendarmes of private property . . . the enemies of the revolution." [*Documents of the Fourth International* (New York: Pathfinder Press, 1973), p. 232]

But we do not necessarily share in the remarks made by Jaber, to the effect that Trotsky's error lies in not having understood that no urban insurrection could triumph in China, not even in 1926-27, without the prior existence of a fundamentally peasant Red Army. That is undoubtedly true for the 1930s *after* the historic defeat of 1927, the destruction of the working-class organizations, and, later, the dismantling of the industrial apparatus after the Japanese occupation, and the drastic reduction in the social weight of the proletariat.

On the contrary, in 1927 real potentialities existed, and the defeat was not inevitable: it was fundamentally the product of the policy carried out by the Chinese Communist Party leadership under pressure from the Kremlin. No one can claim that a revolutionary orientation, such as Trotsky advocated, would have guaranteed the victory of the revolution; yet the fact remains that the situation might have developed differently.

**B**UT LET us return to the subject of our article.

The one-sided or incorrect premises that led to our delay in understanding the Yugoslav revolution had a similar effect with respect to the Chinese revolution, including its final phase. The resolutions of the Third World Congress — which we should recall, was held nearly two years after the overthrow of the Kuomintang regime — state that the new China is no longer part of the capitalist world market. The resolutions included China, like the USSR and "people's democracies," among the countries imperialism is getting ready to launch a war against and took an unambiguous position in favor of its defense. Despite this, the resolutions remain rather vague on the definition of the new regime, speaking of the "Mao Tse-tung regime" and of consolidation of the gains of the revolution. The congress manifesto calls on the Chinese workers to "pursue their struggle up to the complete destruction of bourgeois power, and the establishment of a genuine dictatorship of the proletariat, based on committees democratically elected by the workers and poor peasants."[6]

It was not until the May 1952 International Executive Committee (IEC) Plenum that the problem of characterizing the new China was explicitly dealt with. As with Yugoslavia, the plenum resolution used the concept of the workers' and peasants' government as expressed in the Transitional Program ("the 'workers' and peasants' government' . . . would represent merely a short episode on the road to the actual dictatorship of the proletariat" — [*Documents of the Fourth International*,

). 203]). At the same time, it introduces the notion of a "special" dual power, a "symbiosis between the central political power, controlled on he national scale by the CP and its armies, and the economic power vhich is still predominantly in the hands of the bourgeoisie."

But the equivalence that is made between "duality" and "symbiosis" — two concepts that are far from interchangeable! — is in itself revealing of the ambiguity that exists. The report approved by a wide majority vas still more explicit. It projected the future outbreak of class contradictions within Chinese society, as well as major "turns" in Chinese Communist Party policy. That is precisely why — the reporter explained — "we refrain for the moment from characterizing the Chinese state as a proletarian dictatorship."

As for use of the "workers' and peasants' government" formula, it vas justified mainly by two arguments:

1. The state apparatus has not yet undergone substantial transformations; "*only* (my emphasis) the armed power has been completely recast and represents an armed power with a different social character." It is because of the "special conditions of this *state apparatus* that the bourgeois property which survives takes on exceptional significance."

2. If we characterize China as already being a dictatorship of the proletariat, "how would we characterize this decisive phase which lies ahead of us . . . in which not only will the bourgeois representatives be truly eliminated from the central government and the old bourgeois apparatus in the south destroyed, but in which undoubtedly and for the first time the proletariat will in action assert *as a class* its leading role in the revolution." [Excerpts from the IEC report by Ernest Germain in Joseph Hansen, *The Workers and Farmers Government* (New York: Pathfinder Press, 1974), p. 56]

As we see, there was an underestimation of what the revolution had already accomplished. In fact, the class character of the political power had already changed through the vehicle of a leadership that was proletarian despite its bureaucratic deformations. The bourgeoisie as a class had already been given a death blow, and the basic economic levers were already in the hands of the new power. This underestimation went hand in hand with an overestimation of the turn that the Chinese Communist Party was still supposed to make in order to insure the transition from the workers' and peasants' government to the workers' state. The plenum resolution explicitly linked this turn to the prospect of war.[7]

Conclusion: in the case of China, the mistakes and ambiguities in the analysis and the errors of methodology were even more serious than in the case of Yugoslavia. The fact that we did not make an explicit self-criticism in time had the result of making later errors easier. Adoption of the concept of a special dual power with regard to the Nicaraguan revolution is the clearest example of this.[8]

## The Cuban revolution and Joe Hansen's characterizations

FIRST, IT should be recalled that in contrast to the Socialist Workers Party the leadership of the Fourth International never used the concept of a workers' and peasants' government with regard to Cuba. This is not necessarily to its credit, since up to October 1960 the International Secretariat took no position on characterizing the new regime. We had, of course, understood that a dynamic of permanent revolution was developing.[9] But the social and political origins of the July 26th Movement and its leadership, the ideology that leadership had expressed before and after January 1959, and the composition of the first revolutionary government impelled us to caution, in fact, to avoiding any precise characterization.

It was only after the radical measures of October 1960 that the International Secretariat wrote the document later adopted at the Sixth World Congress, defining Cuba as a workers' state. This document described three phases of the revolution, on the socioeconomic as well as on the political level, with the growing over into a socialist revolution occurring in the third phase (after the break with the representatives of the bourgeoisie). It pointed out that the revolution "essentially destroyed" the bourgeois state apparatus, but that Cuba became a workers' state only by carrying out the expropriations of October 1960.

It was unquestionably Joe Hansen who made the most efforts to analyze and characterize the different phases of the Cuban revolution. On the formation of the workers' state, he had the same position as the International Secretariat: Cuba became a workers' state after the measures of August-October 1960.

But to define the preceding period, after the departure of Urrutia and the replacement of Felipe Pazos at the head of the National Bank, Hansen used the characterization of a workers' and peasants' government. It is worth the trouble to go over this point, even taking up some of Jaber's quotations, since we are dealing with the most systematic attempt to explain the concept of a workers' and peasants' government and the criteria for applying it.

In a July 1960 article, Hansen, after having summarized the gains of the revolution and pointing out the dynamic of the Castroist leadership, concluded that "the new Cuban government is a workers' and farmers' government of the kind defined in our Transitional Program as a 'government independent of the bourgeoisie.'" But why not simply call it a workers' state?

Two arguments are put forward to explain this:

1. The regime that was established remained "highly contradictory and highly unstable, subject to pressures and impulses that can move it

forward or backward. . . . As a petty-bourgeois formation, it can retrogress." All of the measures necessary to overturn bourgeois economic and social relations had not yet been taken.

2. "The regime lacks the socialist consciousness (program) to accomplish this. Even if it carries out extensive expropriations, these, precisely because of the lack of socialist consciousness, are not so assured as to be considered a permanent foundation of the state."[10]

Later, Hansen explained that the decisive element is not the scope of the expropriation measures at a given stage, but the overall dynamic. This, in the final analysis, is guaranteed only by the socialist consciousness of the leadership, which is, therefore, the decisive criterion.[11]

This approach is confirmed by the arguments Hansen raises to refute a comrade's theory that the workers' state arose in Cuba in October 1959 after the formation of militias. If we take the criterion of the nature of the armed forces as decisive — he writes — why not date the formation of the workers' state from January 1, 1959, especially since at that date, the bourgeoisie's instrument of repression had been effectively destroyed? The answer is clear: what prevented the comrade in question from drawing that conclusion is that "the revolution at that time lacked socialist consciousness."[12]

Second question: is the workers' and peasants' government "a necessary link in the revolutionary process"?

Hansen correctly points out, in a July 1970 letter, that in our theoretical tradition the answer would be no.[13] In an August 1969 report to the SWP convention, he had already explained in regard to China that the workers' and peasants' government had indeed been the "link" that had made possible "the qualitative leap in the revolutionary process," that is, its socialist transformation.[14] In the letter, he does not hesitate to state that a workers' and peasants' government existed in Russia after the October revolution "before a workers' state was actually established." With all due respect to the comrades who point to Hansen in arguing against the Socialist Workers Party's present course: with such analyses Hansen opened the door to the theories of Jack Barnes and Mary-Alice Waters; even if, it goes without saying, the general approach, and especially the conclusions, are not the same. In 1978, moreover, Hansen asked the following question: "What is the first form of government we can expect to see appear after a victorious anticapitalist revolution, and what is the link between it and the previous struggle to win power?" It's clear that for him, that "first form of government" — *after*, not *before* the victory of the revolution — is the workers' and peasants' government. It follows that we must project two very different phases of the revolution. The transition to the second phase, i.e., the establishment of a workers' state, would be marked essentially by socioeconomic measures.

Finally, there is a third question which, while it has a broader application, may be pertinently raised here. Is it correct to use the characterization of petty-bourgeois for leaderships or political formations that are at the head of workers' and peasants' governments?

We might be tempted to answer that it is precisely to the extent that one feels leaderships or political formations are petty-bourgeois that one resorts to the more cautious formulation "workers' and peasants' government" rather than the formulation "workers' state." But that is not the case. There are, in fact, revolutionary Marxists who believe that a petty-bourgeois leadership may even go so far as to establish a workers' state. Hansen says so explicitly with regard to the Chinese revolution, and, in a more qualified way, with regard to the Cuban revolution also.[15]

Use of the characterization of certain leaderships and formations as petty-bourgeois has a twofold origin in our movement. First, in a number of documents, including the Transitional Program, the Stalinized Communist parties are defined as "petty-bourgeois." In our view this is an incorrect or at least confusing definition. It is better to avoid it, and use the characterization of workers' parties for the Communist parties – as for the Social Democratic parties – opportunist, bureaucratized, workers' parties, of course.[16]

Second, this characterization was used to refer to the Cuban leadership. Indeed, that leadership has a petty-bourgeois origin, dominant composition, and ideology. But inasmuch as it has understood since 1953 what the fundamental motor forces of the revolution are, has linked itself ever more closely with the exploited masses, and struggles consistently to defend their interests and aspirations, it has undergone a transformation, indeed, a "growing over"; and regardless of the level of consciousness reached at one or another moment, has basically functioned as a proletarian revolutionary leadership: that is the main thing.[17] Contrary to what some revolutionary Marxists thought and think, history has produced no petty-bourgeois leadership that has led a proletarian revolution.[18]

## On the revolution in Indochina

FOR AN entire period, the positions taken on the revolution in Indochina were much more general than on the Yugoslav or Chinese revolutions. For example, the resolution of the Fifth World Congress (1957) on the colonial revolution limits itself to stating that, as in North Korea and China, the revolution won in Vietnam as a "proletarian revolution" under the leadership of a "workers' party of Stalinist origin." If memory serves, there is no other document of the time that puts forth a clearer analysis.

Fifteen years later, a resolution of the International Executive Committee took up the new phase of the revolution growing in South Vietnam despite U.S. imperialism's intervention. The problem we are dealing with in this article is not discussed in that resolution either. But it is nonetheless useful to mention that resolution, because it contains an important and still valid clarification regarding coalition governments with bourgeois representatives. The resolution said:

"But this principled opposition to any coalition government with the bourgeoisie does not entitle us automatically to define all cases of such governments as popular-front regimes stabilizing and defending the economic rule and the state of the possessing classes.

"History offers us the example of France and Spain in 1936, France, Italy, Greece, Indonesia, and elsewhere at the end of the Second World War, where this was the case. But it was not the case in Yugoslavia, Czechoslovakia, and China, where the presence of bourgeois ministers in the central government did not prevent the socialist transformation of the revolutionary process from occurring. The decisive thing is the nature of the state, that is, the class character of those who control the armed forces. If the bourgeoisie is in reality disarmed, then the bourgeois ministers are hostages of the proletarian state (whether bureaucratically deformed or not). If the proletariat and poor peasantry are in reality disarmed, then the revolution has suffered defeat. If both the proletariat and the bourgeoisie retain their arms, then the 'government' structure of 'national coalition' can only be an expression of dual power; that is, it represents but a momentary hiatus in an ongoing civil war that can be ended only by the victory of one or the other existing camp of class antagonists."[19]

It is too bad that such clearly defined criteria should be forgotten a few years later when the revolutionary victory occurred in Nicaragua!

Just before the fall of Saigon, a resolution of the United Secretariat hailed the great victories won by the peoples of Indochina, while at the same time explaining: "The military victory of the forces of the PRG over the Saigon puppets would, of course, not in itself guarantee the socialist growing over of the revolution in South Vietnam; the revolution's consolidation in the cities will depend on a series of social, political and economic measures." Regarding Cambodia – Phnom Penh had already fallen – the resolution explains: "What is on the agenda in Cambodia today is the socialist revolution. The character of the Cambodian revolution is nevertheless not yet decided definitely. The consolidation of a new workers' state in Asia will in fact require a series of deep economic, political, and social measures."[20]

Here, it seems that the criterion of "the class character of those who control the armed forces" is no longer considered decisive in itself: the character of the revolution is not yet "decided," and a workers' state does not yet exist either in Vietnam or in Cambodia.[21]

It was during a discussion of Vietnam's intervention in Cambodia in

1979 that opposing positions were defined. Ernest Mandel, expressing the views of the United Secretariat majority, explained that workers' states had arisen in Vietnam and Cambodia in the aftermath of the final defeat of the proimperialist regimes in Saigon and Phnom Penh. This means that contrary to the approach it took with regard to the Yugoslav and Chinese revolutions, the international majority never used the workers' and peasants' government formulation with regard to the revolution in Indochina. On the other hand, the comrades representing the views of the Socialist Workers Party not only resorted again to this formulation, but they even introduced a third phase — before the workers' and peasants' government phase (after August 1975) and the phase of the workers' state (since March 1978) — between the overturn of the proimperialist regime and the establishment of a workers' and peasants' government. As for Cambodia, it remained quite simply a capitalist state.[22] We do not need to reiterate the arguments that Mandel and Jaber have already raised against such fantasies.[23]

## Nicaragua: falling back into old ruts

THE DEBATE on Indochina seemed to warrant the conclusion that the majority of the Fourth International's leadership had evolved in a positive way in their understanding and characterization of the phases of a revolutionary process, despite the few uncertainties that remained. It had, for instance, reaffirmed that "the character of the state power — that is, the class character of those who hold armed power" is the determining factor, and had not clung to the "workers' and peasants' government" formula to overcome difficulties in interpreting the first phase of a revolution.

Unfortunately, through a sort of methodological backtracking that was all the more strange in that it took place in the space of a few months, what had seemingly been assimilated with regard to Indochina was forgotten in the analysis of the Nicaraguan revolution.

The comrades of the Socialist Workers Party did not have much of a problem. After some hesitation, they applied the criteria they had developed in the Indochina polemic and explained that a workers' and peasants' government had existed in Nicaragua since July 19. From their standpoint, this was logical. It is also logical that they are still using that formulation now, rejecting the definition of workers' state — because the old ruling classes were only partially expropriated — and claiming that the Nicaraguan state remains bourgeois.

The majority rejected the "workers' and peasants' government" formulation, not because it believed that Somoza's overthrow marked the birth of a workers' state, but because it thought that even to speak of a workers' and peasants' government was not justified. "Although generally dismembered" — the majority's resolution at the 1979 world congress states — "a bourgeois state persists, with its fundamental laws that protect private ownership of the means of production (land property, industry), hence capitalist accumulation" [*1979 World Congress of the Fourth International* (New York: Intercontinental Press, 1980), p. 162]. What is more, it brings back from oblivion the concept of a special type of dual power used — as we saw — with regard to the Chinese revolution, that is, a type of dual power that rests fundamentally on the fact that the insurrection changed the political relationship of forces, while the bourgeoisie still holds the bulk of economic power.

We do not know if someone put forward or approved such an analysis with the 1952 precedent in mind; in any event, it is significant that nearly thirty years later the same key to interpretation was adopted.

Ten months after the eleventh world congress, the majority also adopted the workers' and peasants' government formulation. In order to take refuge in the orthodoxy of the Transitional Program, it took the precaution of explaining that this was "a brief episode on the way toward the installation of the dictatorship of the proletariat." But that explanation was qualified to a large extent by the fact that the United Secretariat resolution states immediately afterward: "In effect, the decisive test of strength between the classes has still not taken place. The resolution of the specific situation of dual power — which would imply a change in the class nature of the state power, socialization of the principal means of production, and the planned centralization of accumulation — is still to come."[24]

Here, different things are mingled, with a tendency to make the same mistake for which the Socialist Workers Party was criticized — correctly — during the Indochina debate. In any case, there are not many people in the Fourth International today who think that a change in the class character of the state had not yet taken place by September 1980, and that in that sense, "the decisive test of strength between the classes" was still before us.

This new slip was determined, in our opinion, both by a mistaken assessment of the true nature of the government established in Managua on July 19, and by a misunderstanding of the crucial fact that the FSLN was a proletarian revolutionary leadership. Indeed, our memory failed us on three counts. We forgot that it is the change in political (political-military) power that is decisive. We forgot what we ourselves said about the nature of a coalition government in a context like that of the Nicaraguan revolutionary process. We forgot what we knew at the end of the 1960s and beginning of the 1970s about the revolutionary nature of the FSLN.

Here is a realization that should push us to think more about the source of certain errors and the use of certain concepts and formulations.

### A few words on the 'negative example'of Algeria

With regard to Algeria, we should first recall that in addition to the February 1964 United Secretariat resolution, which is the current reference, a resolution exists that was adopted by the same body after the decrees of March 1963 and ratified by the world congress that same year. This resolution does not explicitly conclude that a workers' and peasants' government existed in Algeria, but it develops the same analysis as the 1964 resolution.[25]

That resolution deserves to be mentioned because — if memory serves — it is the only document of the International that explicitly states the criteria for the characterization of a workers' and peasants' government, namely: (1) removal from the government of representatives characterized as belonging to the bourgeoisie; (2) change in the nature of the army; (3) adoption of measures that begin to undermine the capitalist socioeconomic framework. In other words, the document relies exactly on the criteria given by the Fourth Congress of the Communist International (1922).

The fundamental error we made at the time is indicated — but without all the consequences being drawn — in a self-critical resolution passed by the International Executive Committee in December 1969. [Available in Hansen, *The Workers and Farmers Government,* pp. 59-64.] Contrary to what we had thought, the National Liberation Army, headed by Boumedienne, was in no sense a people's revolutionary army. There now exists an entire literature on this subject that leaves not the slightest doubt on the question.[26] In the final analysis, it was the analogy with the Cuban revolution that led us astray. Once again, we must draw the fundamental lesson that each revolutionary process must be studied on its own, according to its specific features. Analogies are merely a secondary analytical tool, to be used with extreme caution.

## PRELIMINARY CONCLUSIONS

WE WOULD like, finally, to outline some conclusions on the problems that we have raised and that our movement should continue to discuss.

### Should we give up the concept of a workers' and peasants' government?

First, we should recall that during the early years of Soviet power and the Communist International, this formula was used only to refer to the government established by the October revolution, and, more broadly, as a synonym for dictatorship of the proletariat. It is not difficult to understand why. There could not be the slightest doubt that in October 1917 the bourgeois state apparatus had been overthrown and replaced by a new power based on soviets. The revolutionary process had unfolded under the leadership of a revolutionary workers' party that had won hegemony in the mass movement through its consistent struggle for the immediate demands and the historic goals of the proletariat, which it explicitly asserted.

The early congresses of the Communist International — inspired by the idea of the universal application of the lessons of October — started from the crisis of the world capitalist system and the outbreak of revolutionary crises in a number of countries to explain that the conquest of power by the proletariat was on the agenda, and that Communist parties already formed or in the process of forming would lead revolutionary struggles and guarantee their victorious outcome.

But when the fourth congress met in November 1922, the leadership of the International understood that the bourgeoisie still possessed greater room for maneuver than had been thought previously; that the conquest of power was not necessarily a short-term prospect, and above all, that the Communist parties were not about to become the majority in most countries. It is in that context that even before the fourth congress, the International had already developed the policy of the united front.

The fourth congress document — so often quoted in our movement — mentions, it is true, that "a genuine proletarian workers' government . . . in its pure form, can only be represented by a Communist Party." But at the same time, applying the principles of the united front at the governmental level, it puts forward the hypothesis of workers' governments that are not yet the dictatorship of the proletariat, and do not constitute "a necessary form of transition toward the dictatorship" but simply "can serve as a point of departure for attaining this dictatorship." Hence, what is involved is a "possibility." The document is clear by itself, but the discussion that took place at the time of its passage clarifies it further. In the words of a delegate, quoted by Radek, it is "not a historic necessity but a historical possibility," or to quote the reporter Zinoviev, "an exceptional possibility."

The authors of the document, moreover, did not claim to give a priori a very precise content to the formula it proposes. This is shown, for instance, by the fact that, in their view, the basic tasks that would be accomplished by a workers' government — before the dictatorship of the proletariat is established — do not differ tremendously from what a dictatorship of the proletariat would do ("arming the proletariat, disarming the counterrevolutionary bourgeois organizations, installing supervision over production, insuring that the main burden of taxation falls on the rich, and smashing the resistance of the bourgeois counterrevolution"[27]).

Moreover, a revolutionary upsurge capable of leading to the formation of a government that acts from such a perspective would inevitably run up against fierce resistance from the ruling classes, which would use every means to oppose it. In fact, the question of state power would be posed from the beginning.[28]

*In any case, one fact is clear: the Communist International never applied the formula of a "workers' government" or "workers' and peasants' government" to a given real situation.* It raised it again at the time of its bureaucratization, while at the same time resurrecting Lenin's old formulation of a "democratic dictatorship of the proletariat and peasantry." But raising it in that way had nothing in common with the fourth congress resolution: it was merely a cover for the neo-Menshevik conception of the revolution by stages that had been formulated in connection with the second Chinese revolution.[29]

As we saw in the second part of this article, the Fourth International itself used the formula "workers' and peasants' government" several times in analyzing revolutionary processes at the end of World War II and in the following decades. *But a second fact is clear; let us say so without flinching: this use was always wrong.* With regard to the Chinese and Yugoslav revolutions, as well as the Cuban and Nicaraguan revolutions, we spoke of a workers' and peasants' government, whereas we should have spoken of a workers' state. In the case of Algeria, the workers' and peasants' government did not actually exist.

We made mistakes on the analytical level through ignorance of insufficient knowledge of the facts (Yugoslavia and China, for instance) or through "forgetfulness" (for instance, Nicaragua). But we also made theoretical or methodological errors, namely:

• We too often tended to analyze new revolutionary processes from the standpoint of the "model" of the October revolution and to picture those that deviated from it as "exceptional," while doing conceptual and/or terminological gymnastics in order to interpret them.[30]

• We were guilty of being too schematic in analyzing the real content of coalition governments, even after major rectifications and clear methodological adjustments. In particular, an entire section of our movement was obsessed by Trotsky's famous passage on the harmful effects of the presence of the "shadow" of the bourgeoisie in the popular front government in Spain. They did not understand that Trotsky did not claim to offer a universal key to interpretation; he was describing a particular process at work.

In some cases, indeed, the shadow of the bourgeoisie can play a decisive role, while in others, even bourgeois figures representing real forces may be merely hostages (i.e., Nicaragua). Everything depends on the total relationship of forces, and even more on the policy carried out by the workng-class leaderships to exploit this relationship to the advantage of the proletariat (after all, even the passage mentioned says the same thing: the "shadow" had weight because of the policy of the Spanish workers' parties and the bureaucratized Communist International).

• For an entire period, we had schematic and simplistic ideas about the Stalinist Communist parties, or those of Stalinist origin, which we considered incapable under any circumstances of leading a revolutionary process to victory, and we lagged in understanding the real role and dynamic of revolutionary formations such as the July 26th Movement and the FSLN.

Let us repeat even more explicitly: on several occasions we used the formula "workers' and peasants' government" not because it corresponded to a real situation or dynamic but because we had not understood — or understood in time — what had happened or was happening. The workers' and peasants' government formula appeared to be more cautious and less predictive of the future than the workers' state formula!

From everything we have just said, must we draw the conclusion that the category of a workers' and peasants' government has neither theoretical value nor practical utility (except as a synonym for dictatorship of the proletariat, or as a formula for propaganda and agitation), and that it is better to simply give it up? If we are not mistaken, that is the conclusion, at least implicitly, of Comrade Jaber's article.

For our part, as long as it is clear that what is involved is an "exceptional possibility," we are not so categorical.

One of Trotsky's writings from 1923 can help us to explain our view. Trotsky asks "is a workers' government realizable in France in any form except that of a Communist dictatorship"? His answer is yes. In the context of a "violent political crisis" and a powerful mass mobilization that would make it impossible for other formations in the workers' movement to bloc with the bourgeoisie against the Communists, "it will be possible ... to form a coalition workers' government."[31] The emergence of such a government would not depend upon the overthrow of the bourgeoisie's political power; hence, that workers' government would not be a dictatorship of the proletariat but would represent a "necessary transition" to it.

If we consider the current composition of the workers' movement in many countries we cannot rule out the hypothesis that in a revolutionary crisis conditions such as those described by Trotsky might appear, and that the revolutionary party might participate in a government in which it would not have hegemony or at least would have to collaborate with other parties, while preparing in this way for the "transition" to a workers' state.

### What are the criteria for a workers' state

THE CRITERIA for defining a workers' and peasants' government are tied, in the final analysis, to the criteria for defining a workers' state. We saw that at least in some cases we came to the conclusion that it was nec essary to speak of a workers' and peasants' government, not because we had well-defined criteria for the elements that make up such a govern ment, but because the criteria for a workers' state did not seem applica ble to us. Especially after the debates on Nicaragua, we became con vinced that a clarification is necessary on two points.

For the comrades of the minority, whose ideas we have already out lined, there are not too many problems: every revolutionary process was and will be characterized by quite distinct phases and by two qualitative leaps.

In our view, the possible formation of a workers' and peasants' gov ernment in — we emphasize once again — the exceptional cases tha might be envisioned on the basis of the hypotheses of the Communist In ternational would not mark a qualitative leap, since the bourgeois state apparatus would not be overturned.

The definition of the elements making up a workers' state does no raise major difficulties either. These elements are threefold: (a) estab lishment of a new political power after destruction of the bourgeois po litical power; (b) qualitative changes in the relationships of production (regardless of the pace and specific forms); (c) dismantling of the bourgeoisie as a ruling social class. There should be a broad consensu on this.[32]

To the contrary, the definition of the qualitative leap — after which a workers' state exists — is a trickier question.

This task may be relatively simple after the events, especially with the hindsight of the historian. The entire course of the revolutionary proces is known, and it is therefore possible to see how the qualitative leap de termines the subsequent phases. But at the beginning and in the course o the process, the difficulty lies in the fact that different potentialities re main, and the outcome is not necessarily given in advance.

The criteria that have been advanced all contain difficulties, even con tradictions. The minority's theory leads to a variant of the revolution by stages and implies the nonsensical conclusion that in all proletarian rev olutions the state apparatus would remain bourgeois after the politica overthrow of the ruling classes (until the expropriation of most capitalis property). Jaber's criticisms on this point are entirely pertinent.

The theory that singles out the criterion of political power may pose questions in specific cases, such as Nicaragua.

This is a specific case which is new relative to other revolutionary pro cesses, in the sense that five years after the victory of July 19, the bourgeoisie as a social class maintains considerable strength and con trols not marginal — or in any case, minority — sectors but sectors vita to the economy of the country as a whole (this is true in the context, o course, of very broad state powers in the area of investments, choice of priorities, foreign trade, and so on).

The Nicaraguan leaders have explained on several occasions that, in their opinion, this situation might well still continue for a long period (they have even talked of fifteen or twenty years). If this were the case, we would have a workers' state that would maintain predominantly capitalist relations of production for two decades. This would not, in our view, pose problems of characterization.

Of course, one may think that this hypothesis will not come to pass. That is precisely our opinion. The survival of such a broad capitalist sector constantly generates conflicts and contradictions, and, in the final analysis, prevents any kind of real planning. Hence the possibility of social and political frictions between the Sandinista regime and sectors of the masses that have always supported it.

Moreover, the bourgeoisie does not feel that its future is secure. It would like "guarantees"; it strives to translate its economic weight into political terms. This inevitably leads it to challenge the central political power, hence to set for itself the prospect of counterrevolution. Beyond the tactical differences, that is precisely the goal for which the bourgeoisie is working in its majority. Even more clearly, that is the prospect for which imperialism is working. The contradictions of a transitional society are going to erupt much more quickly than the Sandinistas would like, and they will have no choice but to use their political power to overcome them.

That is why we feel, while being conscious of the difficulties, that the criterion of power is decisive in this case also, and that Nicaragua is a workers' state, even if it has not yet been consolidated in all the elements making up a workers' state.

## A necessary discussion

Our DISCUSSION of the problems of power and the transitional phase from capitalism to socialism must continue. Is this a Byzantine discussion without any practical use?

Only narrow pragmatists could think so. After all, if we had dealt with these questions better in the past, we would have avoided a good many errors.

Concerning those errors, it should be clear that there is nothing surprising in the fact that theory should be fine-tuned or even overhauled after events that that theory should have helped us to understand. The Marxist theory of the state was perfected only after the Paris Commune. Lenin wrote *State and Revolution* during the 1917 revolution, and Trotsky made his contribution on the transitional society after Stalin's victory. Nor is it too serious that we did not grasp in time the revolutionary qualitative leaps. Nonetheless, we cannot gloss over the fact that we often made mistakes after the fact as well, and, what is more, that we were incapable of understanding real revolutionary processes. This could not fail to have major practical implications.

Our discussion should and will enable us not only to assess our mistakes, but also, and *especially*, to understand the reasons for them, to grasp the factors that muddled our analyses and distorted our conclusions. This will enable us in the future to see revolutionary processes more clearly, in time, and to be able to participate in them better and contribute better to the defense and flowering of the revolutions that have already succeeded.

January 5, 1985

# Notes

1. See, for instance, Mary-Alice Waters's article "The Workers' and Farmers' Government: A Popular Revolutionary Dictatorship," in *New International*, vol. 1, no. 3, Spring-Summer 1984.

2. Here is the exact quote from Trotsky: "The nationalization of the land, the means of industrial production, transport and exchange, together with the monopoly of foreign trade, constitute the basis of the soviet social structure. Through these relations, established by the proletarian revolution, the nature of the Soviet Union as a proletarian state is for us basically defined." [Leon Trotsky, *The Revolution Betrayed* (New York: Pathfinder Press, 1972), p. 248.]

3. We agree with what Jaber writes about a "lesser phase of dual power" and about Ernest Mandel's "extreme variant." Mandel, moreover, describes three types of "dual power situations" (see *Intercontinental Press*, May 4, 1981, pp. 457-58). Unfortunately, the Fourth International and Mandel himself have theorized about a fourth type, which is precisely the one we have just mentioned and which must be rejected. We will come back to this problem later.

4. In the Second World Congress resolution (April 1948) on the Eastern European countries — which were called "the Soviet buffer countries" at the time — it is explained that the state remains bourgeois because "its structure remains bourgeois: nowhere has the old bureaucratic machinery of the bourgeois state been destroyed" and because "its function remains bourgeois.... It defends a kind of property which, despite its various and hybrid forms, remains fundamentally bourgeois in nature."

5. "The Yugoslav Revolution," in *Class, Party, and State and the Eastern European Revolution* (New York: Pathfinder Press, 1969), p. 56. In a 1949 discussion, Michel Pablo defended the position that Yugoslavia was a workers' state, without, however, defining the point of qualitative leap and without mentioning a workers' and peasants' government. Ernest Mandel, meanwhile, wrote: "The definition we could give of Yugoslavia between 1944 and 1948 is that of a country where a stalled proletarian revolution did not lead to building a new type of state apparatus, but where the extraordinary weakness of the

bourgeoisie did not permit rebuilding of the bourgeois state power either. In other words, we have a typical example of that workers' and peasants' government, the possible existence of which was theoretically recognized by our Transitional Program but which it defined as having to be a brief transition to the dictatorship of the proletariat." In the polemic on Indochina that we will mention below, the same comrade basically clings to the analysis of the 1951 world congress, stating that the workers' and peasants' government lasted for only six months in 1945.

6. See *Quatrième Internationale*, August-October 1951, pp. 25, 26, 32, and 40. [The major resolutions and reports from the Third World Congress were published in English in the November-December 1951 issue of *Fourth International*. The manifesto was printed in the October 8, 1951, *Militant*.]

7. "The outbreak of world war will probably be the beginning of a fundamental turn of the CP away from capitalism, resulting in the liquidation of the dual power in all echelons of the state apparatus." (See *Fourth International*, July-August 1952, p. 116.)

8. I agree with Jaber that we must recognize, at least in retrospect, that at the 1952 plenum it was Favre-Bleibtreu who was right on the nature of the Chinese state. Anything Bleibtreu may have said and done since then does not wipe out this unquestionable fact. Mandel expressed his opinion on the subject in the polemic on Indochina (see *Intercontinental Press*, May 4, 1981, p. 464), where he maintained that a workers' and peasants' government had existed in China (during a period between "six months and one year," in 1949-50).

9. A section on Cuba was inserted into a draft document on the colonial revolution written in mid-1959 (mistakenly published in the January 1961 issue of *Quatrième Internationale*, although it should have been deleted since a specific document on Cuba already existed). This document fairly well reflects the judgments we made at the time it was written, and the prudence of our conclusions. From the standpoint of criteria, it is useful to recall the following passage: "What counts at the current stage is not so much the completion of the economic and social measures that will seal the overturn of the feudal-capitalist regime, but the organization of a proletarian political power, through extension of the militias, the people's tribunals, and organization of the communes and committees as organs of local power." In other words, the priority of the political criterion over the socioeconomic criterion is affirmed.

10. See Joseph Hansen, *Dynamics of the Cuban Revolution* (New York: Pathfinder Press, 1978), pp. 67, 68.

11. In a letter to Bob Chester (July 1970), Hansen writes: "If a revolutionary-Marxist party exists, and gains governmental power under the impulsion of a revolution, there is no question as to the subsequent dynamics. The party assures it through its program, through the cadres imbued with that program, and through the experience gained in the living class struggle that finally puts it in power." [Joseph Hansen, *The Workers and Farmers Government* (New York: Pathfinder Press, 1974), p. 35.] There is something more substantial than mere consciousness!

12. Hansen, *Dynamics*, p. 126. It should be added, however, that even in his letter Hansen alternately projects two arguments: "Once we are forced by reality itself to reject January 1, 1959, as the point of qualitative change," he

explains, "we are compelled to await either the appearance of socialist consciousness or of economic institutions that in and of themselves are socialist in
principle." (p. 127) This confirms, in any case, that the concept of a workers'
and peasants' government is used in place of a workers' state when there is no
conscious socialist leadership (or we do not yet have sufficient information to
say that it exists). This obviously restricts the value of the concept of a workers'
and peasants' government.

13.  See one of the letters to Bob Chester [Hansen, *The Workers and Farmers
Government*, pp. 33-38]. From this letter in particular, it appears that Hansen
was quite conscious of the difficulty we encounter in defining the concept of a
workers' and peasants' government and its applications.

14.  See a report he gave in August 1969 on the Ninth World Congress [Han-
sen, "The Social Transformations in Eastern Europe, China, and Cuba," in *The
Workers and Farmers Government*, pp. 20-30].

15.  See his above mentioned report of August 1969.

16.  In Lenin and Trotsky, we can find various characterizations of the opportunist workers' parties: workers', petty-bourgeois, bourgeois, or bourgeois
workers' parties, depending on the context and the needs of the polemic. But basically, they make a qualitative distinction between those parties and the
bourgeois or petty-bourgeois parties in the strict sense (I touched on this problem
in *Dinamica delle classi sociali in Italia*, Rome, 1976). Let us add that the characterization of the Soviet bureaucracy as petty-bourgeois is also wrong. We
agree with what Mandel says in this regard (see *Intercontinental Press*, May 4,
1981, p. 469), with the reservation that in our view, it is necessary to say more
explicitly that this is a characterization not to be used. Indeed, it blurs the historically original nature of the bureaucratic caste — a social formation belonging to
the phase of transition from capitalism to socialism — and has created a lot of
confusion in our ranks.

17.  This interpretation is already put forward in the Sixth World Congress
document on Cuba (point 7) [*Fourth International* (Rome), No. 12, Winter
1960-61, pp. 48-50].

18.  Jaber reproaches me for having used the nationalizations in Eastern
Europe as an argument in order to "infer by analogy the possibility that Egypt
has become a workers' state in a 'cold' way." In fact, in outlining a new theoretical hypothesis, we made other, more pertinent arguments, and the reference to
Eastern Europe was made only in answer to comrades claiming that "history had
shown no example of a country that became a workers' state without a thoroughgoing popular revolution." No doubt we missed a fine opportunity to keep silent
at the time. But in discussions among revolutionaries you have to take risks
sometimes if you don't want to settle for warmed-over soup.

19.  See *Intercontinental Press*, January 19, 1973, pp. 27-29.

20.  See *Intercontinental Press*, May 5, 1975, pp. 601, 599.

21.  It is true that the document speaks of "consolidation" and not establishment of workers' states through economic, political, and social measures. But
on the one hand, it does not say that workers' states have actually appeared, and,
on the other hand, it explains that the growing over of a revolution is not guaranteed. Pierre Rousset, meanwhile, wrote after the fall of Saigon that "there will be
neither a bourgeois state nor a new revolution between the liberation of Saigon

and the reunification of a united socialist Vietnam," which is, of course, more correct. (See *Inprecor*, no. 26, May 22, 1975).

22. For this discussion, see the February 26, April 9, May 14, 1979, and May 4, 1981, issues of *Intercontinental Press* and the Summer 1980 issue of *Inprecor*. See also the resolutions submitted to the Eleventh World Congress (in *1979 World Congress of the Fourth International* [New York: *Intercontinental Press*, 1980]).

23. In their resolution submitted to the Eleventh World Congress, the comrades of the minority reiterated the arguments raised in the polemic mentioned above. The majority document explains that "the April 1975 victory . . . opened the way for the establishment of a workers' state in South Vietnam" (p. 187), and uses the same term in regard to Cambodia (p. 188). Mandel, meanwhile, wrote that South Vietnam became a workers' state "if not after the capture of Saigon by the armed revolutionary forces, then certainly at the moment of the formal unification of North and South Vietnam into a single state." (*Intercontinental Press*, April 9, 1979, p. 342) As we see, the moment of the qualitative leap remains nebulous.

24. See *Intercontinental Press*, November 24, 1980, p. 1228. Members of the United Secretariat including the author of this article, had proposed adopting the "workers' and peasants' government" formula in July 1980, explaining that the departure of the ministers representing the bourgeoisie was what marked the turning-point. Although they did not use in their analysis formulas such as "the decisive test of strength between the classes has still not taken place," their position was also wrong.

25. See *Fourth International* (Paris), October-December 1963, pp. 73-74. The 1963 resolution says, among other things: "As a result of recent measures adopted and in the process of being applied, Algeria has entered an eminently transitory phase from the standpoint of the economic and social structures, a phase that will culminate in establishment of a workers' state." The February 1964 United Secretariat resolution is reprinted as an appendix to Jack Barnes, *For a Workers' and Farmers' Government in the United States* (New York: Pathfinder Press, 1985), p. 46.

26. The most important contribution — as Jaber also points out — was that of Mohammed Habri. As a mitigating circumstance for us, we should recall that nothing of the kind existed in 1963-64. Even those who helped to clarify things later on did not have exactly the same views at the time.

27. Hansen, *The Workers and Farmers Government*, pp. 39, 40, 41, 43.

28. An executive committee plenum of June 1923 returns to the question of the workers' and peasants' government. But this debate was aimed essentially at drawing the Communist parties' attention to the peasant question. [The June 1923 report and resolution are reprinted in Barnes, *For a Workers' and Farmers' Government*, pp. 48-52.]

29. See, in this regard, the Transitional Program and Trotsky's polemic with Radek in Leon Trotsky's *The Permanent Revolution* (New York: Pathfinder Press, 1969).

30. Our rejection of a key to interpretation of revolutionary processes based on the Russian "model" — like our rejection of the "detour" notion to explain the real course of the world revolution — does not lead us to accept Jaber's rather

abridged arguments on this point (see pp. 71 and 72). It is undeniable that we have seen victorious proletarian revolutions without "the central role of the soviets and without Bolshevism in its pure form." We are convinced, moreover, that probably no revolution will follow the same course as the Russian revolution from the standpoint of the formation of soviets, the rise of the peasant movement, the crisis in the armed forces, the conquest of hegemony within the mass movement by the Bolsheviks, forms of dual power, and so on.

Nonetheless, it is the experience of October that sheds light on the necessity for a revolutionary overthrow of bourgeois power, the irreplaceable role of a revolutionary leadership, the function of revolutionary democracy, the concrete impact of internationalism. The same cannot be said for any of the revolutionary experiences that have occurred since. In that sense, it retains its universal value.

31. Hansen, *The Workers and Farmers Government*, p. 46.

32. Ernest Mandel, for instance, wrote in one of his articles on Indochina: "A workers' state exists when and if the previously existing bourgeois state machine has been smashed, the existing bourgeois class has lost its political and economic power, and when the economy based upon new production and property relations, of a noncapitalist nature, evolves according to laws of motion that are not those discovered by Marx in *Capital* as being characteristic of the capitalist mode of production." (*Intercontinental Press,* April 9, 1979, p. 338).